ELEMENTS OF PHILOSOPHY,

COMPRISING

LOGIC AND ONTOLOGY

OR

GENERAL METAPHYSICS.

BY

REV. W. H. HILL, S. J.,

PROFESSOR OF PHILOSOPHY IN THE ST. LOUIS UNIVERSITY.

BALTIMORE:

PUBLISHED BY JOHN MURPHY & COMPANY,

NO. 182 BALTIMORE STREET.

LONDON: R. WASHBURNE, 18 PATERNOSTER ROW.

1873.

PREFACE.

The following elementary work, though primarily intended for learners, will, it is believed, be found by the general reader of philosophy to contain things which are new, as regards works of the kind published in the English language.

In order to render the Logic more easy and more practical, *First*, the author has omitted the perplexed, undiscussed and indeterminate Greek derivatives, which give vagueness or obscurity to the matter contained in many popular text books on Logic; and he has aimed to use in their stead the most plain and simple terminology. This perpetual multiplication of indefinite and unintelligible technicalities, which are devised as if to embody new forms of thought, helps much to render the study of Logic and Philosophy discouraging, and their very names repulsive, even to the most ambitious and the most intelligent young minds that attempt to master the established elementary principles of these all-important branches of a good education. The introduction of a new term into a book on Philosophy, does not necessarily imply the actual discovery of a new truth. It is a significant fact that, while eccentric thought and novel phraseology possess a peculiar charm for ill-educated, rambling and superficial minds; yet, the language which remains in prevailing use, is the embodiment of deep and true philosophy; and the words as well as the conclusions, which convey what is absurd or preposterous, it must necessarily repudiate, by the general law of human thought.

Second: It was judged best, also, for the interests of learners in general, to omit the discussion of the *modes* and *figures* of the syllogism; for, in practice they are not attended to, even by those who actually argue in form, the simple rules of demonstration sufficing for all practical purposes, and being all that is even really useful in the strictest argumentation. On the other hand, it was deemed expedient to introduce some matters that pertain to branches of Philosophy, whose full treatment is appropriate to another volume; e. g., certain subjects which strictly belong to Psychology, Cosmology and Natural Theology.

The author derived much help from notes taken in private study years ago, but which were prepared with no thought of ever employing them for any other purpose than his own instruction. It is hoped that the acknowledgment of having made a free use of what was then obtained from the best works within his reach, will excuse the omission of more frequent reference to them in the margin.

In disposing the matter, the method employed in the most approved text books used in the schools of Philosophy is generally followed. In such works the definitions of terms, many important propositions of Logic and Metaphysics, even with the chief arguments for them, are treated as common property; as happens, for example, with certain definitions and theorems of geometry, originally from *Euclid*, but which are now the recognized property of all geometricians.

In order to secure brevity, after having indicated succinctly, but, as he trusts, clearly and comprehensively, the theories and the salient points of the matters treated, he has been compelled, in many instances, to leave their development to the instructor, or to the reader for himself.

The writer flatters himself that the treatises on certainty, and its motives and principles; on sensible and intellectual cognition; the objective reality of ideas; the principle of causation; will, perhaps, be found to possess special value, more particularly for those who are not familiar with the language of the schools.

It was deemed expedient to insert on the margin, here and there, some suggestive axioms, brief distinctions and explanations, taken from the *Latin* authors, among whom they pass for established doctrine, and are usually enunciated nearly in the same terms. The *Latin* of the schools, besides being brief, is also peculiarly capable of expressing precisely, clearly, and comprehensively, matters which it is difficult to utter through the less accurate vernacular, in terms that are neither obscure nor ambiguous. Though they are not essential to the text of the work, yet, for the convenience of the reader who is not familiar with the Latin language, the translation is subjoined to these citations. It was, however, found no easy task, in some instances, to reproduce them with fidelity in English phraseology, as the classic scholar will readily see from the result, and know how to judge benignantly.

If the offering which is herewith respectfully made to the cause of education meet with public favor, it is designed to complete the philosophical course by adding to the present work treatises on Cosmology, Psychology, Theodicea, and Ethics or Moral Philosophy. Whether this part of the undertaking be well or ill done—and, doubtless, many errors and imperfections have escaped notice—it may, nevertheless, fairly be taken as a specimen of what the whole is likely to be; and, even if it prove to possess but indifferent merit, still it is the fruit of much toil, and the result of the writer's best possible effort, done, as it was, during intervals between various daily duties. With this candid statement, the work is sent forth with the hope that kind suggestions and ingenuous criticism may contribute to improve, and perfect it for the object intended; i. e., an aid for the study of Philosophy.

ST. LOUIS UNIVERSITY,
February 10th, 1873.

INTRODUCTION.

PHILOSOPHY; ITS OBJECT.

The word *Philosophy*, according to the sense in which Pythagoras applied it to his school, means the love, desire and pursuit of wisdom. Philosophy, as a science, is the knowledge of things in their highest and most universal causes, so far as such knowledge is attainable by the light of natural reason. Its object, therefore, includes the world or universe, man, God, in their most essential relations to each other.*

It is not without propriety, then, that Philosophy, when compared to the whole collection of human sciences, is pronounced to be, "as the sun in the planetary system, the light of all." Without some adequate acquaintance, at least with the body of its established doctrine, even a liberal education is incomplete or partial, if, indeed, it be not superficial or unsound.

The *knowledge* of a thing, even when it is *scientific*, stops with the immediate or proximate causes of that thing; but *wisdom*, which is *philosophical knowledge*, refers the same thing

*"Rerum divinarum atque humanarum causarumque quibus continentur cognitio." The knowledge of human and divine things, and of the causes by which they are related to each other.

to its still higher and more universal causes; that is, it seeks to understand and explain it in its essence as it absolutely is, and must be. Other science acquaints us with things as they are directly and extrinsically known through the senses, or other powers of cognition; but philosophy, by means of higher scientific knowledge, proceeds further, and explains the *intrinsic nature* of those things, and their relation to still more universal truths. For example: *Physiology*, as a science, explains the whole economy of the living human body, its organism, the functions of its tissues, the relations and connexions of its members, and the like; and that science is wholly limited to this positive object, to this view of organic beings. Philosophy proceeds much farther; it explains the *nature of man* as a rational animal, or as consisting of an organized body and a living soul in union by composition; and it answers the questions, "what is life? what is the nature of the soul? what essentially constitutes the union of the soul and body? can material organs, by any possibility, elicit acts of intelligence?" etc.

It is manifest, therefore, that Philosophy is superior in its aim and objects to all other human sciences. It treats of its matter on *metaphysical principles;* that is, it explains objects in their *essence*, employing for that purpose *necessary*, *immutable* and *absolute truths;* which preserve the understanding from error, not only in these elevated matters, but also in the study of facts, no less than the conclusions from those facts.

The subjects that are now usually treated in a course of

Philosophy, are Logic, Ontology, Cosmology, Psychology, Natural Theology, and Moral Philosophy or Ethics.

Logic explains the laws of right reasoning; it is, when considered under different respects, both a natural gift, and the result of art. Artificial Logic derives its value from the natural, whose principles it aims to express in a few clear and invariable formulæ. Logic, considered as practically directing the mind in reasoning, is an art; but inasmuch as it explains and proves the precepts of correct argument by their reasons, furnishes the means and the criteria of certainty, or propounds the truth of cognition, it is a science.

Ontology, or General Metaphysics, has for its object the essential predicates of all things; and it, therefore, deals with truths which are strictly absolute and universal. It is the most completely generalized system of knowledge which it is possible for the human intellect to form by its highest power of analysis.

Cosmology treats of the visible world; its origin by creation, the nature of the material substance of which it is made, of what constitutes the essence of inorganic, organic, and living forms of material substance.

Psychology has for its end to explain the human soul, considered both as the vital principle in the human compound, and as a spiritual substance capable of existing *per se*, or separate from the body, together with its nature, operations, its essential immateriality, and indestructibility.

Natural Theology treats of God as the first and unproduced

cause of all that exists out of him; his nature, attributes or perfections, so far as they can be known by mere reason.

Moral Philosophy or Ethics has for its object moral good; and man as a moral being, his relation to the natural law of right and wrong, the ultimate end of his being, what constitutes his chief good, *summum bonum*. When limited rigorously to its sphere, Moral Philosophy prescinds from Revelation; or, in other words, it presents its subject matter only in a philosophical light. But, because there can be no disagreement between natural and supernatural truth, God being the author of both;* and, also, since the light of revelation perfects even the knowledge which is acquired by the light of natural reason, it is not wonderful that much of the matter which is usually contained in works on Moral Philosophy should really be derived, directly or indirectly, from revelation; for, indeed, all human science has been benefited, in one respect or another, by supernatural truth.

*"Principiorum naturaliter notorum cognitio nobis divinitus indita est, cum ipse Deus sit auctor nostræ naturæ. Quidquid igitur principiis hujusmodi contrarium est, divinæ sapientiæ contrarium est, non igitur a Deo esse potest. Ea igitur quae ex revelatione divina per fidem tenentur, non possunt naturali cognitioni esse contraria." (Div. Th., contr. gent. lib. I. c. 7.) The knowledge of principles known naturally is divinely put into us, since God himself is the author of our nature. Whatever, therefore, is contrary to these principles, is contrary to the Divine wisdom, and on that account cannot be from God. Those things, therefore, from Divine revelation, which are held by faith, cannot be contrary to natural knowledge.

CONTENTS.

LOGIC: FIRST PART.

CHAPTER I.

CHAPTER II.

CHAPTER III.

CHAPTER IV.

LOGIC: SECOND PART; OR, LOGIC APPLIED.

CHAPTER I.

CHAPTER II.

MEANS OR SOURCES OF CERTAINTY.

APPENDIX.

ONTOLOGY; OR, GENERAL METAPHYSICS.

CHAPTER I.

CHAPTER II.

CHAPTER III.

LOGIC: FIRST PART

OR

DIALECTICS.

ELEMENTS OF LOGIC.

THEORETICAL AND APPLIED.

CHAPTER I.

As the end of Logic is to direct the mind in reasoning, it has for its object: 1st. To explain the operations of the mind so far as they are directly related to that end; 2d. The rules and precepts that govern these operations.

Some of its principles prevent error in the process of reasoning, that is, in the *form* of argument; others guard against deception in the *subject matter*, that is, in the *truths* or *facts* that are compared.

Hence, Logic may be conveniently divided into two parts: into Theoretical Logic or Dialectics, and Applied Logic.

In the first, the operations of the mind in right reasoning are described, and the rules are given which direct it in the *form* of reasoning. In the second part of Logic, those principles are considered in their practical application to the objects of reasoning, that is, to the *matter* or the *logical truth* of propositions.

Observe, then, that Logic is not limited in its scope or general aim to the mere *form* of arguments; for this is, in fact, only a part of its proper object. It teaches also the means of attaining truth of cognition, since it lays down principles that preserve the mind from error in judging and assenting to the motives of certainty. By explaining and prescribing the rules of definition, division and ratiocination, it gives light and method to all the sciences; and, because its true and proper end is to expound and direct the acts of reason, it is itself correctly styled by philosophers *the science of reason.*

ARTICLE I.

SIMPLE APPREHENSION.

There are three acts or operations of the mind which are to be treated in the first part of Logic, namely, *simple apprehension*, *judgment*, and *reasoning*.

Apprehension, from the Latin word, *apprehendere*, *to take hold of*, *as with the hand*, in its widest sense, includes all those acts of cognition which precede *judgment*. Hence, even the *senses* may be said to *apprehend* their objects; the fancy *apprehends* by means of its images; the intellect *apprehends* the *intelligible essence*, after the concrete or singular realities of the objects which are presented by the sensible organs are dropped. The intellect expresses what it thus *apprehends* or *conceives* in the *verbum mentis*, or *concept*, or by these acts it forms its *idea* of the object. All these acts of *simple knowledge* are included under the general name, *simple apprehension*. We may regard the idea, or concept, as the *term* of all these *apprehensive acts*, since it is their last immediate result. It is manifest that the object conceived or apprehended may be either *complex* or *incomplex*; v. g., "learned man, man," "stone house, stone;" but so long as there is no judgment affirmed by the mind, the acts all pertain to *apprehensive knowledge*, or they are acts of *simple apprehension*. When the mind actually *compounds* or *divides* two concepts, as predicate and subject, it *judges* or formally and explicitly *affirms* truth, and this judgment or explicit affirmation, being *enunciated* or expressed in language, is a *proposition*. The truth contained in this judgment is *implicitly* contained in the acts of simple apprehension, but it is *explicitly* in the judgment alone, for, as is manifest, it is only judgment that can *properly* be said to *affirm* truth.

Simple apprehension, in the more special sense in which the expression is generally used, is an act of the *intellect*, by which it takes notice of an object and acquires some knowledge of it, but without any judgment or explicit affirmation; or, in other words, by this act it merely perceives or sees the object, without proceeding to form a judgment.

The object of the apprehension may be either a *singular* and individual thing, or a *relation* between two or more things.

The knowledge or cognition acquired by this act is called, indiscriminately, a *concept* or an *idea*, and it is the result or *fruit* of the simple apprehension. Take care not to confound *idea*, which is mental, with the *image* or *phantasma* in the imagination, which is *organic*, and which we have in common with the brute. The thing apprehended, as it is in itself, with its qualities and attributes, is the *material object;* the object, with its constituent *marks* or *properties* as *expressed in the mind*, is the *formal object* of the apprehension; this *formal object* is also called the *mental term* of the apprehension, and *verbum mentis*, or mental word. The *oral term* is the *word* which is employed in language to express *orally* the name of the *mental term*, *concept*, or *idea.*

The *formal* concept,* is the actual mental word by which the intellect *formally*, i. e., actually, perceives or sees the thing known, or it is the intrinsic or formal term of mental conception. The concept is so called on account of its being, as it were, the *offspring* of the intellect. The *objective* concept is the *thing*, whatever it be, which is known or represented by means of the *formal* concept;† v. g., when we mentally conceive "*man*," the act in the intellect by which we do this is the *formal* concept, but "*man*," as known and represented in that act, is the *objective* concept. The *formal* concept is always a singular and individual thing, because it is an act in the intellect; but the *objective* concept may be a *universal*, a confused object, a common or general thing; as *animal*, *substance ;* or, what is the most universal of all objective concepts, *being.*

* Vide Suarez's Metaphysics, Disp. 2, Sect. 2.

† "Objectum est determinans; intellectus, determinabile ad concipiendum." The object is that which determines; and the intellect is that which can be determined to conceive an object.

ARTICLE II.

TERMS; COMPREHENSION AND EXTENSION OF TERMS; DEFINITION OF OTHER TERMS.

Oral terms are the names in language for ideas or concepts, and, therefore, represent them, or stand for them.

A term may be considered in connexion with the constituent marks or properties contained in its object; v. g., *man*, as expressing intelligence, mortality, stature, complexion, etc.; in this case the *comprehension* of the term *man* is attended to. The *comprehension* of a term, therefore, expresses all the marks or constituent properties of the object for which that term stands.

If we consider the number of individuals to which the term may be applied, we then regard the *extension* of that term; v. g., *intelligence*, extends to more individuals than the term *man*, for it belongs, also, to angels Hence, the *extension* of a term expresses the greater or less number of individuals to which it applies.

The *comprehension* of a term decreases as its *extension* increases; and, *vice versa*, the *comprehension* increases as the *extension* decreases; v. g., the term *substance* expresses but one *mark* or *attribute* of beings, for its *comprehension;* but its *extension* is very great. Now, if another property or mark be added to it its *comprehension* is increased, but its *extension* is diminished; v. g., *corporeal substance* has greater *comprehension*, but less *extension*, than *substance* without any mark or property added to it.

Attention is an act of the mind by which it is directed to some object or objects, to which it adheres, for a time. This act is either *voluntary* or *spontaneous.* There is some degree of *spontaneous attention* in every act of cognition which the understanding elicits. *Voluntary attention* may last for a greater or a less time, and may consist of one or more acts.

Abstraction is a species of Attention by which the mind separates (withdraws) one thing from others with which it is connected, and contemplates *that*, to the exclusion of the others; v. g., to think of the *eye* without attending to the other parts of man.*

Reflexion is also an exercise of attention, by which the mind contemplates its own acts, or considers its concepts or ideas of objects.

ARTICLE III.

THE OBJECTS OF IDEAS OR CONCEPTS; DEFINITION OF OTHER TERMS.

In reference to their objects, ideas are divided into *concrete* and *abstract*, *universal* and *particular*, etc. *Concrete ideas* are those whose objects are conceived as actually or physically existing; as Peter, those books, etc. The *abstract idea* has for its object a form or quality separated from its subject; as *whiteness*, *roundness*, *wisdom*, etc. A *univervsal idea* is one whose object is a mark or property which is common to a whole class of objects and can be affirmed of each one; as "man, animal," etc. The objects included under it are called its *subjects* or *inferiors*. A *particular* idea has for its object only a part of the objects to which a universal is applicable, or it is a common or universal limited to a part only of its extension; as "a soldier, some men, some trees," etc.

A term is *singular* when it applies to but one concrete and actual individual; as "Cæsar, this apple," etc. A term is *common* when it may be applied to many; as "father, substance, just," etc.

* "Abstrahentium non est mendacium." Abstraction is not falsehood.

"Id cognoscitur *abstractive* quod non cognoscitur *praesens; intuitive*, quando cognoscitur *praesens*. Seu cognitio *abstractiva* est cognitio rei in alio tanquam in medio prius cognito ut *quod* seu *in quo:* e. gr. Videre *partem* in toto; *parietem* in domo, objectum repræsentatum in speculo, causam in effectu, etc. Cognitio intuitiva est cognitio *immediata* seu a tali medio independens." That is known *abstractly* which is not known as *present;* it is known *intuitively* when known as *present;* or, *abstract* knowledge is the knowledge of one thing in another as in a medium previously known; v. g., to see a *part* in the *whole*, a wall in the house, an object imaged in the mirror, cause in the effect, etc. *Intuitive* knowledge is *immediate* knowledge, or it is independent of such medium.

Transcendental ideas are those whose objects *transcend* all classification of genus and species, being the common attributes of all things; as "*being, essence, one, true, good.*"

The idea, considered as expressing its object, is either *adequate* or *inadequate;* the *adequate* includes not only all that is of the essence, but all accidents and relations of its object; it is *inadequate* when it does not include all, absolutely, that is true of its object.

Terms, considered in respect to their objects, are *real* and *logical;* of the *first* and *second intention;* *absolute* and *connotative.*

The object of the *real term* actually exists outside of the mind; it is a real or actual object, or, at least, really possible; as "this horse, a star, a planet." The *logical* term has for its object a concept or idea, which, though founded upon real objects, does not itself express anything really existing out of the mind; v. g., the terms *genus, species,* and all *universals.* *Terms of the first and second intention* have the same objects, respectively, as *real* and *logical* terms; a term of the *first intention* expresses the object as seen by the *first* and direct act of the mind, in which act the object is affirmed by its *real predicates.* A term of the *second intention* stands for another concept which the mind forms by a *second* and reflex act, in which second act *logical* or universal predicates are attributed; v. g., the terms *genus, species, transcendentals,* are terms of the *second intention,* because their objects are not *real,* but *logical* only.

A term is *absolute* when there is not directly implied in the idea of its object any *dependence* on, or *relation* to, another object; e. g., such *substantives* as gold, apples, etc.; also, adjectives used *absolutely;* as *the good, the true,* etc.

The *connotative* term stands for an object, in the very idea of which is directly implied an *adjacent object* on which it depends or to which it is related; as *white, heavy, living, rapid,* and all *adjectives* and *adjunctives,* as also such substantives as *professor, musician, artist,* etc.

Signs are either *natural,* as sighs, groans, laughter; or *sup-*

positive, as articulate sounds forming words or terms, which are conventional signs for things. *Supposition* here means merely *the conventional use of a term or sign for a thing.* Aristotle observes (Elench. lib. i., c. i.), that since we cannot have all objects physically in our presence when arguing, we employ *in their stead names* as *signs* for them. In the well known saying, "*words* are the *counters* of wise men; they are the *money* of fools," it is meant that *words suppose* or *stand for* different objects with two classes of men.

Terms are *univocal* or *equivocal;* a term is *univocal* which, being applied to different objects, has the same signification or expresses the same quality or essence; thus, *animal* is *univocal* when applied to *man* and *brute*, because, in each case, its meaning is the same.

A term is *equivocal* when, being applied to different objects, it does not express the same quality or essence in each; thus "*light* is the opposite of darkness; feathers are *light.*" Equivocal terms often subserve the designs of sophistry; they are also frequently employed for comparison and metaphor, giving to style one of its chief ornaments.

A term is used in a *material* sense, or the *supposition* is *material*, when the word is used merely as a word; as "*Cicero* is a word of three syllables." It has a *formal supposition*, or is used in its *formal sense*, when it is employed to express the object for which it stands, as "*Cicero* was an orator."

Analogy is a certain agreement or remote relation that one object bears to another. *Analogy* is either that of *attribution*, or that of *proportion.*

In the *analogy* of *attribution* a predicate that belongs *primarily* and *properly* to one object is *attributed* to another, owing to some relation between them or aptitude of one for the other; thus *healthy* is *primarily* and *properly* a predicate of the animal body; but we say *healthy food*, *healthy complexion*, *healthy climate*, from the relation which these things have to *health* in its primary meaning.

Analogy of proportion is founded on a resemblance of proportion which is in the substance or in a quality of objects that are of a different species. It imports a certain agreement in the effects produced by causes which are otherwise quite dissimilar, or it is a certain agreement in the manner in which objects are related to or referred to other objects. Owing to this agreement, the *term* that expresses the relation in one set of objects is applied to the other related objects; v. g., "bread is the *staff* of life;" "the Scipios were *thunderbolts* of war." The terms "staff" and "thunderbolts" here have an *analogical* sense; they are not used either in a *univocal* or an *equivocal* sense, but in a sense that is between them as extremes. This analogy of proportion is the basis of *tropes* and *metaphors;* "Cicero was a *pillar* of the state;" "*voice* of the waters;" "*music* of the spheres," etc.

Analogy must not be confounded with *parity* or *equality of ratios in proportion;* v. g., "a mile is the *third part* of a league," "four months are the *third part* of a year;" in real parity of the kind the terms expressing it are used *univocally;* "*third part*" is univocal in the examples given.

ARTICLE IV.

GENUS, SPECIES, DIFFERENCE, ATTRIBUTE, ACCIDENT.

Species includes all that is necessary to constitute the *essence** of many individuals, and the *essence* includes all that is necessary for a thing *to exist* or without which it cannot be conceived

* "Est *essentia* in ordine ad *esse; natura,* prout *principium operationis.*" What we term *essence* in respect to *existence* is called *nature,* when it is regarded as *operative.*

"*Species* immediate subjicitur generi, *individuum,* mediante specie; genus de specie immediate prædicatur, et ea mediante de individuo." *Species* is immediately subject to genus; the *individual* is subject to genus through the medium of species; genus is predicated immediately of species, and *mediately* through species of the individual.

"Est *differentia* per quam species excedit suum genus. Plus continetur *actu* in specie quam in genere; plus autem continetur *potentia* in genere quam in specie, quia genus *potentia* omnem continet inferiorem differentiam." *Difference* is that by which the species exceeds its genus; more is *actually* contained in species than in genus; but more is *potentially* in genus than in species, for genus *potentially* contains every inferior difference in its extension.

by the mind. Now, that cannot be *conceived by the mind* which is absolutely false, absurd, or impossible, and the mind can really and properly conceive nothing but truth, or that which is, and it can form some concept of any real object that is presented to it. Therefore, that which cannot be conceived by the mind is, more strictly, *nothing*. Hence, essence is all *that*, without which a thing cannot exist, cannot be the object of a *concept*,* or is *nothing*. The species is the answer to the question, "what is it?" "what is man?" "Man is a rational animal;" this is an answer which assigns the species of man by its essential constituents.

Genus expresses an attribute or essential property which is common to many species; v. g., *material*, *animal*, which are common to many species of bodies and living things. *Genus* does not express determinately the *whole essence* of its inferiors; while *species* does *express* the *whole essence* of its individuals.

Difference is an attribute or essential property which, when added to the *genus*, along with it constitutes a species; v. g., *rational*, being added to *animal*, constitutes the *species man*. It is here properly called *difference*, because *animal* in general, and *man* in particular, DIFFER by the essential constituent, *rational*.

The *extension* of an idea increases as we ascend from individuals to their species, or from species to its genus; while the *comprehension* decreases; but the *comprehension* increases as we pass from *genus* to *species*, or *species* to *individuals;* while the *extension* decreases. A genus has more *extension* than any of its species, but the species have more *comprehension;* that is, more essential properties.

In respect to *genera*, the *species* may be treated as *individuals;* and similarly genera for still higher genera.

Aristotle's ten *categories*, or ten highest genera, that include all real things, are "substance, quantity, relation, quality, action, passion (action received), place, time, posture, habiliment (cov-

* Do not confound *concept* in the understanding with *image* in the imagination; there are many *concepts* in the intellect of whose objects no real images can be formed by the fancy.

ering or clothing, ornament, armor, etc.)" The categories are the classification into genera and species of all things, according to their mode of existence; "sunt modi existendi."*

The five universals or predicables, genus, difference, species, property or attribute, and accident, are capable of being affirmed, or predicated, of individual inferiors, in all those supreme genera.

The following table, figured as the Porphyrian Tree, exhibits to the eye, genus, species and individuals, as they are respectively related to each other.

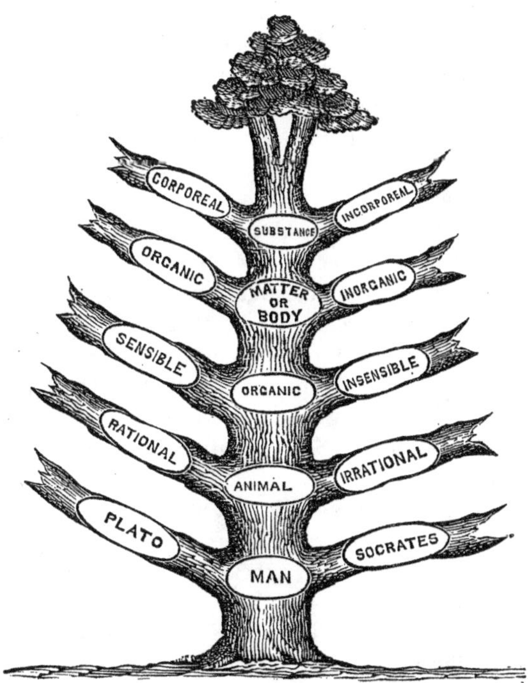

THE PORPHYRIAN TREE.

* "Categoriæ seu prædicamenta sunt ordo seu series generum, specierum et individuorum." "Res prædicamentales seu prædicamenta considerantur a *Logico*, prout *secundis intentionibus* subjacent; spectantur a *Metaphysico*, quatenus *reales*." The categories or predicaments are the order or series of the genera, species and individuals. The things in those categories are considered by the *Logician* as subject to the *second intention;* by the *Metaphysician* they are regarded as *real*. (Vid. p. 20.)

In like manner, each of the ten genera may be resolved into its subjects by adding the respective *specific differences ;* v. g.,

QUANTITY.

DISCRETE.......................CONTINUOUS.

CONTINUOUS.

SURFACE.............................LINE.

SURFACE.

CURVED.............................PLANE.

ETC.

Attributes or properties, and accidents, are found in all the species which are formed out of the genera; and hence, since the five universals are *predicables* of *all* the categories, they are properly denominated *universals ;* and, as there is no other *predicable* that applies to all the categories, they are the *only universals.*

Supreme, or *ultimate genera*, are those which are the highest, and, therefore, cannot be made the species of other genera; v. g., *substance*, which has no superior genus. *Being* (*ens*) is a *transcendental;* it is not a genus, but it is common to every genus, species, and difference; it is, therefore, a common predicate of all things, and for that reason can have no sub-species, for it is not *univocally* predicated of its inferiors, as is required for *genus* or *species.*

As above indicated, the *ultimate genera* are usually called the *categories*, or *predicaments.*

The *proximate*, or *lowest genus*, is that which contains species whose subjects or inferiors are *individuals ;* v. g., *animal* in respect to *man*, for *man* is one species, whose subjects or inferiors are *individual men.*

*Attribute** is a property that necessarily results from the essence of the object to which it belongs; as "the power of rational speech, laughter;" or, what is still more intrinsic, "intelligence, liberty," etc.

* "Proprium est quod prædicatur de pluribus in quale quid seu in quale necessario." Property is that which is predicated of many in what is *essential.*

"Proprium seu attributum est quod convenit speciei omni, soli et semper." Property or attribute is what pertains always and exclusively to the inferiors of the whole species.

Essential attributes, or such as necessarily and always follow the essence of every individual belonging to the species of objects, are absolutely inseparable from the objects to whose essence they belong. All other properties or qualities, though they may be necessary in different degrees for the integrity or perfection of the objects in which they inhere or to which they pertain, are absolutely separable from them, as will be explained in another part of this work.

*Accident** is anything whose presence in the object, or absence from it, does not destroy, or even change the essence of the object; as *learning* in man, *roundness* in marble: the essence of man is not intrinsically changed by the possession or the want of *learning*, nor that of marble by any *particular shape* of it.

ARTICLE V.

DIVISION.

Division † and Definition are employed to facilitate clearness of matter and distinctness of thought, by preventing all confusion arising from multiplicity in the objects of thought and ambiguity in the use of terms.

Division is the separation of a whole into its component parts; a *whole* is that which is one, and yet is capable of this resolution into parts. A *whole* is either *actual* or *logical;* in the first, the parts are *physical* or *real;* as "man's *soul* and *body;*" in the second, they are *metaphysical;* v. g., the *species* and *difference* of objects are only *metaphysically* distinct.

Again, parts are *essential;* as *body* and *soul* in man; or *integral;* as *hands* and *feet* in man. All *universals*, in respect

*"*Accidens* est quod prædicatur de pluribus in quale contingenter. Quod adest et abest sine interitu subjecti." *Accident* is that which is predicated of many in what is *contingent;* it is what may be present or absent without destroying its subject.

† "Bene docet qui bene distinguit." He teaches well, who distinguishes well.

"Per id res constituitur per quod et distinguitur." That which constitutes a thing, is that by which it is also distinguished.

to their extension, may be regarded as logical *wholes;* as also *genus* in respect to the *species*, which it includes; and *species* in respect to its *individuals.* Hence, division is also either *physical* or *metaphysical.*

Logical divisions are, first, of genus into its species; as *animal* into *rational* and *irrational;* second, species into its individuals; as Peter, John, Greeks, Romans, etc.; third, of substance into essential constituents, attributes, accidents; or into essential properties, and qualities which are not essential.

An *attribute*, as already observed, is a property or power that flows immediately from the essence of a thing; as, intelligence in man, freedom, risibility; an *accident* is that which may or may not exist in the subject, and whose presence or absence does not change the essence of its subject, as this color, size, etc.

RULES OF DIVISION.

First—The division must be *adequate*, that is, the sum of the members or parts must be equal to the *whole.* This rule may be violated by *excess*, or by *defect;* by excess, as, v. g., when the ancient philosophers divided souls into "rational, irrational and vegetable;" by defect, v. g., if we divide the motives of human action into "love of glory and love of money."

Second—No member of a division must equal the whole; still less must it exceed the whole; for example, to divide animals into "those endowed with reason, and those endowed with senses," is a violation of this rule; and still more faulty would be a division of trees into "fruit-bearing, and those that are not fruit-bearing, and trees that vegetate."

Third—One member of the division must not include another; as, to divide animals into "rational, irrational and mortal," which is also a violation of the preceding rule.

Fourth—Division should be made, first, into the proximate or immediate members; then, if necessary, into others by subdivision; as in the "porphyrian tree," viz., substance into corporeal and incorporeal; then corporeal into organic and inorganic; organic into vegetable and animal, etc. Any other method would produce confusion rather than clearness.

ARTICLE VI.

DEFINITION.

Division gives the extension of an idea; *definition* its comprehension. *Definition*, then, is a true and complete notion of a thing expressed in words. But definition is twofold—first, *nominal*, that is, of a word; second, *real*, that is, of a thing. Definition of a word is either by its synonym, or by its derivatives or components, or by a periphrasis of its import. General usage determines the signification of words; but when they are *equivocal* a distinct meaning may be attributed to them arbitrarily.

A definition is *real*, first, when it is essential, that is, when it expresses the *essence* or nature of the thing defined; this is done by enumerating the attributes or essential properties of the thing. The essential parts of a thing are either *physical* or *metaphysical;* v. g., man may be defined by his physical essence "*a being composed of a rational soul and an organized body;*" and, again, he may be defined by his essence, metaphysically considered, to be a *rational animal.* A logical definition is one in which the proximate or nearest genus and the specific difference are given; v. g., *a brute is an irrational animal.* Here *brute* is the thing defined; *animal* is the proximate or immediate genus; and *irrational* is the specific difference.

A *descriptive* definition is one in which no genus or species is assigned, but only some accidental circumstances with a general term as a quasi genus; this is resorted to when the object defined transcends all the genera or categories; v. g., being, goodness, unity, etc.

A *genetic definition* is one in which an effect is explained by its cause; v. g., "a *lunar eclipse* is an occultation of the moon, which is caused by the earth directly intervening between the moon and the sun;" "*brass* is a metal produced by the fusion of copper and zinc together."

RULES OF A GOOD DEFINITION.*

First—It must not be more nor less extensive than the thing

* "Una unius definitio est."—Of *one* thing there is but *one definition*.

defined; v. g., if man be defined, "an intelligent being;" the definition is too general, for it includes angel; if he be defined, "a rational being who knows how to read," the definition is faulty, for it is applicable to some men only.

Second—The definition must be clearer than the thing defined; hence, the definition must contain no vague, obscure or equivocal words; v. g., "logwood is a species of wood; life is vitality," are offences against this rule.

Third—A definition must not be negative; for in such a case the definition would not declare what the thing defined is, but only what it is not; v. g., "a bird is a creature that is not rational." But if two contraries, between which there is no medium, are to be defined, when one is positively defined the other may be given as its negative or opposite; v. g., "a compound is that which consists of parts; a simple substance is that which does not consist of parts."

Fourth—A substance must be defined in itself; accidents may be defined by the substance in which they adhere; v. g., "man is a rational animal; motion is change of place by a body."

Fifth—Habits and powers must be defined by their acts, or by the objects of those acts; v. g., "Meekness is the virtue by which we restrain the motions of anger; the will is the power of choosing between things that are judged to be good; sight, the power of distinguishing objects by figure and color."

CHAPTER II.

ARTICLE I.

JUDGMENT.

Judgment is an act of the mind, by which it affirms the agreement or disagreement of two concepts or ideas. When they are affirmed to agree, the judgment is *affirmative;* when they are affirmed to disagree, the judgment is *negative;* v. g., "The soul is a spirit; God is not a creature."

These two judgments by which the mind affirms the identity or diversity of two ideas by conjoining or separating them are termed respectively *composition* and *division* in respect to the ideas, which are the matter or elements; and they are also *affirmation* or *negation*, in respect to the identity or diversity of the things compared.

When the identity or diversity of the ideas is self-evident, or one is seen to be necessarily included in the other, it is a *judgment a priori;* v. g., "the sum of the parts is equal to the whole; a part is not equal to the whole." Such judgments are also often termed *necessary*, *metaphysical*, *pure* or *analytical* judgments. But when the identity or diversity in the objects of those ideas is learned solely by experience, then it is a *judgment a posteriori;* v. g., "fire gives pain when it burns." These judgments are also termed *contingent*, *physical*, *empyrical* or *synthetical.*

Judgments, both *a priori* and *a posteriori*, are sometimes *mediate*, sometimes *immediate*, according as they are formed with or without the medium of reasoning. *A priori* judgments suppose a necessary identity or diversity in the objects compared; *a posteriori* judgments suppose a mere contingent relation or connexion, learned only by experience.

ARTICLE II.

PROPOSITIONS.

A proposition is a judgment expressed in words; v. g., "man is mortal; prudence is a virtue." A proposition consists of three parts: the *subject*, *copula*, and *predicate* or *attribute*. The *subject* is that of which something is affirmed; the *predicate* is that which is affirmed; and the *copula* is the term that connects or *couples* the subject and predicate. For example, in the proposition, "*diligence is praiseworthy*," the *subject* is "*diligence*;" the *copula* is the verb "*is*," and the predicate is "*praiseworthy*."

Logic recognizes but one verb, and but one mood and tense, viz.: the verb *to be* in the indicative mood and in the present tense. The reason of this is, the affirmation is always indicative and present; v. g., "Cæsar conquered; James writes," are equivalent to the affirmation; that which is expressed by "*conquered*" is predicated of Cæsar, etc. All that is not expressed by this verb belongs to the predicate, for it is *attributed* to the subject.

Propositions may be considered in respect to their *quality* and their *quantity* or extension. The two concepts compared to each other are the *matter;* the *perceiving* of their agreement or disagreement is the *form* of the proposition; since the copula either affirms or denies agreement, the *quality* and *form* of a proposition are indeed the same.

Propositions as to their *form* or quality are either *affirmative* or *negative*. In an *affirmative* proposition the predicate is declared to agree with the subject. In the *negative* proposition the predicate *is denied* or declared *not* to agree with the subject.

In an affirmative proposition the predicate is taken according to the whole of its comprehension; but not according to the whole of its extension. In the proposition, "*air is a body*," the predicate "*body*" is taken according to the whole of its *comprehension;* that is, all the attributes or essential properties included in *body*, as such, are predicated of *air*, or said to be verified in *air;* but, as there are many objects besides *air* which are *body*, the *predicate*, *body*, is not taken in its whole *extension;* and it is, therefore, said to be *particular* in affirmative propositions.

In such propositions as this, "man is a rational animal," the predicate is commensurate in comprehension with the subject; not, however, in virtue of the form, but by accidental coincidence. Good definitions are thus convertible and true.

In a negative proposition the predicate is taken according to the whole of its extension; v. g., "matter is not intelligent;" that is, matter is not one of those objects of which *intelligence* can ever be predicated.

When any term is thus taken, according to the whole of its extension, or universally, it is said to be *distributed.* Therefore, in a negative proposition the predicate is always distributed; that is, is taken as universal, or in all its extent.

In an affirmative proposition, the predicate is *particular*, as already observed. The subject of a proposition is distributed if taken as a universal; as "every man is mortal;" "no metal has sensation."

Quantity or extension of propositions: quantity or extension regards the *extent* of the propositions; that is, as being *universal* or *particular;* when universal, the subject of the proposition is taken according to its entire extension; v. g., "all men are mortal." It is particular when the subject is taken according to a part only of its extension; v. g., "some men are learned."

Universality, in reference to the matter of the proposition, may be, first, *metaphysical*, as when the proposition expresses a judgment *a priori;* v. g., "a part is less than the whole;" second, it may be *physical*, as when it is according to the laws of nature, which, however, are contingent; v. g., "the dead do not return to life;" third, it may be a *moral* universality, that is, when it is taken according to the ordinary action of moral causes; v. g., "a mother loves her child." In respect to the last two, exception is not *absolutely* impossible.

A proposition is either *categorical* or *hypothetical.* It is *categorical* when it positively and unconditionally affirms the agreement or disagreement of the predicate with the subject.

A *hypothetical* proposition affirms conditionally; v. g., "if you are virtuous, you will be rewarded." This species of enunciation *implies an argument;* and under that respect it may be regarded as pertaining to the third operation of the intellect; i. e., to *reasoning*. It consists of two propositions; the first, or *antecedent*, which affirms the condition; the second is the *consequent*, whose truth depends on the verification of the *antecedent.* A hypothetical proposition is true, if the connexion between the antecedent and consequent be true. It is sometimes disjunctive in form; "every body is either in motion, or at rest." Such a disjunctive is not true when there is a medium; v. g., "John must either write or come to see me." It is possible that he may do neither.

A term, or a proposition, is taken *reduplicatively*, or by *reduplication*, when any particles or clauses are annexed to it which have the effect of *doubling* or *repeating* it, in order that the sense in which it is used may be rigorously defined; v. g., "all substance *as* substance, is good;" "a being, *so far forth* as it is free, is necessarily intelligent;" "water, *as such*, is composed of eight parts of oxygen with one part of hydrogen." When a term is used *reduplicatively*, it is restricted to a precise signification; the limiting words and phrases are, *as such*, *as*, *so far forth*, *precisely taken*, and the like.

ARTICLE III.

OPPOSITION.

For *opposition** between two propositions, first, they must have the same subject; secondly, they must have the same predicate; thirdly, one must, in some sense of the terms, affirm what the other denies. Hence, opposition is a mutual *repugnance* between two propositions, arising from the affirmation and negation of the same thing in the same respect.

* "Oppositio est affirmatio et negatio ejusdem de eodem." Opposition is the affirmation and negation of the same thing in regard to the same object.

This opposition is twofold, first, of *contradiction;* second, of *contrariety;* in *contradictory* propositions, one simply denies the other; v. g., "all souls are substance;" the contradictory, "not all souls are substance." A negative prefixed to any affirmative proposition forms its contradictory, because any particular and negative proposition is the contradictory of the opposite universal proposition.

Contrary* propositions are both of them extreme; that is, what one of them affirms as universal, the other denies with equal universality; v. g., "*no miser* is happy;" the contrary, "*all misers* are happy."

Hence, a contradictory merely denies its opposite, while the contrary goes further, and affirms its equally general opposite.

Of two contradictories, one is necessarily true and the other false; two contraries cannot, at the same time, be true; but both of them may be false; v. g., "all good men are prosperous in this world; no good man is prosperous in this world;" these propositions are both false.

Subcontrary propositions are both *particular*, and they differ in *quality;* that is, one is affirmative and the other negative; as, "some men are honored;" "some men are not honored." Subcontraries may both be true, but they cannot both be false; for, if both were false, they would make two contradictories to be both false, which cannot be; v. g., "some men are learned;" "some men are not learned." It is evident that both of these propositions cannot be false.

* "Contraria juxta se posita magis lucescunt." When contraries are put near to each other they become clearer.

"Contraria versantur circa idem." Contraries regard the same thing.

CHAPTER III.

ARTICLE I.

REASONING.

The power in the soul by which it *perceives*, *judges*, *reasons*, is termed the *understanding*, the *judgment*, the *reason*, according to the act which it performs; yet, it is one and the same power that *understands*, *judges* and *reasons*. All the powers of the soul that are concerned in the acts of *knowing*, when taken collectively, constitute the *mind;* hence, the *soul* is the spiritual substance with its perfections; the *mind* is the aggregate of its powers or faculties, the understanding, consciousness, will and memory; but *mind*, more particularly, stands for the power in the soul of *knowing*.

Every process of reasoning is reducible to *an act* of the mind by which it determines the agreement or disagreement, the identity or diversity of two things, by comparing them to a third; v. g., "that which is designed is the work of an intelligent cause; the world shows design; therefore, the world is the work of an intelligent cause." The two things here compared to a third, are the "world" and "the work of an intelligent cause;" and the third thing to which they are compared is that which is "*designed*," with which they both agree, and, therefore, they agree with each other.

All reasoning or argument rests on this self-evident principle: "when two things are each equal to a third thing, they are equal to each other;" "when one of two things is equal, and the other unequal to a third thing, they are unequal to each other." Take care to observe, however, that when the two things are *both unequal* to a third, it does not follow that they are either equal or unequal to each other.

The truth of this agreement or disagreement of two things, following from their relation to a third, is termed the *consequence* or *sequence;* and the proposition which expresses that agreement or disagreement, as following from the comparison, is called the *conclusion* or *consequent.*

Hence, an act of reasoning, or an argument expressed in full, consists of three judgments or propositions; the first two are a comparison; and the third, or conclusion, affirms the consequent which follows from this comparison; v. g.,

> "All virtue is commendable;
> Diligence is a virtue;
> Therefore, diligence is commendable."

Here "diligence" and "commendable" are both compared to "virtue," and judged to agree with it; the agreement of "diligence" and "commendable" is perceived *to follow* from their agreement with "virtue"; and the truth of that agreement thus following, is the *sequence* or *consequence* which is declared in the third proposition or conclusion, "diligence is commendable." *Sequence,* therefore, expresses the *dependence* of the conclusion on the premises; and is truly there when the conclusion or *consequent really follows* from the premises.

ARTICLE II.

THE SYLLOGISM AND ITS LAWS.

An argument expressed in the preceding form is termed a *syllogism;* hence, a syllogism is defined to be "an argument consisting of three propositions so related to each other that, the first two being granted, the third necessarily follows from them." The first two propositions are sometimes termed the *antecedent;* also, the *premises;* and the *conclusion* is sometimes termed the *consequent;* which, however, must not be confounded with *consequence* or *sequence.*

The peculiar and specific act of *reason,* by which its nature is defined, is, the *knowing of one thing from another; i. e.*, reason is the power of deriving the knowledge of one thing from the knowledge of another by means of the relation between the two. (*Vide rule fifth for a good definition.*)

The syllogism is the *formula* for the act of deriving the knowledge of one thing from that of another by means of their relation to each other. There is no other mode of learning truth proper to *reason* as such; for, it belongs only to *intelligence* to perceive truth directly in itself, and not by means of its relation to other truth. To reject the syllogism, therefore, as a mode of acquiring truth, is to reject reason itself. Nor, in fact, is it possible to state an argument against the syllogism without virtually employing that very form itself; for the argument itself would be an exercise of *reason*, inasmuch as it would be a formal effort to derive the knowledge of one thing from that of another to which it was assumed to be related.

When the propositions of a syllogism are *categorical*, the syllogism is *categorical;* and when they are *hypothetical*, it also is *hypothetical.*

A syllogism consists of three propositions, each containing two terms, and each one of these terms is named twice in the syllogism: these terms are the *subjects* and *predicates* of the propositions.

The subject and predicate of the conclusion are the *extremes*, the former being the *minor extreme* or *term*, and the latter the *major extreme* or *term.*

The *major premise* is strictly the one which contains the *major extreme;* and the *minor premise* the one which contains the *minor extreme.* But in *practice*, the premise which comes first is generally termed the *major*, and the other the *minor* premise.

The term twice named in the *premises* to which the *extremes* are compared is called the *middle term;* in the preceding syllogism "diligence" is the minor extreme, because it is the subject of the conclusion; "commendable" is the major extreme, because it is the predicate of the conclusion; and "virtue" is the *middle term*, because it is the one to which the two others are compared.

The *rectitude* of the conclusion, as already observed, depends on its *sequence;* that is, on its *following* from the premises; its *truth* depends on the nature of the *matter.*

Observe, that in the following syllogism—

"Every virtue is hateful;
Patience is a virtue;
Therefore, patience is hateful;"

There is *rectitude* of conclusion, but it has not *truth,* because one premise is false in matter.

The conclusion may express truth, and yet not follow from the premises; v. g.,

"All virtue is good;
Health is not a virtue;
Therefore, health is good."

Here there is truth of matter, but not *rectitude* or *sequence* of conclusion.

The requisites of a correct, simple or categorical syllogism are expressed in the following rules or canons:

Rule First: The syllogism must contain three, and only three, terms.

Rule Second: No term can have greater *extension* in the conclusion than it had in the premises.

Rule Third: The conclusion must never contain the middle term.

Rule Fourth: The middle term must be, at least once, distributed; that is, it must be, at least once, taken according to the whole of its *extension.*

Rule Fifth: A negative conclusion cannot follow from two affirmative premises.

Rule Sixth: No conclusion follows from two negative premises.

Rule Seventh: The conclusion follows the less *worthy* premise.

Rule Eighth: No conclusion follows from two particular premises.

First Rule: The reason of this rule is obvious, if we reflect that a syllogism is founded on a comparison of two terms with a third; and, hence, if there were four terms, it would not be a syllogism, but several comparisons from which there could follow no certain conclusion; since the terms might agree in pairs, or disagree, without any relation to a *third term*. There may be four terms *explicitly* or *implicitly;* v. g.,

> "Diligence is commendable;
> But anger is not a virtue;
> Therefore, anger is not commendable."

This syllogism contains four terms *explicitly*. But when four terms are used, it is generally done by employing the middle term in two senses:

> '*Cæsar* is a word of two syllables;
> But Brutus killed Cæsar;
> Therefore, Brutus killed a word of two syllables."

In this syllogism *Cæsar* is used in two senses—as a *word* and for a *person*; hence, when the middle term is ambiguous, it is equivalent to two terms.

Second Rule: If a term have greater extent in the conclusion than it had in the premises, there would then be inferred from the premises what is not contained in them; but the conclusion, from its nature, is that which *follows* from the premises; v. g.,

> "Every animal is a substance;
> No tree is an animal;
> Therefore, a tree is not a substance."

In this syllogism "substance" is a *particular* term in the premises, while it is universal in the conclusion; that is, in the premises "substance" is compared to the middle term only as to a part of its extent; while in the conclusion it is denied of "tree," according to its whole extension.

Hence the conclusion, as such, can have no greater extension than its premises.

The fact that we frequently derive the knowledge of that which is greater from the knowledge of that which is less, as, for example, when from their relation we infer a cause from an effect, which, as such, is inferior to it, is not adverse to this rule when rightly understood. The conclusion must not have greater *extension* than the premises; but it may have more *comprehension;* nay, its terms, in some sense, *must* have greater comprehension; for the conclusion is the synthesis of a subject and predicate which is not made in the premises.*

THIRD RULE: If the middle term be used in the conclusion, nothing would be inferred; since the conclusion in that case would be but a repetition, in some shape, of one premise, and, therefore, it would not express a *sequence;* v. g.,

> "All virtue is commendable;
> Kindness is a virtue;
> Therefore, virtue is commendable."

FOURTH RULE: If the middle term be not, at least once, distributed; that is, be not at least once a universal, it would be equivalent to two terms; for it might be taken, according to one part of its extent, in one premise, and according to another part in the other; whence the major and minor terms would be compared to two things instead of one; v. g.,

> "Every man is an *animal;*
> Every bird is an *animal;*
> Therefore, every man is a bird."

In this syllogism "man" is compared to "animal," taken according to one part of its extension, and "bird," according to another part; whence, as the two extremes are not compared to the same term, no conclusion legitimately follows.

The *subject* of every *universal* proposition is distributed, and it is not distributed in any other than a universal proposition; the *predicate* of every *negative* proposition is distributed, and it is not distributed in any but a negative proposition.

FIFTH RULE: A negative conclusion cannot follow from two affirmative premises; for, when they affirm the agreement of the major and minor terms with the middle, the conclusion must affirm the consequent agreement of the major and minor; v. g., "a substance whose action, or mode of operation, exceeds

* "Semper enim est potior causa suo effectu."—Div. Th. 1, 2, p. q. 66, a. 1. The cause is always superior, in some respect, to its effect.

the powers of matter, is above matter; the actions of the human soul transcend the powers of matter; therefore, the human soul is a substance which is superior to matter," is a correct syllogism by this rule.

SIXTH RULE: When the premises deny the agreement of both the major and minor terms with the middle term, then nothing is affirmed as to the identity or diversity of the major and minor; it is only declared that they do not agree with the middle term; hence, when both extremes disagree with the middle term, they may either agree or disagree with each other; v. g.,

> "A reptile is not a bird;
> A snake is not a bird;
> Therefore, a snake is not a reptile."

This conclusion, though false in matter, derives neither truth nor falsehood from the premises.

> "A bird is not a reptile;
> A tree is not a reptile;
> Therefore, a tree is not a bird."

This conclusion is true in matter, but it does not follow from the premises.

SEVENTH RULE: The unworthy premise is that which is *negative*, in respect to that which is *affirmative;* and that which is *particular*, in respect to that which is *universal.* The reason of the rule will become obvious if it be observed that when one premise affirms the agreement of its extreme term with the middle term, and the agreement of the other term with the middle is denied in the remaining premise, it follows that the extremes disagree with each other; v. g.,

> "If A is equal to B,
> And C is not equal to B;
> Then C is not equal to A."

Or

> "None but organized, living, corporeal beings are mortal;
> Angels are not corporeal beings;
> Therefore, angels are not mortal."

Again, if a term which is particular in the premises, be made universal in the conclusion, in such case, an agreement will be affirmed in the conclusion which is not implied in the premises; v. g.,

> "All virtue is commendable;
> Some parsimony is a virtue;
> Therefore, all parsimony is commendable."

Here the conclusion affirms that *all* parsimony agrees with "commendable," though in the premises it is only said that *some* parsimony agrees with "virtue," the middle term. Hence, this is, at the same time, a fault against the second rule.

EIGHTH RULE: When both premises are particular, neither term is distributed; and hence the extremes may be actually compared to different parts of the same extension; v. g.,

> "Some Cretans were liars;
> Some Romans were liars;
> Therefore, some Cretans were Romans."

This is a vicious syllogism; for the major and minor terms agree with "liars" in different parts of its extension; therefore, since they are not compared to the same thing, it does not follow from the premises either that they agree or that they disagree with each other. This syllogism is wrong by rule the fourth also, since the middle term is not distributed. Yet, even when the terms are all singular, the conclusion may be valid; v. g.,

> "Romulus was the founder of Rome;
> The first king of Rome was Romulus
> Therefore, the first king of Rome was the founder of Rome."

Here the conclusion is really consequent, for the middle term, "Romulus," may be considered as virtually a common term taken according to its whole extent and including "founder of Rome," and "first king of Rome;" this is termed by the old philosophers, an *expository syllogism*. It is an apparent exception to the eighth rule. When the three terms are *really singular*, they may be identical as to their *object;* and then it is not a real argument, but a sort of definition, by synonyms; v. g.,

> "Man is a rational animal;
> Man consists of soul and body;
> Therefore, a rational animal consists of soul and body.

This also is an *expository syllogism*.

ARTICLE III.

HYPOTHETICAL OR CONDITIONAL SYLLOGISMS; THE DISJUNCTIVE SYLLOGISM.

A hypothetical syllogism is one in which a categorical conclusion is deduced from a hypothetical premise. In a hypothetical proposition, the conclusion or consequent is verified when the condition is verified; hence, when the major proposition is conditional, i. e., has a condition which is expressed by "if," or its equivalent, in the minor the truth of the condition is affirmed as a categorical proposition, from which the truth of the conclusion follows; or the truth of the *consequent* is denied; whence the falsity of the condition will result; v. g.,

> "If Brutus killed Cæsar, then Cæsar is dead;
> But Brutus did kill Cæsar;
> Therefore, Cæsar is dead."

In such syllogisms, then, the minor premise may either affirm the truth of the condition, or deny the truth of the conclusion; in the first case, the consequent will be the conclusion of the syllogism; v. g., "Cæsar is dead;" in the second, the denial of the condition will be the conclusion of the syllogism; v. g., "Brutus did not kill Cæsar;" and in both cases, the argument will be *in form*, that is, *consequent.*

But, as regards the *matter*, it does not follow that if the condition be false, the consequent is therefore false; for it may be true for some other reason; v. g., even if Brutus did not kill Cæsar, still Cæsar may be dead from some other cause.

Again, it does not follow that if the consequent be true the condition is therefore true, for the consequent might be verified by a different condition; v. g., though it may be granted that Cæsar is dead, it does not therefore follow that he was *killed.*

In such hypothetical enunciations as the following, "if man is a *mineral,* he does not *feel;*" the *consequent* has not *real,* but only *suppositive* truth, for the antecedent is merely an arbitrary *supposition.*

Hence, when, in a conditional proposition, the truth of the

affirmative *consequent* is really dependent on that of the affirmative *antecedent;* or, also, when the *antecedent* is so included in the *consequent*, that the denial of the *consequent* necessarily implies the denial of the *antecedent*, we have for the conditional argument the following

RULE: First, In the affirmative conditional, the minor premise must affirm the *antecedent*, and the conclusion must affirm the *consequent;* v. g., "if the soul reasons, it is a simple substance; but the soul does reason; therefore the soul is a simple substance." Second, In the *negative conditional*, the minor premise must deny the *consequent*, and the conclusion must deny the *antecedent*, observing that two negatives in English are equivalent to an affirmative; v. g., "if the soul perishes when the body dies, then the soul is not a spiritual substance; but the soul is (*is not not*) a spiritual substance; therefore, the soul does *not* perish when the body dies."

As regards the *form* of the hypothetical or conditional argument the preceding rule is absolute, or it admits no exception. But it may happen by *accident*, or in virtue of the *matter*, that the conclusion is true, even when these rules are inverted; as, for example, when the *antecedent* is the *sufficient reason* of the *consequent;* if the *antecedent is denied*, the *consequent* may also be denied; v. g., "if the sun is at the meridian, it is noon; *but the sun is not at the meridian;* therefore, it is *not noon.*" This conclusion is true, not in virtue of the *form*, but on account of the *matter;* in other words, it is not *logically consequent*, though it is *materially true.*

Also, when the *condition* and *consequent* are in matter *identical* and co-extensive, by accident, and not in virtue of the form, the falsity of the condition infers the falsity of the conclusion; v. g., "if Apollo was not a man, then he was not a rational animal; but he was a man; therefore, he was a rational animal": "if man is immortal, he will not die; but he is not immortal; therefore, he will die." As the condition and conditionate are identical, the falsity of one always infers, necessarily, the falsity of the other, on account of that *identity.* This species of argument, for its brevity, is used in practice; and when the *matter* is true, the proof of the *condition* is the proof, also, of the *conditionate;* or *vice versa.* The *same* thing which is misunderstood or denied under one form of expression, may be seen and admitted under another; hence, this mode of proof is legitimate, and may be useful in some cases.

A syllogism is *disjunctive* when it proceeds from a disjunctive proposition. The disjunction of the antecedent and consequent is perfect when they divide the whole matter so as to admit no medium; v. g., "man is either mortal, or not mortal;" in man there can be no medium between mortality and immortality. The truth or rectitude of the disjunction is determined by the matter. In the completely disjunctive syllogism, the admission of one member of the disjunction requires the denial of the other; v. g., "either man is mortal, or he is immortal; but he is mortal; therefore, he is *not* immortal;" "the honor of first discovering America belongs either to Americus or to Columbus; it belongs to Columbus; therefore, it does not belong to Americus." When one member of a disjunctive premise is merely the contradictory of the other, if the affirmative one be granted, the negative one has a double negation, which is really an affirmative; v. g., "either it rains, or it does not rain; it does rain; therefore, it does *not not* rain;" i. e., it does rain.

ARTICLE IV.

OTHER FORMS OF ARGUMENT WHICH MAY BE REDUCED TO THE SYLLOGISTIC FORM.

The *enthymeme* is a syllogism, one of whose premises is not expressed; v. g., "the poor are men; therefore, they are not to be contemned." The sorites is a series of propositions in which the predicate of the first is the subject of the second, the predicate of the second is the subject of the third, and so on till the last or conclusion, in which the predicate of the last proposition is conjoined to the subject of the first proposition;

v. g., "he who does not restrain his passions, has many violent desires; he that has many violent desires, is unquiet; he that is unquiet, is miserable; therefore, he that does not restrain his passions is miserable." Both these forms of argument consist of abridged syllogisms.

The *epycherema* is a syllogism in which one or both of the premises are proved, each by its reason; or it has its reason annexed to it in the syllogism; v. g., "every spiritual substance is incorruptible, since it neither has parts nor depends on matter; but the human soul is a spiritual substance, since it is intelligent; therefore, the human soul is incorruptible."

The *dilemma* is a compound argument which consists of two members proposed disjunctively, and so related that the legitimate conclusion from either member, or *horn*, is a refutation of the adversary; v. g., "the skeptic's denial of all certainty is either true or false; if true, then that is certain; if false, still more is there certainty; therefore, in either supposition, scepticism is false."

This argument is called a *dilemma*, because it consists of but *two members*. The *trilemma* and *quadrilemma* are too complicated to be ordinarily useful in reasoning.

A dilemma is faulty; 1st, If the division of the matter made by the disjunctive be not *complete;* in other words, if there be a medium of escape from it. The dilemma put into the mouth of Socrates when dying, has this fault: "Death is either a sweet sleep, or it is a transition to the happy companionship of Orpheus and Ulysses; in either case, therefore, it is good to die." Between "sleep" and the "society of Ulysses," there is a wide medium. But when the early Christians said to the Roman tyrant, "either we are innocent, or we are guilty; if innocent, why condemn us? if guilty, why refuse us a lawful trial?" between men's *innocence and guilt*, and also between the corresponding provisions of the law, there is no medium. 2d, The *conclusion* derived from one, or each member of the dilemma, may not be *legitimate;* in this case, it not only proves nothing, but it may be *retorted;* v. g., it was said to a judge, who was about to enter into office, "you will administer the laws either well or ill; if well, you will displease the people; if ill, you will displease the gods;" he retorted, "I will administer the laws justly or unjustly; if justly, I shall not displease the gods; if unjustly, I shall not displease the people."

Another example of the dilemma which may be retorted: Protagoras bargained to educate Euathlus for the law, half of the money to be paid when his studies were finished, the rest when Euathlus gained his *first suit;* after some time Protagoras sued Euathlus, and this was the first case for Euathlus. Protagoras thus argued: "Either Euathlus will lose or gain this case; if he lose it, then the money is to be paid me by the *decision of the court;* if he gain it, then he must pay me by our *contract.*" Euathlus retorted: "If the decision is in my favor, then I will pay nothing by the *sentence of the court;* if against me, I will pay nothing according to the *contract*, since I will not have gained my *first case.*" The fallacy really arises from Protagoras having, *by the contract*, no right to bring the suit, as he was to wait till Euathlus *gained his first case;* hence, the disjunction did not include *the whole matter.* Euathlus' dilemma was at fault, because he assumed that the judge's decision would annul the contract, or exempt him from paying, if he gained the suit; and Protagoras was wrong for assuming the canceling of the contract, in case the decision of the judge was adverse to his disciple.

A sophist argued: "You say that you *lie;* and if you speak the truth, then you do *lie;* if you say *falsely* that you *lie*, then also you *lie;* therefore, whether you speak truly or falsely, you *lie.*" He does "lie" in each case, but not about the same thing, and under the same respect.

CHAPTER IV.

ARTICLE I.

SCIENTIFIC METHOD: ANALYSIS AND SYNTHESIS, IN THEIR RELATION BOTH TO PARTICULAR SCIENTIFIC COGNITIONS, AND TO SYSTEMS OF SUCH COGNITIONS.

There are two methods which the mind follows in acquiring or imparting knowledge by reasoning; namely, *Analysis* and *Synthesis.* In *analysis* the mind proceeds from the compound to its simple components, from the particular object to the general truth; but in *synthesis* this order is inverted, and the mind proceeds from the simple to the compound, from the general to the particular.

The particular, *as this man*, *this rose*, is compound, or has many component *marks* or *properties*, while the universal has but *one mark;* hence, the process of going from a particular object or truth to the general or universal, is *analysis.* When we say that the particular is compound, we regard the *comprehension* of the term. The more general the term is, the greater its *extension*, but the less its *comprehension;* v. g., the term *man* includes many *marks*, as, "substance," "animal," "rational"; the term *being* includes but *one mark*, but, as to its extension, it is applicable to all things.

When by argument we proceed from a subject to a predicate, the method of reasoning is *analytical;* when the reasoning is from the predicate to the subject, the method is *synthetical.* A simple syllogism is synthetical; a sorites may combine in it both synthesis and analysis. But *analysis* and *synthesis* may also regard the general method by which a series of cognitions, a particular system of knowledge or a particular science is acquired or taught; however, they are always distinguished from each other in the same manner. By *analysis* we resolve what is complex into its simple constituents; by *synthesis* we form one whole out of many constituents. By analysis we find the *extension* of terms, ideas or propositions; by synthesis we find their *comprehension*.*

In all lengthy trains of reasoning both synthesis and analysis may occur, whether the *general method* be conducted according to the one or the other. Induction, as a *method* of acquiring science, is *analysis;* regarded as a *syllogism*, it is *synthesis;* for, as a general method of scientific reasoning, it deduces universal principles from particular facts, and this is analysis. When its *conclusions* are *finally* established, it is by one argument concerning the *whole class* in which a law or property is *predicated* of them; this is synthesis, and yet it pertains to the induction. When a property is deduced from a substance; when algebraic formulæ are resolved by transformation into more general formulæ; the process in each case is analysis; for, in these instances, the *universal* is deduced from the *particular*. When we predicate the effect of the cause, or pass from the general truth to the particular object, the process is synthesis. Analysis is called, also, the method of *invention;* synthesis the method of *discipline*, or *instruction*.

Observe, however, that in *education*, considered as to its general scope and progress, knowledge advances by *analysis;* for the progress of the mind in education thus generally understood, is from the particular to the universal; from what is less universal to what is more universal; but yet the *particular* steps or acts of cognition by which the mind proceeds, are, as already remarked, both those of synthesis and those of analysis. This will be easily understood if it be kept in mind that to *deduce* a *general property* from its subject is *analysis;* to *predicate* is *synthesis*. The mind, by the law of its nature, begins with the knowledge of physical and sensible objects, reasons to their general properties; it passes from quantity to its general properties, and finally attains to strictly metaphysical truth;

* "Multa ex uno analysis, unum ex multis efficit synthesis." Analysis makes many out of one; synthesis makes one out of many.

i. e., to the most absolute and universal truth. This progress of the intellect, considered as to its general method and final result, is *analytical.* But the particular arguments or acts of reasoning in this advance of the intellect towards what is most universal, are sometimes synthetical, sometimes analytical, in their method; v. g., when the universal axioms of geometry are proved to be verified in particular figures, or parts of quantity, this is synthesis; but when, by comparing the parts or divisions of particular figures, general conclusions are deduced from them, this is analysis.

If we conceive *genus* as *composed* of species, and *species* as *composed* of individuals, then to resolve *genus* into its species thus assumed to be its components, and resolve *species* into individuals, is *analysis.* But this, however, would not be a strictly correct mode of conceiving the *universals*, genus and species. Since analysis is the resolution of that which is *compounded* into its constituents, it properly regards the *comprehension* of its object, not the *extension.* Yet, it may sometimes be convenient to conceive *extension* as consisting of component parts of quantity; in which case it is to be regarded as capable of *analysis*, in a wider sense of the term.

ARTICLE II.

DEMONSTRATION.

Demonstration is a legitimate argument in which an evident conclusion necessarily follows from evident premises. Its premises are either *immediately* evident in themselves; or they are *mediately* evident as necessary conclusions from other premises, which are evident. Such demonstration is *simple* when it contains but one argument, or syllogism; it is *complex* when it contains two or more arguments. The premises are *prior* to the conclusion; they are the *cause* of the conclusion; they are better *known* than the conclusion.

A demonstration is *direct* when the conclusion is evident from the agreement of the subject and predicate; v. g., "the first cause must be independent of any preceding cause; now, God is the first cause; therefore, God is independent of all preceding cause."

The demonstration is *indirect* when it is shown that the contradictory of a proposition necessarily leads to an absurdity; v. g., "God is either eternal, or he is not;" to say that "God is not eternal," is to affirm a proposition that leads to absurdity; for that which is not eternal is produced by some cause; but by the hypothesis, "God is not eternal;" therefore God, the first cause, is produced by some cause; which is absurd.

A demonstration may be either *a priori* or *a posteriori*. When the truth of the conclusion depends upon, and proceeds from, the truth of its evident premises, as its necessary cause, the argument is *a priori;* but when the truth of the premises logically depends upon the truth of the conclusion, then the argument is *a posteriori;* in the first case the reasoning is from principles to their results, or this is to reason *a priori;* but in *a posteriori* reasoning, the process is from the results to the principles or causes.

It is to be observed that the *a priori* method of argument regards truths taken in their *ontological* order; the *ontological* order proceeds according to the real relation which they bear to each other as cause and effect, in themselves considered; and in this respect the cause is *prior* to the *effect*. The *logical* or *psychological* order regards the relation to each other in which we first *know* or *learn* them; which, in many cases, is in the reverse order; that is, by passing from the knowledge of the effects to the knowledge of their causes: taking truths in this order, is to learn or reason *a posteriori*.

A thing may be *prior* to another, either *physically* or *metaphysically;* a thing is *physically prior* to another, when it is the real cause of the other; it is *metaphysically prior*, when it is an *essence* from which *attributes** are conceived as emanating; or in which they are conceived as inhering; for essence is *metaphysically* prior to *attribute* or *quality* of any kind.

* "Proprium seu attributum est quod fluit ab essentia ratione formæ." Property or attribute is what flows from essence in virtue of the formal principle in that essence.

ARTICLE III.

INDUCTION.

Induction is an argument in which we conclude that, because some property or law is true of each individual of a class, or, at least, of a large number of them, it is necessarily a property or law of the whole class. An inductive argument, in form, would run thus: "a property, or law, that is common to each individual of a class, belongs to all the class; but it is a law of each heavy body to gravitate towards the centre of the earth; therefore, etc."

The force of the conclusion depends on the uniformity and universality of the facts observed; it affords certainty for many physical laws of material objects; because the action of such agents is physically necessary, and is, circumstances being the same, constant and uniform. But as regards the laws of still more strictly contingent beings; that is, things that really depend on mutable *free agency* for their existence, or, as to whether they will happen or not, the conclusion can seldom strictly afford more than probable or conjectural certainty.

There are few classes of real objects in respect to which one mind, or even several minds, can actually make a complete induction. But the general observation of mankind, extending through a great length of time, affords proof that is, in many cases, perfectly conclusive, both as to facts and their obvious causes. The induction from facts universally attested, is sometimes first formally made by one superior mind; as, when Newton inferred the law of gravitation, the general induction being suggested by the falling of an apple from the tree. It is a law or rule that all heavy objects near the earth's surface gravitate towards its centre, whatever may be the hypothesis employed to explain the cause.

Some predicates can be affirmed of a class distributively, but not collectively; and *vice versa*, some can be affirmed of it collectively, but not distributively. When a predicate pertains to a part, or a member, or some members, of a class, *only as such*, then such predicate cannot be affirmed of the whole class. For example, "a part of a class is incomplete; therefore, the whole class is incomplete." Here, *incomplete* is predicated of a part, *as such*, or by *reduplication*, as it is termed. A similar remark applies to predicates which can be affirmed of the whole class, *only as such:* "a hundred years make a century; therefore, each year of the hundred makes a century;" which is absurd.

Induction affords a prudent rule for the observation and study of natural phenomena; but it is neither a new nor a distinct method of acquiring or imparting science; since man has observed facts and drawn conclusions from his observations ever since the days of Adam. Though Lord Bacon made no new discovery in Logic or Philosophy when he explained induction, and insisted so much on the extensive and accurate observation of facts, before laying down their principles; yet his writings stimulated scientific research and helped much to the advancement of physical science.

ARTICLE IV.

PROBABLE ARGUMENT.

Probability in objects of cognition is an appearance of truth, coming from a greater force of argument on one side, which inclines the mind to assent to that side as true, but yet leaving room for doubt or fear that the opposite may be true. Both sides of a proposition may, in respect to our knowledge, be truly probable.

An argument is merely *probable* when *one* of its premises is only *probable;* for a still greater reason, it is merely *probable* when both premises are only probable. A proposition is *probable* only, when there are good reasons for assenting to it, yet there is a *possibility*, amounting to any *degree of probability*, that its opposite may be true. For probability, as such, is essentially different from certainty.

It is manifest that truth, when considered in itself objectively or *a parte rei*, is incapable of mere probability, which, by its nature, pertains to finite cognition only.

The conclusion follows the weaker premise, according to the seventh rule of the syllogism; hence, while evident premises give a certain and evident conclusion, one *probable* premise renders the *conclusion only probable.*

The argument is probable; 1st, when we reason from remote and imperfect *analogy* or indeterminate *resemblance*; 2d, when the reasoning is upon some *hypothesis*. *Analogy* is a likeness, or a certain agreement of relation or proportion, between objects of different species, on account of which the one suggests the other, and hence, from one similarity, another one is inferred. (*Vide Chap.* 1. *Art.* 3.)

Identity includes all that likeness, or sameness of attributes or qualities, found in objects of the same species. *Similarity* implies an identical quality, or some identical qualities, in objects that are otherwise different; v. g., same color, shape, etc.

The force of argument founded on *analogy*, or resemblances, depends upon such general principles as the following: "similar causes produce similar effects; things that are seen to be similar in nearly every respect, are wholly similar," etc.

Analogy *can* found strict demonstration or give a conclusion which is scientific; v. g., when we demonstrate the existence of *God* from the *creation*. The *extremes* agree with the *medium*, in this case, by analogy only.

The *hypothesis*, or *supposition*, is a "*proposition, which, though not yet demonstrated, is assumed to be true, because it affords a satisfactory explanation of many facts.*" For example, to assert that "there is a subtile fluid diffused throughout the universe whose undulations explain the phenomena of light." To this class may be referred many of the theories adopted for the explanation of natural phenomena. An *hypothesis* is more or less probable, according to the number of facts or phenomena which it satisfactorily explains. Its logical value never exceeds probability; or it remains only an *opinion* until truly demonstrated. An *opinion* is a judgment which is assented to, but with some hesitancy or fear, as to its objective certainty. An *hypothesis* that is demonstrated, is thereby changed into a *thesis*, and ceases to be an *hypothesis*.

Between the extremes of attaching too much importance to analogical reasoning and hypothetical theories on the one hand and pronouncing them valueless on the other, is the wiser middle course of estimating them according to the degree of probability which their arguments furnish.

ARTICLE V.

SOPHISMS OR FALLACIES.

A *sophism*, or *fallacy*, is an apparent argument, which, under the specious form of truth, leads to a false or absurd conclusion. The following are the fallacies which most frequently occur: 1st, the *equivocation*, or *ambiguous middle;* 2d, the fallacy of *composition* and *division;* 3d, of the *accident;* 4th, *dictum simpliciter et secundum quid;* or, *confounding what can be said absolutely with what can be said under a particular respect only;* 5th, the *ignoratio elenchi*, or *ignoring the question;* 6th, the *petitio principii*, *begging the question*, or, *the vicious circle;* 7th, *non causa ut causa: no cause at all for a cause*, or *the fictitious cause.*

The *equivocation*, or ambiguous middle, is a fallacy arising from the use of a term of more meanings than one; attributing to it a different signification in each premise, but drawing a conclusion that supposes the two meanings to be identical; v. g., the Romans equivocated, when, after Antiochus had stipulated to surrender *half* his navy, they compelled him to divide each vessel into *halves*, and then deliver up the *half* of his navy by giving them the *half* of each ship.

Ambiguity arises, then, from the fact that a proposition is capable of having two meanings; for example, when the priestess of Apollo said to Pyrrhus, who consulted her when he was about to invade Rome: "I say, Pyrrhus, you the Romans will conquer;" her credit was saved in either event; whether Pyrrhus or the Romans were victorious.

This fallacy, or the double *middle term*, is of the most frequent occurrence, perhaps, of all the errors in reasoning.

Composition and *division:* this fallacy is committed if, when two predicates, taken separately or one at a time, agree with the same subject, it is inferred that they agree with it when they are taken conjointly; v. g., "Peter can walk and Peter can lie down; therefore, Peter can at the same time lie down and walk." Peter can walk, and lie down *by division*, is true; otherwise, it is not true. Or, *vice versa*, if they agree when taken *conjointly*, and it be inferred that they agree when taken *separately*; v. g., "man has a body and soul, or is a rational animal; therefore, matter is man, and spirit is man;" which is incorrect.

Fallacia accidentis: the fallacy of the *accident* arises from confounding those predicates that *essentially* belong to the subject with those that *accidentally* belong to it; or, in other words, from not distinguishing between what is *essential*, and what is *accidental* to the subject; v. g., "that is bad from which evil comes; but evil comes from the study of philosophy, medicine, the physical sciences, etc.; therefore, the study of those things is bad." "Evil" comes by *accident*, to this or that person, owing to intellectual or moral defects, and erroneous reasoning; but it does not thence follow that the well directed study of those sciences is bad. Again, "the exact *site* of an ancient city is not surely known; therefore, that city never existed."

The fallacy termed *dictum simpliciter et secundum quid* (of confounding what is *simply* true with what is true *in a certain respect only*): a predicate is affirmed *simpliciter*, i. e., simply or absolutely, when it is affirmed without any limiting word or phrase joined to it; as, "Plato is learned." Here the predicate, "learned," is not restricted to any particular object; but when the predicate is affirmed *secundum quid*, or, in a certain respect, there is a limiting adjunct to it; v. g., "Peter is learned *in Botany;*" here, "learned," is restricted to a particular object, "Botany." The fallacy arises from arguing that, because the predicate agrees with the subject in one of the senses, it therefore agrees with it in the other; v. g., "he that throws goods into the sea, *wills* the destruction of them; but the master of a vessel, in a storm, throws goods into the sea; therefore, he *wills* the destruction of them." He *wills* the destruction of them in a certain respect, as a means to an end necessary, and not otherwise to be attained, it is true; that he *wishes* to destroy them *simply*, or absolutely and directly, is not true. The fallacy termed, *dictum simpliciter et secundum quid*, or, of what is said *simply* and absolutely, or relatively and under a certain respect, is like to that termed, *accidentis*. "A man eats what he buys in the market; he buys *raw* meat in the market; therefore, a man eats *raw* meat."

Ignoratio elenchi, or *ignoring the question;* in familiar language, often termed "*evading the question;*" or, "*changing the question.*"

Ignoratio elenchi, or *ignoring the question*, is an evasion of the real question in dispute, and attempting to prove something else that apparently includes the thing in dispute; v. g., if a certain *means* to an *end* were denied to be just, one should prove that the *end is good*, and thereby seem to justify the means; or, if the *immortality* of the soul were proved, and one should answer as if the *eternity* of the soul, or *its having no beginning*, were the question. The *ignoratio elenchi*, or *ignoring the question*, is sometimes from real, not simulated ignorance of the state of the question; it may also come from obtuseness of the understanding; but it is often the artifice of a crafty and sophistical mind, which is wanting in moral rectitude. This fallacy occurs frequently in the harangues of demagogues; as does also the *assertion* by means of *interrogatory*.

To the "ignoratio elenchi" may be referred the error which consists in "proving too much;" of which it is justly said, "he that proves too much, proves nothing;" v. g., if one should attempt to demonstrate that the *human soul* is a *substance*, and his arguments went to show that *man's soul* has the properties of *matter*, he would then commit the error of "*proving too much.*"

Petitio principii, or *begging the question*, under which may be included the *vicious circle** and the *false supposition*, is the ***as-sumption*** of what is in *question;* v. g., if it be the *question* in dispute as to whether a particular substance have *weight*, and it be answered, "that has *weight* which is *ponderable*, the substance in question is *ponderable;* therefore, it has *weight;*" this would be the *petitio principii*, or *begging the question*. If it should be argued that "the earth turns on its axis *because the sun is stationary;* and, on the other hand, the *sun is stationary, because the earth turns on its axis;*" this would be to reason in a vicious circle, or to prove two propositions, the one by the other, as a reason. If it be said, "Pompey did not return to Rome after the death of Cæsar," this would be a *false supposition*, or a *false assumption;* namely, *falsely assuming* it to be a fact that Pompey was alive at Cæsar's death. The argument may falsely suppose or assume either a fact or a principle; the fallacy is the same in all these cases, and consists in assuming in the argument something that is in question.

This fallacy is sometimes concealed under a proverb; v. g., "the *exception* confirms the *rule;*" i. e., the *formal exception*, or one properly so-called, proves the *existence* of its *co-related rule*. For instance, if an old charter were found, exempting a certain family, for special reasons, from military tax, this exemption or exception in their favor, would prove the existence of a general law imposing such tax. But this axiom is sometimes misapplied; as v. g., when *counter* facts or *contrary* instances are adduced to prove the *non-existence* of a rule, then in answer, they are *preposterously assumed* to be *exceptions* which prove the *existence* of the rule. This is *false assumption;* and, when viewed under another respect, it is also the fallacy of the *double middle*.

Non causa pro causa, no cause at all as a cause, is a fallacy, in which that, which is *no cause at all*, is assumed to produce an effect, simply because the two are contiguous in time and place; or from some other mere coincidence or circumstance. The Pagans ascribed "the downfall of the Roman Empire to the

* "Circulus non est vitiosus in relativis." Illation from one co-relative to another is not a vicious circle.

rise of Christianity," when, perhaps, the converse was more nearly true. "Comets cause wars, plagues and other calamities." Or this fallacy may be committed by attributing effects to vague and fanciful agents; as *fate*, *luck*, *fortune*, or other superstitious causes. They are all the same fallacy, and from such delusions even educated minds are not all exempt. The origin of such errors is ignorance, along with an instinctive desire to know the cause of strange or terrible events.

"*Post hoc ergo propter hoc;*" or, "*a thing happened after another, therefore, it was caused by it;*" is obviously false, and is a form of expression which, on that account, is often employed in answer to the fallacy, "*non causa pro causa.*"

Of the seven fallacies above described, the first two are *verbal* fallacies; the remaining five, are *material* fallacies; or, they arise from the *matter* or *truth* of the propositions being at fault.

Mere sophistry is unworthy of a candid mind; but even vigorous and truthful intellects may, by mistake, employ inconsequent argument. The most ordinary fallacy that leads to unintentional error in reasoning, is *the complex or ambiguous middle term*, which is not accurately distinguished, so that what is false may be rejected, while that which is true is admitted.

Examples of inconsequent argument: "as the body is composed of many members, so the soul is composed of many powers; therefore, since the former can be divided into its component parts, so can the latter." Here distinguish between *compound* objects which possess members that are *really distinct*, and, therefore, *separable;* and objects that are *simple*, having powers *not really distinct* from them as parts; and which are, therefore, *indivisible* substances.

"Whatever is opposed to reason must be rejected; but faith in mysteries is opposed to reason; therefore, faith in mysteries must be rejected;" or, "*faith* in mysteries is *against reason.*" Distinguish what is *above* reason from what is *against* reason; also, *faith* that presupposes *prudent motives of credibility;* and *faith* that rests on *insufficient grounds* or *no grounds at all;* and is, therefore, *unreasonable.* To believe what is *above* reason, when we have valid authority for its truth, is not belief which is *against* reason, though the object is *above* reason; but to believe pretended mysteries, that directly contradict the evident principles of reason, would surely be *against* reason.

It will be found that complex or double middle terms generally contain both truth and error; they must, therefore, be carefully distinguished; the one to be admitted, the other to be rejected.

An ancient sophist puzzled some less acute contemporary logicians with the following objection against the possibility of motion: "A thing cannot move where *it is not;* nor can it move where *it is;* but that which can neither move *where it is, nor where it is not*, cannot move at all; therefore, a thing cannot move at all."

The ingenious reader will readily see that the clause, "where it is," is equivocal; in one sense it means, "where it is *at rest;*" in another it signifies, "where it is *not at rest;*" i. e., where *it is moving.* In this second sense of the words, it may be said that, "a thing moves *where it is.*" It surely cannot move *where it is not*, in the direct and proper sense of the expression.

This sophism, which under a somewhat different form is attributed to Zeno; as also the one devised by him to prove that Achilles could not overtake the turtle which had a given distance the start of him; both rested, in reality, on the *false assumption* that a period of time consists of an infinite number of moments, and that a given distance consists of an infinite number of points; whereas, in truth, time, distance, and simple motion, as such, do not consist of *distinct parts*, for they are *continuous*, and not, as number is, *discrete.*

LOGIC SECOND PART.

LOGIC APPLIED.

Since Logic is chiefly concerned with the acts of the intellect in discourse of reason, or right argumentation, it is manifest that it must include in its object the truth of cognitions, and the means of knowing with certainty; without which all mere *forms* of argument are unmeaning, or nugatory.

Hence, the second part of Logic treats of *logical* truth and certainty; and the means of attaining them. Its object is, therefore, the extrinsic norma of right reasoning; that is, its *matter*.

A genuine or truly valid argument must not only be *in form*, but its judgments must possess *logical truth*.

CHAPTER I.

ARTICLE I.

TRUTH, ERROR AND FALSEHOOD DESCRIBED.

Truth* may be divided into *metaphysical*, *logical* and *moral truth*. *Metaphysical* truth is the agreement of the essential properties of a being among themselves, and with their essential concept or prototype, whether that being be actual or only possible; for, whatever exists, or is only possible, has, in the

* "*Veritas est rerum, cognitionis, et sermonis.*" Truth is of things, of cognition, of language.

essential and eternal archetype of it, the constituents by which it is what it is, and can be nothing else; and it is such independently of our knowledge, though not independently of divine intelligence. But *metaphysical* truth, as such, and truth considered as *transcendental*, pertain to *general metaphysics*, and will be treated in another place.

*Logical truth** is the conformity of the understanding knowing to the thing or object known. The concept or idea may be conceived to be the medium between the object and the intellect, "est medium quo incognito."† *Moral truth*, is the conformity of the language, or signs of thought, to the internal judgment of the person uttering the affirmation of that judgment; or, it is *moral truth*, when the internal judgment is truly expressed. The language or sign expressing the internal judgment may be termed, the *enunciation*. But we must distinguish between the *logical truth* of an *enunciation*, and its *moral* truth; the *enunciation* is *logically* true, when the judgment which it declares is *right;* that is, when the judgment is objectively true; or, expresses a real conformity of the mind to the object known.‡ The *enunciation* is *morally* true, when it declares correctly the internal judgment, such as it is in the mind. When this conformity of the *enunciation* and the *internal judgment* is wanting, then the enunciation is *erroneous*. *Logical* truth of enunciations regards the rectitude or the correctness of the judgment *objectively; moral* truth pertains to the language of the subject uttering the judgment. It is termed *moral* truth, because its right expression, or enunciation, is generally subject to the will, which, being free, attributes to it a moral character.

As concrete truth always implies both an object known, as

* "Veritas est adæquatio intellectus, et rei." Truth is the equation of intellect and object; i. e., it is the conformity of the power as knowing with the object as known.

† "Species intelligibilis (conceptus) est medium *quo* et incognitum ut *quod*." The idea in the mind is the *medium* of knowledge, though it is not seen itself as an *object*, in the act of perceiving.

‡ "Ex eo quod res est vel non est, vera est oratio." According as the object is, or is not, the proposition that enunciates it is true.

one term, and the intellect knowing, as the other term of the relation, truth is sometimes denominated by the *objects*, and is then called truth of the *metaphysical*, *physical* and *moral* order, according to the objects. In this sense we may apply the definition of truth by St. Augustin: "Veritas est quæ ostendit id quod est:" Truth makes known that which is.*

Error is *assent* to what is false, or *dissent* from what is true; it is an act of the mind by which we affirm two things to agree, which do not, in themselves, agree; or, we deny the agreement of two things, which, in themselves, do really agree. As assent, in matters whose evidence does not force the understanding, is a free act of the mind, error may be attributed to the will as its formal or actuating cause; yet the action of the will, in error, is not always *deliberate*.

Falsity: *Falsity* is the opposite of truth; and is, therefore, a want of conformity in the mind to the object of cognition. This want of conformity is either *negative* or *positive*; *negative*, when the concept expresses the object only partially or obscurely; v. g., should it contain nothing more about the moon

* *Truth* is, by its nature, for the intellect, and is its proper object; as *good* is the object of the will, as color and figure constitute the object of sight, or as sound is the object of hearing. Truth, then, is of the intelligible order, or is ordained for the intellect, by its nature; *truth* and *intellect* are connotative, so that the one supposes the other. Truth, in itself, is a *relation*, and is threefold: 1st. The *relation* of agreement between a real being and its *concept*, or its *essential prototype*, according to which it is constituted; like to that, for example, which is between the *idea* of a house in the mind of the architect, and the *real house*, which he forms exactly according to that idea in his mind; or the *idea* in the painter's mind, and the *picture* on canvass, which accurately expresses it. 2d. The *relation* of agreement between the mind knowing an object, and the object itself; v. g., the exact *conformity* of the mind knowing an *orange* to the *real* orange itself. 3d. The *relation* of agreement between the *words or signs* by which we express or manifest the cognitions in our minds, and those *cognitions* as they *really* are in the mind; v. g., "virtue is amiable," are words that express truly a real judgment of your mind, and, therefore, your words agree with the mind, and the relation is real between the cognition and its enunciation.

Truth, then, in its formal entity, is a *relation*; it is threefold, as said above, and it is *totally comprehended* in this threefold division: 1st. The agreement or relation between a thing and the prototype in the concept of its essence or nature, is *metaphysical truth*; 2d. The conformity of the mind knowing, to the object known, is a relation of agreement between them, and is called *logical truth*, or intellectual truth; 3d. The *conformity* or relation of agreement between *words and signs*, used to enunciate or manifest cognitions, and the *cognitions as they actually are in the mind*, is called *moral truth*.

than, that it is a luminary. This is false by *privation*, and is, perhaps, more properly, *ignorance*. *Positive falsity*, is a disagreement of the cognition and its proper object; for, in that case, the mind attributes to the object what does not belong to it, or denies what does belong to it; this is a want of conformity in the understanding, to the proper object of its cognition; v. g., "God is a body; the human soul is material."

It may be said, therefore, that falsity in the mind, when *positive*, is the effect of error in judgment; for, how else can positive falsity be in the mind, or get access thereto?

Simple apprehension cannot, *per se*, *i. e.*, of itself, or of its own proper action, induce error, or *cause falsity* in the mind. A simple apprehension, or perception, is an act of the mind by which it acquires an inchoate cognition; by which it *takes hold* of the object, as it were; or perceives it, and forms for itself an *idea* or *similitude* of it. In this, nothing is explicitly affirmed or denied by the mind; and its conformity to the object is limited to the mere perception; as it does not express a judgment. Hence, the apprehension is a necessary effect of a necessary law, and, therefore, cannot be false. The *judgment*, or the understanding judging, is never *per se* false; but *assent* can be false, by precipitancy, or, by impulse of the will; and, therefore, *positive falsity* in the mind is produced only by error in judgment.

If it be objected that many ideas of rude and uncultivated people are not conformable to their objects; as, v. g., they may conceive "*the sun to be a round plane a few feet in diameter*," etc.; and, since all languages declare the sun to *rise*, and *set*, it would appear that the minds of all men were long *in error* in regard to a *sensible fact*.

We should distinguish: that these ideas may not be conformable to their objects, *negatively*, *i. e.*, by *privation*, is true; but if it be meant that they are not conformable to their objects, *positively*; then we should *subdistinguish*; they may not be really conformable *after a judgment* is formed; but it is not true to say that *before* the judgment there is a *positive falsity*, or want of conformity in the mind to the object. *Language* expresses the *sensible fact* of the sun's *rising* and *setting*, though the philosophical hypothesis formerly employed to explain its *cause* is now known to be untenable; or, in other words, the minds of men did not err in affirming the *fact*, but philosophers erred in giving its explanation.

Mere apprehensions or ideas are true, so far as they express their objects *positively;* since they are produced by the mind and object, operating both naturally and necessarily. Even the intellect cannot be forced to assent to what is *false*, as *false;* but it can, under the command of the will, assent to what is false, in those cases in which the evidence of the truth does not necessitate its decision. Truth, properly so-called, is only in the understanding which judges; and it is only by a certain imitation or analogy, and, therefore, improperly and incompletely, in *sensation* and *simple apprehension*, which are means of knowing truth. Truth is fully and properly only in that act by which the mind is fully conformable to its known object; but the mind is fully and properly conformable to its object only when it *affirms* what the object is; *i. e.*, when it judges. Any preceding act of knowing is preliminary and preparatory to *full* knowledge, or truth, properly so-called.

ARTICLE II.

DIFFERENT STATES OF THE MIND IN RESPECT TO TRUTH.

As the mind attains truth by acquiring ideas conformable to their objects, and by comparing these ideas or concepts to their objects, or among themselves; it is manifest that the mind may by these efforts approach more or less nearly to complete knowledge of things. Hence, the different states of the mind in respect to truth.

The following classification of those states is sufficiently comprehensive: 1st, Ignorance; 2d, Doubt; 3d, Suspicion; 4th, Opinion; 5th, Certainty. They comprehend the different relations the mind may have to the objects of its knowledge, either as ignorant of those objects, or as knowing them in different degrees of perfection, i. e., more or less completely.

Ignorance is the state of the mind when it has no knowledge of an object; v. g., we are ignorant as to whether the number of the stars be *odd* or *even;* or what was the precise number of angels created; or how long the present world will endure.

Doubt is the state of the mind when the judgment is suspended between the two parts of a contradictory; or when the assent of the understanding cannot be determined to either of two contradictory propositions or judgments.

Doubt is either *positive* or *negative; doubt* is *positive* when there are reasons that persuade in favor of each proposition; which, however, do not determine the intellect to assent to either, but leave it, now drawn to one side, now to the other, still hesitating in uncertainty between them.

The *doubt* is *negative* when there are either no reasons at all in favor of either side, or such as are of very little moment.

Suspicion is a propensity or inclination to judge on slight grounds; in it, the judgment is often prompted or impelled by passion or affection in the will; and it is apt to tend rather to the unfavorable side.

*Opinion** is an assent of the understanding to one of two contradictory or opposite propositions; not, however, without fear of the other being true.

For an opinion to be prudent, the following conditions must be fulfilled: 1st, a careful examination of the reasons in favor of each contradictory, must precede the assent of the understanding; 2d, the side embraced must have in its favor a grave motive; and the objections against it, as well as the reasons in favor of the opposite proposition, must be suitably answered; 3d, the assent in favor of the opinion formed must not be more firm than the motive or decisive reason in its favor justifies.

* "Opinio est actus intellectus quo fertur in unam partem contradictionis cum formidine alterius. Assensus probabilis est idem ac opiniativus."—(Vide Div. Thom. P. I.; Qu. 79; Art. 9; Ad. 4.) Opinion is an act of the intellect by which it is borne to one side of a contradictory, but with fear lest the opposite be true. Assent to what is probable is the same as opinion.

An opinion may be *probable*, *more probable*, *most probable*; but an *opinion*, as such, cannot transcend the limits of *probability;* for, if what was an *opinion* be made afterwards *positively certain*, it thereby ceases to be an *opinion*, and becomes a *thesis* or a certain truth. *Probability* and *certainty* differ *essentially*, since they are of different species; and therefore no degree* of probability can constitute certainty.

ARTICLE III.

CERTAINTY; EVIDENCE; SPECIES OF CERTAINTY; THEY DIFFER AS TO INTENSITY.

Certainty is a state of the mind in which it adheres firmly to the truth on account of motives which exclude all doubt, and all fear of the opposite being true.

Certainty, primarily and properly, is in cognitition, and is therefore subjective;† but it is attributed by translation to the object. For the sake of greater clearness, therefore, certainty may be considered both as *objective* and *subjective*.

Objective certainty is the *necessary truth* of the object known as cognoscible; its "*necessitas seu firmitas essendi.*" The *necessity* here meant is, in the case of facts, *consequent;* and it is, therefore, common to all accomplished and actual truth, or to every actual object. *Subjective* certainty is a firm adhesion of the mind to the object as true, which excludes all doubt and all fear of the opposite being true.

* "Gradus non mutat essentiam rei." The degree, i. e., *more* or *less*, does not change the essence of a thing.

† "Certitudo *subjectiva* est firmitas adhæsionis virtutis cognoscitivæ ad suum cognoscibile." Subjective certainty is firmness of adhesion in the power knowing to the object known.

"Objectiva est firma et invariabilis objecti determinatio in suo esse."—(Billuart.) Objective certainty is the firm and invariable determination of the object in being; or, its existence as actual, and, under that respect, both necessary and unchangeable.

"Nihil est adeo contingens, quin in se aliquid necessarium habeat." — (Div. Thom. P. I.; Qu. 86; Art. 4.) Nothing is so absolutely contingent as to be, under no respect, necessary.

The causes of certainty, or the motives that lead to it, may be reduced to two classes; namely, *evidence*, and *authority* or *testimony*.

Certainty which is produced by *evidence** may be distinguished, according to its objects, into three kinds, which differ in the degree of intensity or force with which they necessitate the assent of the intellect: 1st., Certainty, whose object is truth which is known *per se;* i. e., which is *self-evident*, or is seen to be truth, and assented to, so soon as the terms which express it are understood; v. g., "two things which are equal to the same thing, are equal to each other; the shortest distance between two given points is a straight line," etc. 2d., A second kind of the certainty which comes from *evidence*, is furnished by conclusions which follow necessarily from *evident first principles;* this kind is often termed *scientific certainty*. It will be explained more fully in Article VIII of this Chapter. 3d., A third species of certainty is furnished by the objects of internal and external or sensible experience; or, that which is possessed when the power of consciousness and the organs of sense are directly cognizant of their proper objects.

Certainty, whose medium or formal motive is authority or testimony, is either from evident signs or marks, or from witnesses that *evidently testify* to what they know directly and in its objective evidence—*ex evidentia in attestante*—as eye-witnesses, ear-witnesses, and the like; or, it is the certainty which is afforded by *supernatural faith*, in which neither the testimony, nor the object, is evident to the mind assenting;† v. g., when we believe that "that there are three Persons and but one Nature in God, because God revealed it." Here, neither the fact of

*"Omnis certitudo naturalis postulat evidentiam vel in re vel in attestante." All natural certainty requires evidence, either in the object or in the witness; i. e., evidence of the *testimony* that *mediates* between the *mind* and the *object* or truth. But, for the act of supernatural faith, this *evident* medium, witness or testimony (*evidentia in attestante*) is not required, except as a preceding condition.

†"Fides omnis est essentialiter obscura quia nititur medio rei extrinseco, ideoque res manet secundum se ignota, sicut antea."—(Billuart.) All faith is essentially obscure, because it depends on a medium which is extrinsic to the object, and, therefore, the thing remains unknown in itself, even after it is believed.

the revelation having been made, nor the *Trinity* itself, is *evident* to us;* though the revelation itself was, doubtless, evident to many; v. g., to Prophets, Evangelists, etc. In this case, the principles that supply for evidence, are the *light of faith* in the understanding and an *impulse of grace* in the will; hence, *actual* faith is *free*, and it is thereby capable of meriting. But, for supernatural faith, *it is an essential condition*, or prerequisite, that its articles be *evidently credible*.† "Non crederet (quis) nisi videret ea esse credenda, vel propter evidentiam signorum vel aliquid hujusmodi:" *i. e.*, no one can believe without evidence as to the credibility of the truths assented to. (Div. Th. 2, 2, qu. 1, a. 4, ad. 2.) But matters pertaining to supernatural Faith, and the resolution of its act,‡ pertain to the scope of Theology; it is here proposed directly to treat only of natural or philosophical certainty, and its principles or causes. But from what has been said it may be concluded as beyond doubt, that the individual reason can prudently assent to no truth except it either know that truth in its own objective evidence, or have for its assent to the truth a certain and infallible motive, while certainty, as already observed, is primarily in cognition, or is *subjective*. Evidence, on the contrary, is primarily in the object; or, it is most properly the object that is evident; but the light of the object as seen§ or perceived by the cognoscive power, is termed *subjective evidence.*

Evidence is either *immediate*, or *mediate;* truths are *imme-*

*"Motiva credibilitatis præstant evidentiam *consequentiæ*, sed non *consequentis:* probant quod revelatio debet credi sed non dant evidentiam rei revelatæ seu veritatis creditæ." Motives of credibility afford evidence of the *consequence*, but not of the *consequent:* they prove that revelation ought to be believed, but they do not give evidence of the thing revealed, or the truth believed.

†Suarez, De Virt. Theolog., Disp. 4, Sect. 6, says that the intellect does not doubt in matters of faith without rejecting their credibility as not evident.

‡The "*resolution of the act of faith,*" is its *analysis*, which is made in order to distinguish clearly all that is necessary to the act, whether as *conditio sine qua non*, as directive of it, as *formal motive*, as *material object*, etc.

§"Illa dicuntur *videri* quæ *per seipsa* movent intellectum vel sensum ad sui cognitionem, ut sunt prima principia et conclusiones ex ipsis evidenter deductæ, vel sensibilia sensibus debite proposita."—(Billuart, De Fide; Disp. I; Art. 4.) Those things are said to be *seen* which *of themselves* move the intellect or the sense to know them; such are first principles and the conclusions evidently deduced from them, or sensible objects duly proposed to the senses.

diately evident when they are known *per se*, *i. e.*, are *self-evident.* The objects of the senses and those of consciousness may also be regarded, when actually observed, as *immediately* evident to these cognoscive powers. Truths are *mediately evident*, when the mind comes to the certain knowledge of them only through the *medium* of reasoning; or, when it knows them only as *evident deductions* from their principles.

Evidence may also be considered as either *intrinsic*, or *extrinsic.* It is *intrinsic*, in self-evident truths, in the demonstrated conclusions from evident premises, and in the proper objects of the senses and consiousness. Evidence is *extrinsic* when it is not derived immediately from the object or truth, but passes through the medium of testimony, and is thereby indirect and and reflected light of the objective truth. Objects thus known are not said to be *evident*, but *believed*, or they are objects of *faith.* A preceding and evident judgment of their credibility gives just grounds from which is inferred, or may be inferred, the necessary truth of the objects in themselves. Hence, distinguish between what is *evidently true*, and what is only *evidently credible;* in the first, the object is *evident;* in the second, the object is *obscure.*

A high degree of *probability* is sometimes termed *moral certainty.* But *probability* and *certainty* differ in species or essence; and, therefore, in strictness, no degree of probability can equal real certainty; or, no number of probabilities can constitute certainty.

The main theory of evidence and the certainty which is founded upon it may be briefly summed up as follows:

Evidence, in its general sense, includes not only the capability in the object of being *seen*, or clearly known, *i. e.*, its cognoscibility; but, also, the capability* in an agent of seeing it, together with the exhibition of the object to the mind, or the act of seeing it to be what it is, and that it cannot

* "Evidentia *objecti* est capacitas in objecto apparendi nostro intellectui si eidem objiciatur; apparentia objecti in *intellectu* est evidentia subjectiva." *Objective evidence* is the capability in the object of being seen by the intellect if presented to it; the manifestation of the object *in the intellect* is *subjective evidence.*

be otherwise than it is seen. It is manifest, then, that evidence may be considered as both objective and subjective.

The cognoscibility of the object, or objective evidence, presupposes objective certainty, and is caused by it. Hence, it may be said that objective certainty is the origin of objective evidence; objective evidence is the proximate cause of subjective evidence, and the subjective evidence produces subjective certainty. Therefore, in the order of cause and effect, *objective* certainty is first, *subjective* certainty is last, and *evidence* is the medium between them.

Certainty, when considered according to its objects, and the medium by which they produce certainty in the mind, is *metaphysical*, *physical* or *moral*. The three kinds of certainty thus denominated differ in their species or essence; because their objects differ specifically. These kinds of certainty differ in species; for, acts are specified by their objects, and the objects give determinate species not only to the acts, but to those things that are consequent upon acts, as the states produced by those acts. The acts of knowing *metaphysical* truth, *physical* truth, and *moral* truth, have *objective principles*, which, it is clear, differ *essentially;* for the *metaphysical* is purely of intellect, the *physical* implies the *sensible*, and the object of *moral* certainty is inevident, or essentially obscure. Hence, metaphysical, physical and moral certainty all differ specifically, because their objects differ in species.

In order to perceive the conclusiveness of the preceding reasoning, it is necessary to understand the force, and to see the truth of the philosophical axiom, "acts* are specified by their objects." It means about the same thing as saying, "effects derive their species or essence from their causes; or, effects depend for their species or essence on their causes; or, effects *really* proceed from their causes;" which is evidently true. Now, regarding the act as an *effect*, the object of the act is one of its causes, as well as the agent that puts that act. Hence,

* "Actus specificantur ab objectis." Acts are specified by their objects; or, acts derive their species from their objects.

when it is said, "action* is specified by the agent; passion is specified by the term;" or, "operations, and habits, and powers, are specified by their objects;" or, "all operation is specified by the *form* (*by the specific nature*), which is the principle of the operation;" all these expressions really convey the same truth, though they present it under different respects. An agent specifies its acts, because it gives to the acts which it puts, their determinate nature; powers, habits, etc., are specified by their objects; for, since their objects determine them to act, the objects are also *principles* or *causes* of action, and, on that acccount, attribute to the acts something which is essential to them as effects produced by the objects. *Colors* cannot be *heard; sounds* cannot be *seen;* but color and figure determine or specify vision, or *the act* of seeing; sounds determine the *specific acts* of hearing. Hence, because objects are *principles* that determine acts in the agents to which those objects are connatural, they also *specify* those acts.

Intensity, or force of the assent: The *assent* of the mind differs in its *intensity*, according to the different species of certainty; or, according to the objects which, through their proper mediums, produce certainty in the mind.

Observe that *assent* is an act of the *intellect*, as *consent* is an act of the *will*. The intellect *assents* to truth; *i. e.*, agrees to, admits, takes the truth: 1st, through the *immediate evidence* of the truth, as in matters which are self-evident, or known *per se;* 2d, through *mediate evidence*, or on account of something else, as, when it *assents* to a demonstrated conclusion on account of the certain premises from which it necessarily follows; 3d, on account of evident testimony to the inevident truth, and also in voluntary obedience to the motives of supernatural faith; 4th, when the motives furnish only probability; in which case the assent is voluntary, and the judgment assented to is only an opinion.

That the assent of the intellect, as thus described, should

* "Actio specificatur ab agente; passio a termino."

"Operationes, et habitus et potentiæ specificantur ex objectis." (Div. Th. Mem. Lect. 1, Sect. 2.)

"Omnis operatio specificatur per formam, quæ est principium operationis."

have different degrees of intensity or strength, according to its motives, and the principles that produce it, is both natural, and just to truth itself: 1st, because the objects which produce different kinds and degrees of assent differ in their nature; 2d, because truth in the mind is in conformity with the objects.

As to *intensity in assent*, there are three principal degrees of the *subjective* certainty that is merely human or natural; corresponding to the three species of *objective* certainty, or three species of objects: 1st, *metaphysical* certainty, whose object is necessary and immutable, i. e., *metaphysical* truth; 2d, *physical* certainty, whose object is *physical truth*, i. e., the existence and the positive laws of created or contingent beings; 3d, *moral certainty*, whose object is truth known by the testimony of witnesses, or the moral laws that universally govern man.

Metaphysical certainty has for its object, either truth that is *a priori*, and absolutely necessary; or truth that is derived from it by demonstrative reasoning; the certainty in us caused by the latter is less intense than that which is caused by the former.

We have *physical* certainty, when the object known is a *fact*, or is something actually and physically existing, and *is evident* to our cognoscive powers; v. g., we have physical certainty that the sun now shines, or does not; or other facts of sense, and consciousness.

Certainty is styled *moral* when its *medium* is that testimony which depends for its significance and truth on the knowledge and veracity of an intelligent and *free* witness. This testimony may be manifested either by words, modes of action, or any other signs of conscious thought or affection. Hence, any manifestation of truth by means of signs, which are intelligent and *free* in their cause, pertains to that testimony which is the medium of *moral certainty*.

We have *moral* certainty when a sufficient number of reliable witnesses all concur in testifying to a sensible fact; v. g., "London exists." We have *moral* certainty, in a less strict sense of the words, *moral certainty*, that "all mothers love their children;" in this latter case, exception is absolutely possible.

When we possess *metaphysical*, or *physical* certainty, we are said to *know the truth* that causes it, or is its object; but when our knowledge comes through the testimony of others, we are said to *believe* the truth of which we thus become certain.

In moral certainty we must distinguish between the object or truth testified to, and the testimony itself: the object is essentially inevident or obscure; but the testimony, at least as a natural medium of certainty,* must be evident.

The manner in which natural faith and supernatural or divine faith are respectively related to their mediums or motives of assent, will be rendered more clear by means of an example: "Hannibal defeated the Romans in the battle of Cannæ," is a historical fact which is believed on its testimony. Those to whom the fact of the defeat was evident in itself, were the first witnesses, and they *knew* the fact in its own objective evidence. Through them as eye-witnesses it became generally credited or believed as made certain by their testimony; through writings and other means of tradition it has come down to the present time. All the testimony, from that of the eye-witnesses, as descending to the present time, constitutes, when it is all taken together, the *medium* which in some manner unites our minds with the fact, and this *medium* is *evident* in itself to us; for, we actually *know it* in existing history and tradition. Our assent to the fact, "Hannibal defeated the Romans in the battle of Cannæ," is on account of this *evident medium* as extending from the present time to the period when it occurred.

The proposition, "God is Triune," is believed as an article of divine faith. There is likewise in this case an evident tradition or medium of testimony, clearly traceable back to the days of the Messias himself, that this Messias explicitly affirmed and taught "God to be Triune." This *medium*, as in the other case, connects us in some manner with the Messias revealing that article of faith; but our assent, as an act of *divine faith*, is not on account of that medium or tradition which is evident to us and certain, for such a medium constitutes only a natural

* "*Evidentia in attestante:* quando evidenter constat de dicente." It is *evidence in the witness*, when the witness is *evidently known* as such.

principle of assent; our assent, as an act of *supernatural faith*, is only and exclusively *because God revealed it.* The existence of the evident medium is an essential prerequisite for this act of faith, and is a demonstrative proof that it is prudent to elicit it; but it is not itself any part of the formal motive for the act, that formal motive being, God said it, or God revealed it; in such manner, however, that both the *motive* and the *assent* are alike supernatural, and totally distinct from the natural medium.

The further explanation and proof of this, we remit to the theologian.

What is here said suffices, it is believed, for a correct understanding of philosophical certainty as related to that of supernatural faith, and as distinguished from it in its principles; and this much was also judged necessary for the adequate treatment of the matter proper to the present article.

As a mode of knowing truth, the intellectual vision, or the distinct, evident perception of truth in its own objective evidence, is more perfect than knowing it by the medium of faith; but yet, divine faith* is more noble in respect to its object, which is the truth of God himself, than any natural knowledge, whose medium is evidence or the testimony of creatures.

The intensest natural certainty is that which is caused by metaphysical truth, because the object is necessary and immutable. *Physical* certainty is next in the degree of its intensity or force; though its object is *contingent* truth, yet, it is made evident to us, and the certainty in the mind corresponds to the principles that produce it. A *contingent* being is one that can exist, or cease to exist, according to the free choice of its cause; or, it is one that depends on a free agent for its existence. *Moral* certainty is the least intense: 1st, because its

* "Fides est nobilior quam scientia ex parte objecti; quia ejus objectum est veritas prima; sed scientia habet perfectiorem modum cognoscendi, qui non repugnat perfectioni beatitudinis, scilicet visioni, sicut ei repugnat modus fidei." (Div. Thom. I, 2 P.; Qu. 67; Art. 3; ad. 1.) Faith is more noble than knowledge as regards its object, because its object is the First Truth; but knowledge is a more perfect mode of cognition, because it is not repugnant to beatitude, namely, to *vision;* to which, however, the mode of knowing by faith is repugnant.

object is obscure or is known indirectly and mediately only; 2d, because the morals and actions of men are more mutable, and more purely contingent, than are the laws of physical nature, or the acts of natural agents, and the truth in the mind is in conformity to the objects.

Both *metaphysical* and *physical* evidence always *necessitate* assent. Testimony, also, when fortified with certain conditions, v. g., as when it refers to a *sensible fact*, when many witnesses agree, and collusion is impossible, in such adjuncts necessitates assent; yet, in many cases, it is possible to dissent, even when this refusal of assent to the testimony is most imprudent; in other words, the assent of the understanding to the truth is, in such instances, under the control of the will. This happens more especially when the object is wholly obscure; or, when both the object and the testimony are inevident.

Though certainty is perfect in its species when its motive is the evidence that the object is what it is, and that it can be nothing else; yet, within its species, the evidence can be of a higher or lower degree in different minds, or in the same mind under different circumstances. Hence, the certainty with regard to the same truths may be *more or less intense*, according to those conditions.

Supernatural Faith* is, in itself, simply and absolutely more certain than any natural cognition; but it is not thus as regards us.

The *certainty* here meant is the firmness with which the cognoscive power adheres to its cognoscible object. This firm adhesion of the mind may arise from the action of the

* "Nihil prohibet id, quod est certius secundum naturam, esse quoad nos minus certum propter debilitatem intellectus nostri: qui se habet ad manifestissima naturæ sicut oculus noctuæ ad lumen solis. Unde dubitatio quæ accidit in aliquibus circa articulos fidei, non est propter incertitudinem rei, sed propter debilitatem intellectus humani." (Div. Thom., 1 P., Qu. 1; Art. 5, ad 1: et I, 2; Qu. 4; Art. 8.) Nothing prevents that which is more certain according to its nature from being less so in regard to us, owing to the weakness of our intellects, which, in regard to things the most manifest in themselves, are like the eye of the owl in the light of the sun. Hence, the doubts which come to some persons about articles of faith are not owing to uncertainty in the object, but to the weakness of the human intellect.

will determining the intellect to adhere, independently of any legitimate motive of assent, to its object; this actually happens in obstinate error. But tenacious adhesion of the mind from such a motive cannot be properly termed certainty; more correctly, it is pertinacity. Again, this firm adhesion may arise from a *true medium* of certainty, and yet derive its efficacy both from the intellect and the will. Now, divine faith derives its certainty from the divine veracity, the First Truth, which infinitely exceeds all created mediums of certainty or truth, as is self-evident. Hence, faith, in respect to its object, is the highest and most perfect motive of certainty which the human mind has in our present state of existence.

As regards our minds, or considered subjectively: that is more certain, in respect to us, which the intellect can more fully possess, which is more connatural and proportioned to it, which more completely satisfies and quiets it; though, in other respects its assent through a connatural motive be, in itself, not the most certain. This is what actually happens in that certainty which we posess concerning objects which are *evident* to us, as compared to the certainty which we have through the medium of divine faith.* Hence, although faith, in respect to its motive, gives the highest and intensest certainty; yet, in the subject, *i. e.*, in our minds, there may spring up indeliberate doubt; for, the debilitated intellect, like the owl at noonday, "sicut oculus noctuæ ad lumen solis," is unable to see by light so superior as that of divine faith. This faith is in itself absolutely the most certain; but the disposition of the subject renders doubt possible.

* "Ipsum testimonium primæ veritatis se habet in fide, ut principium in scientiis demonstrativis." The *testimony* of the First Truth is, in matters of faith, like the *principle*, in scientific demonstration.

ARTICLE IV.

ULTIMATE CRITERION OF TRUTH; OR, ULTIMATE MOTIVE OF CERTAINTY.

A criterion of truth is a rule or standard by which truth is unerringly known and distinguished from falsehood and error. Also, because certainty in the mind is the legitimate result of truth thus known, it follows that the criterion of truth is, at the same time, the criterion of certainty. This criterion, in its last reason or motive, is evidence in concrete. In other words, all certainty supposes evidence, either as its formal motive, or as a preceding *conditio sine qua non, an indispensable condition*, to which the mind finally reverts in order to dismiss all doubt.* Hence, it will be seen why the sounder philosophers so universally insist on the truth of the proposition, "Evidence is the ultimate criterion of truth, or is the ultimate motive of certainty."

Evidence is said to be the *ultimate* criterion of certainty or truth; because, when the motives and principles of certainty are examined *reflexively*, or by their analysis, evidence is the *last* reason or principle which is dwelt on by the mind, in determining the admissibility, or the validity of all the motives for its assent furnished by any object. In the *direct* acquisition of certainty, *evidence* may be considered as, under some respect, the first principle or motive of assent. Hence, then, evidence is termed, under different respects, both the *first principle* and *ultimate motive* of certainty.

The following are essential requisites for the *ultimate criterion* of truth: 1st. It should not require *demonstration;* for, all demonstration supposes something more known, from which another truth is deduced, and which thereby becomes also known; hence, if this principle or criterion were demonstrable, the truth from which it is deduced, would be the *ultimate* standard in question; or, if it were not *self-evident* or known *per se*, the *medium* through which it is known, would be that

* "Evidentia est ultimum in quo quiescit intellectus noster." (Billuart, T. 1; Proem. Dissert. 1; Art. 7.) In evidence the intellect finally rests quiet.

standard. 2d. This ultimate standard must be *internal*, not an *external* rule; or, it must be *intrinsic* to the mind. An *extrinsic* standard of truth can be known only by its medium; or, it must be recognized by the individual reason, "*per lumen rationis naturale*," through the evidence, that it is a medium of certainty. In other words, in order to follow any external criterion of truth, or assent to it with certainty, an *evident judgment* of its reliability is an essential prerequisite; i. e., ultimately this external standard must be tested as a medium or law of certainty by *evidence* in concrete, or formal evidence, which is an *internal* principle. The mind must first be certain that this external criterion exists; that it is true; and it can know this truth, which is external to itself, only by the evidence of it in the mind.

This standard cannot be divine faith: for faith presupposes the knowledge that there is a God, who is true; and it is an essential prerequisite that Revelation, or the truths proposed for belief be *evidently* credible; otherwise there could be no rational assent. Hence, divine faith cannot be either the *first* or the *only* motive of certainty; since it has essential *prerequisites* to it, which must be known by their evidence.

The criterion of certainty cannot be the common consent of men, as some authors erroneously maintain; for the admission of such a standard of truth, which, like divine faith, is *external*, presupposes the evident knowledge that men exist, attest, attach a definite meaning to their words; that they agree, etc.; all these truths suppose an internal principle of the mind which is their criterion, or is the standard by which they are ultimately tested; i. e., evidence in the concrete is the ultimate criterion of all truth, or the ultimate motive of certainty.

It follows from what has been said, that error in a sane mind is never physically necessary; for assent is necessitated only by perfect evidence, and, in all other cases, it is caused by the will, to which, therefore, must be referred assent or dissent, when the understanding is not compelled by the evidence.

ARTICLE V.

PRIMITIVE TRUTHS; THEY ARE NOT DEMONSTRABLE.

Primitive truths are such as neither require nor admit of proof, either because they are *per se** known, i. e., *known of themselves*, without the aid of other truths from which they are deduced, or by which they are proved; or, because they are facts of experience, known directly through our cognoscive powers.

To begin reasoning or philosophising with universal doubt, is simply absurd; for doubt, as such, can give neither evidence nor certainty of anything deduced from it, since the conclusion has the nature of the premises. It is but little less absurd, to begin with admitting the testimony of consciousness (*cogito ergo sum*, I think, or *am* thinking, therefore, I exist, which is a *petitio principii*), and doubting that of other powers, the external senses, etc.; for all these powers, taken together, constitute our only natural means of knowing; and it is as legitimate and reasonable to deny or doubt the truth of one natural faculty or power in respect to its own proper objects as that of another.

From consciousness, which is purely subjective, to the objective, is not a valid illation, since no power or faculty can transcend its own order of objects, and pass without a medium, to a class specifically different, or really *separated* from it.

But sound philosophy must begin with, as admitted, because undeniable, the truths or principles that are known to reason, without argument, of themselves, and which need no proof, and admit none, and require no other reason for an assent, than

* "Propositio *per se nota est*, quando ea est connexio prædicati cum subjecto, ut penetrari subjectum nequeat, quin ea connexio deprehendatur in ipsa ratione subjecti. Seu propositio *per se nota* dicitur cujus veritas per se et sine medio a se distincto innotescit: sic lux dicitur per se visibilis, quia eaipsa et non per medium magis lucidum videtur." A proposition is *per se* known, or is *self-evident*, when the connexion of the predicate with the subject is such, that the subject cannot be understood, without the connexion being perceived in the very nature of the subject. Or, a proposition is said to be *per se* known, or *self-evident*, whose truth is known in itself and without any medium which is distinct from it: thus light is *per se* visible, for it is seen in itself, and not by means of another medium more distinct than itself.

their own self-evidence. With regard to *empirical* knowledge, or that acquired by experience, we must also admit, without other proof, the evident perceptions of the mind, through the senses and consciousness; since these, too, are direct cognitions of *evident* truth: nature, of itself, cannot err.* Nor do we thereby *assume* truth *on faith in natural law*. No; we assent to it, because it is evident; and it is evident because it is truth, or that which is, and we *know* it to be such as we *see* it to be.

Hence, then, our own existence, our perceptions of external objects, the acts of consciousness, truths known *per se*, as, "it cannot be that the same thing exists, and does not exist, at the same time;" and the like, are truths that are admitted as absolutely certain, and incapable of logical proof; since that alone is capable of proof which can be made more evident by another truth still more evident, from which it is evidently deduced.

Therefore, genuine philosophy begins, not with doubt or negation; but with certain first truth, immediately evident without demonstrative proof, and the affirmation of it.

This question, as to primitive truths, should not be confounded with the question, as to the *origin of ideas;* this latter subject pertains to *psychology*, or the philosophy of the mind, but yet it will be briefly treated in a subsequent part of this work.

The importance of the foregoing doctrine will be appreciated if it be remembered that, as said by an illustrious author (D. Th. de veritate, a. 1). "the certainty of knowledge comes from the certainty of its principles; for, the certainty of inferences or conclusions is known only when they are resolved into their principles."

Observe, also, that inferences or conclusions, as such, partake in some mode of the nature of their premises; for they are caused by them. Hence, principles or premises that are evident and absolute, furnish conclusions which are necessary and evident in virtue of those premises.

*"Natura non deficit in necessariis." Nature is not deficient in what is necessary.

CHAPTER II.

MEANS OF ATTAINING TRUTH WITH CERTAINTY.

The means of attaining truth may be classified under the following heads, viz.: 1st, the faculty of consciousness; 2d, the internal senses and the external senses; 3d, the ideas which the mind has acquired, and which it compares among themselves, or, simple Apprehension, Judgment and Reasoning; 4th, Testimony or Authority, which exacts rational assent.

ARTICLE I.

THE POWER OF CONSCIOUSNESS.

The word consciousness is here used to signify the power or faculty of the mind to reflect on its own modifications or operations, together with the act of thus reflexively seeing what is within itself. In this sense it corresponds to the Latin phrases, *sensus intimus*, *conscientia reflexa*, and is, therefore, not only the power, but includes the act of the mind by which it sees and recognizes what happens within itself, *as its own*. Hence, it has for its immediate object *internal facts; i. e.*, 1st, the modifications of the mind alone, as ideas, judgments, acts of volition; 2d, modifications of the human compound, as grief, gladness, cold, hunger. The act or modification of the mind is not anything really distinct from the mind itself; it is the mind acting within itself as subject and object. In an act of consciousness two things are always seen, at least confusedly, viz., the impression, and the subject of it; for the impression is always perceived in concrete, as it is; therefore, it is seen not as abstract or separate from the mind, but in the mind itself. For the mind knows itself as a living principle of action, by its own operations; *i. e.*, it knows its acts, *as its own*. The faculty or power of consciousness does not attain physically and immediately to external objects; but it becomes cognizant of them only as they are presented through the action of the senses, the imagination, and as seen through the ideas or concepts in the intellect, but without directly perceiving the internal *medium*. (Vide page 62, *note*.) Without this power of the mind we could have no reflex knowledge of anything; even evidence itself can only become a motive of philosophical certainty when it is an object of consciousness; or is reflexively seen as such. The action of consciousness is implied in all judgments; for it is the directing and controlling influence in all the mind's completely rational action.

Consciousness, therefore, affords an unerring motive of certainty, as to the truth of its objects; that is, both of our existence and the mind's own modifications.

This proposition cannot be logically demonstrated, since the formal argument would explicitly assume what is in question; but, on the other hand, we cannot conceive or declare a doubt of it, except on its own testimony. All demonstration presupposes some truths that are known *per se*, that is, evident in themselves without proof; or, such as are known through our cognoscive powers by their own objective evidence, as facts which neither require nor admit any demonstration; what we know by the direct and immediate act of consciousness is an evident fact of this kind. It neither admits nor requires demonstration; for, the understanding clearly perceives the truth in the objects of its own acts, as self-evident; and it is absurd either to doubt or to attempt the *a priori* proof of what is self-evident. To deny the absolute certainty of its testimony is to reject all certainty, and the right use of reason, and logic itself; which would be either intellectual blindness or moral perversity.

The fact that persons who are delirious, or dream, do not

have normal action of consciousness, and do not thereby either perceive or acquire truth, does not militate against the thesis, that consciousness affords an infallible motive of certainty as to its own objects. In such conditions the mind perceives and judges by the phantoms of a disturbed imagination. This organ, in those states, has none but disordered action; for, when diseased or disturbed, the imagination cannot coöperate in rational thought, as will be more fully explained in another place. As disturbed water reflects images in distorted fragments; so, when the fancy is in an abnormal state, its action is morbid and disorderly, and its imagery is in undistinguishable confusion.

When this organ is so diseased or disordered as not to have normal action, the intellect is thereby more or less completely shut off, according to the extent and nature of the affection, from the entire world of realities, with which the fancy, as will be again remarked in the next article, is its essential medium of communication; and, in this state of seclusion, it is either wholly or partially unable to distinguish what is merely of the sickly fancy, from what is objectively real. In such case, this organ either forms no image at all of objects acting on the external senses, or those images are distorted and confused. Even in dreams, the action of the external senses being suspended, and those senses thereby ceasing to present real objects to the imagination, it is not then a medium of rational communication for the soul with real or actual objects; which strikingly shows how entirely dependent the intellect is on the imagination, for all the objects of its action.

By the power of consciousness it is sometimes difficult to distinguish in impressions that are even but recently *past*, whether they were acts of the will, or acts of the soul as not free; especially since the acts and affections of the will are, by their nature, more obscure than are the acts of direct perception or judgment. But even in this and analogous cases, in which truth may be difficult of attainment, close observation of what actually occurs in the mind, with careful reflection, secures the judgment from *error*, especially if the mind merely affirms what it perceives, and as it perceives it.

Abnormal action of the faculties proceeds from a disturbed condition of the bodily organs, and is an exceptional case, that properly has nothing to do with the thesis; for it has reference to the operations of the mind only in its sound condition. The causes of diseased mental action properly pertain to another science for their analysis.

ARTICLE II.

THE SENSES; THE NATURE AND FUNCTION OF ORGANIC POWERS.

The senses, sensation, the nature of organic action, also the nature and specific objects of intellectual action, are explained somewhat diffusely in this article and the succeeding one; because a clear distinction between *organic* action and *intellectual* action is of the utmost importance, even for the very beginning of philosophic study. That distinction is ignored in some popular works on philosophy, and is directly denied in others, either because their authors had made no careful and considerate examination of the subject, or because it was their pleasure to teach an hypothesis which identifies matter and intellect.

The old philosophers classified the senses as *internal* and *external.* The *internal* senses are, *imagination; sensile memory; potentia æstimativa*, or power of estimating material things, as good or evil for sensible appetite; *sensus communis*, "common sense," an organic power, by which the impressions made on the external senses are sensibly distinguished from each other.

A sensible organ, or an organic power, is a member of the living animal compound, i. e., compound of a substantial vital principle, and matter; it is capable of vital action in respect to its proper objects, and is ordained by its nature to sustain and perfect the living organism to which it pertains. Hence, organic power essentially belongs to *animal* nature, and is, therefore, *living*, and *corporeal or material.*

Imagination, and *fancy*, are two names for the same organic power, or internal sense, and are used in this work indiscriminately; the former word is derived from the Latin language; the latter, from the Greek. Imagination is the power of forming and reproducing sensible images made out of the impressions received by the senses from external objects. *Sensile** memory is the organic power by which these impressions are retained, and recognized when they are reproduced; or, more explicitly, sensile memory, which is an organic power, is the faculty of retaining the *quasi concepts* or *intentions* of those impressions and images in the fancy, and sensibly recognizing them when they are reproduced.

If the *reproduction* of the past impression be understood to include the *recalling* of it, then, the *reproduction* of an impression may be referred, under different respects, both to the imagination and the memory.

The *intellectual* memory is not an *organic* power, but is a faculty of the soul itself, having no more direct dependence on the organs of the body than the understanding or will has.

THE CONNEXION OF THE INTERNAL SENSES, AND THEIR DEPENDENCE ON EACH OTHER.

The *potentia æstimativa* is the power of duly *estimating*, i. e., *sensibly appreciating* the fitness or unfitness of an object to satisfy the wants of animal nature, or, as good or harmful for it. The *sensus communis*, which is analogous to the *potentia æstimativa*, is the basis of all the external senses, and is thus *common* to them, somewhat as the sense of touch, under another respect, may be regarded as the basis of all the senses;† but it moreover *distinguishes* the impressions made on the five external senses from one another. It was argued thus: even

*It is manifest that *sensile* is here a more proper term than *sensible, sensitive* or *sentient*, any one of which would be equivocal in this connexion.

†"Omnes alii sensus fundantur supra tactum." (Div. Th., 1 p., qu. 76, a. 5.) All the other senses are founded on that of touch.

the brute animal *feels* that it sees, *feels* that it hears, *feels* that it smells, etc.; but the *eye* cannot distinguish between color and sound, the *ear* cannot distinguish between sound and smell, etc.; therefore, there must be an organic power which receives, feels, and distinguishes all these impressions made upon the external organs. To do this, is the function of the *sensus communis*, or "common sense," so called, because, as already observed, it is the common basis and principle of unity for all the five external senses. The *imagination*, which is also an internal sense, forms its *images* or *phantasmata* from the impressions made through the external senses on the *sensus communis;* the *potentia æstimativa*, i. e., the power of *estimating* or valuing objects as good or hurtful for appetite, makes its appreciation or estimate of its objects *as presented to it by images in the fancy;* and in this act the *potentia æstimativa* forms for itself *quasi* concepts expressing the *uses*, "*intentions*" of sensible objects, and these *quasi* concepts are *retained* by the *sensile memory*. All these powers are purely organic, and are situated in the brain. They are possessed by all the *perfect* animals: i. e., all animals that have *five* external senses.

They discriminate, in certain instances, between the properties of objects presented to them through the external senses; not, however, by way of a formal judgment; but by a true, though *sensible*, *appreciation* of them.*

But the *potentia æstimativa*, as it is in man, is far more perfect than it is in irrational animals. In man it is not limited in its action to merely *appreciating* a sensible object as useful or hurtful for appetite; but it can *compare* particular and singular objects of the kind among themselves, in a manner not unlike to that in which the intellect *compares* universals, and it

* "*Opinio* passionem facit in appetitu, non autem imaginatio; si enim præcise *imaginemur* hostes, non statim timemus aut fugimus; secus vero si *opinemur* præsentes. Ratio est, quod sola apprehensio qualis est in phantasia, non movet appetitum nisi accedat æstimativæ operatio."—Musæum Philos. de Anima. *Opinion* produces passion in the appetite, imagination does not; if we merely *imagine* enemies, we do not at once flee away or fear; it is otherwise though, if we have the *opinion* that they are present. The reason is, that the sole apprehension as it is in the fancy cannot move appetite, unless there accede to it the operation of the *potentia æstimativa*, which reputes the object to be real.

thus approaches to a nearer resemblance of intellectual action. Hence, this power in man, was termed *vis cogitativa*, or *cogitative* power; or, also, *ratio particularis*, or *particular reason;* and it was described by the old philosophers as the connecting link in man between *sense* and *reason*. It is, therefore, under different respects, both the highest power of *sense*, and, in some manner, the lowest power or act of *reason:* yet this power is, in itself, merely *organic*.

The human soul, by the power of consciousness, can *reflect* on its own acts and what affects it, and see these operations as its *own;* but no *sense* or organic power, whether internal or external, can reflect on itself or its own act; this power of reflex action pertains to simple intellectual substance only.

It is, perhaps, not too much to affirm that no other theory as yet proposed by philosophers, so consistently or so satisfactorily explains the phenomena of what may be termed by analogy, the *brute mind*, or which accounts equally well for all that which is merely *sensible* or *organic* operation, in man also.

THIS THEORY FOR THE EXPLANATION OF SENSE COGNITION, ACCOUNTS CONSISTENTLY FOR ALL ITS PHENOMENA.

In order that the limits of purely sensible knowledge may be more distinctly traced, and be more clearly seen, it will be useful to consider this truth, namely, that the doctrine of internal sense, or internal organs of sensible cognition, is in itself not repugnant to the nature of organic power. For since the fact is undeniable that the senses have many virtues or perfections of various species and degrees, we can easily conceive internal ones capable, without at all transcending the specific nature of organic power, of receiving and acting on the impressions conveyed to them by the external senses, as their connatural objects; analogously to the manner in which the external senses receive and act on impressions from their objects.

Since the sense has no reflex action, the impression which is actually in it must be immediately produced by the object and the organ, and as the object is singular, concrete and material, the impression as in the organ, though vitally received by it, must be a *material* effect. Both the organ, and the object are material; therefore, the effect of their combined action is material. The *material* nature or character of the impression in the external sense, is all that is *per se* or necessarily required to constitute it the connatural object of another organic power that is superior to the external sense. That the fancy is an internal organic power of this kind, i. e., that its proper or connatural object is an impression furnished by the external sense, will be rendered more manifest by what is to be shown a little further on.

They who deny or fail to recognize the existence of internal senses, attribute all sensible operation, whose principle is not obvious, or which cannot be explained by the action of external sense alone, either to *instinct* or to *intellect.* Instinct, in such theory, is a vague and indeterminate power which is made to account for all cognoscive operation which transcends the capacity of external sense. But this is to evade the difficulty, not to explain it. Instinct,* more precisely and accurately understood, is a natural impulse and positive tendency to some vital action which is useful or necessary for the individual agent or its species, that *utility* of the action not being *apprehended* or *known* by it as an *end* to be attained. Thus we explain some actions of beavers, ants, migratory birds, etc. They apprehend certain sensible objects, and are moved by them to action; but the design or intention of the *end* in their action, we ascribe, through the law of their nature, to the Author of their being.

Considered in itself, instinct appears to be a virtue or principle of action superadded to nature as operative, over and above appetite and cognition; subserved by them, and directive of them and the subject to which they belong, in certain matters in which those powers are not sufficient for the end to be attained.

In order not to confound merely organic action with intellectual action, we must not lose sight of the truth that their

* Div. Th. 1, 2, p. qu. 40, a. 3.

objects are essentially distinct;* the formal, proper, connatural object of organic power or sense, is the singular, or concrete and *material* reality; that of the intellect, is the abstract, universal or intelligible, which is, of its nature, absolutely *supersensible*, and is therefore *immaterial.*

THE BRUTE SOUL, ANIMA BELLUINA, IS MATERIAL.

Brutes evidently have those cognitions that are perfected in sense alone; though they show no signs whatever that they possess intellect or free will. Their action is physically necessary and uniform, *quid determinatum ad unum*, "what is determined to one mode of action." An agent which is thus limited to that action which is physically necessary has, of course, no rational empire over its own operation, and, therefore, has no intelligent principlc of action.

It cannot be legitimately denied that an agent which depends on matter in all its action, also depends on matter in existing, according to the metaphysical principle, "modus agendi sequitur modum essendi," "action is according to the essence of the agent:" or, that which is material in its action is also material in its essence; and hence, knowing the *action*, we may justly conclude *a posteriori to the essence* or nature of the agent that puts it. This axiom holds true, whether the agent is the *univocal*, or the *equivocal* cause of the effect produced by means of its act.

The argument may be stated more strictly in form, thus: all organic action is material action, because both the organ is material, and its object is *per se* material; the brute mind has none but organic action, and, therefore, it has none but material action.† But that which wholly depends on matter in its

* "Sentire, et consequentes operationes animæ sensitivæ, accidunt cum aliqua corporis immutatione . . intelligere exercetur sine organo corporeo." (Vide Div. Thom. Sum., 1 p., qu. 75, a. 3.) To feel sensibly, and the consequent operations of the sensitive soul, happen with some change in the body . . . to understand, is exercised without a bodily organ.

† "Cum animæ brutorum animalium non *per se* operentur, non sunt subsistentes, similiter enim unumquodque habet esse et operationem." (Div. Th. 1 p. qu. 78, a 3.) Since the souls of brute animals do not operate *per se*, they do not subsist, (or exist alone or apart from matter), for every thing exists and acts in a similar manner.

action, also depends wholly on matter in existing; now, the brute soul is affixed to matter and limited to matter in all its action; it is, therefore, similarly dependent on matter in existing; i. e., it can not exist *per se*, or *alone* and *apart* from matter, but only dependently on it.

The force of this reasoning will be still more clearly perceived, if it be borne in mind that we not only know an agent by its action, and know it only by its action; but its action is, in some proper sense of the words, the *measure* of its essence; "unumquodque agit in quantum est actu, i. e., in quantum forma actuatum;" "every thing has *action*, in proportion as it has *actual essence*."

THE HUMAN SOUL A SPIRITUAL OR IMMATERIAL SUBSTANCE.

By similar reasoning it follows that since the acts of the human soul, intellection and volition, are wholly inorganic, for their objects are wholly immaterial, and the intellect and will elicit their acts *alone*, i. e., without any other second cause as a concurrent principle, the soul is therefore immaterial; or, since the human soul operates *per se*, or without direct dependence on matter, it also can exist *per se*, or is an immaterial substance.

The intellect knows material or sensible things by their intelligible essence;* i. e., by real intellectual types or similitudes of them expressed in concepts of their essence; hence, it knows material things in an immaterial manner, which it is not possible for organic power to do.

The human soul, when existing separate from the body, is said to *subsist incompletely;* because, by its very nature, it is ordained to substantial union with the body. But, considered as a *substance*, it can be said to *exist completely* when in that state, because it exists *per se;* i. e., it, as it were, *stands alone*, or exists without *leaning or depending on another* thing, by inhering in it.

* "Essentiæ rerum materialium sunt in intellectu hominis, vel angeli, ut intellectum est in intelligente, et non secundum suum esse reale." (Sum., 1 P., Qu. 57, Art. 1, Ad. 2.) The essences of material things are in the intellect of man, or the angel, as that which is understood is in that which understands, and not as to their real existence.

It would seem necessarily to follow from what is said above that the brute soul, *anima belluina*, is a substantial and living principle, or, as expressed by the old philosophers, *forma substantialis et principium vivens;* and, in fact, such it evidently must be. Yet, its total dependence on matter in operating proves that it is totally of matter also in existing; it can exist only in union by composition with matter, and it is, therefore, only *incomplete*, and, at the same time, *partial* substance. Besides, even if we conceived it absolutely possible for the brute soul to exist separate from matter, to which it must naturally be affixed in existing, as shown above; then it could have no sensible action, for it would be destitute of an organ; it could have no spiritual action, for it would have no intellect; therefore, its state would be that of mere *potentiality*, or existence without action; i. e., the supposition is absurd.

IS THE IMAGINATION AN ORGANIC POWER; OR, IS THE SUBJECT IN WHICH IT RESIDES, THE SOUL; I. E., THE SPIRITUAL SUBSTANCE AS ESSENTIALLY DISTINGUISHED FROM MATTER?

The imagination or fancy is organic; or, its subject is the living compound, and not the soul or spiritual substance alone; its peculiar function in man is to serve the intellect, or to present objects to it by means of true images of those objects.*

It is an organic power, for the brute animal possesses no higher principle of action than that of sense or organic power, as already seen; but the brute has imagination, and even sensible memory also; for the arguments which prove the existence of fancy in them, at the same time conclusively show them to possess organic or sensible memory. For the *perfect* animal, imagination is physically necessary, since it must know sensible things not only as present and acting on its external organs; but it must know them when they are absent so that it may tend to such objects as are necessary for sustenance,

* "Anima rationalis, licet quamdiu corpus informat, supponat operationem phantasiæ quæ per organum operatur, tamen organo non elicit suam intellectionem." (Irenæus Carmelit, et philosophi passim.) The rational soul, though so long as it informs the body it suppose the operation of fancy which acts through an organ, does not elicit its intellection by an organ.

preservation, etc. But to form and preserve the images of sensible things, to reproduce and recognize them, are respectively the functions of fancy and sensible memory. Since brutes have no intellect, this power must be merely organic in them; it follows, therefore, that the faculty, imagination, is, at least, not *per se*, or necessarily intellectual.

But even in man this power can form the image of no object except one that is either sensible in itself, or which it can represent as invested with sensible forms or qualities. Now, a power that can have no object of action but that which is *sensible*, and, therefore, material, must itself be material; for the *nature* of a power is known by the specific objects of its action, since action follows the nature, or agrees with the nature of the agent. The imagination in man is, therefore, an organic power, or its subject is the living compound of soul and body. Or, in fewer words, the imagination is not an intellectual principle, because its connatural object is only the sensible or material; and, hence, it is *per se*, or *essentially* material or organic.

The imagination in man is sometimes termed "the medium between the senses and the intellect;" "fantasia est media inter sensum et intellectum." Hence, without the action of the external senses, the fancy could form no images of sensible objects; without the action of the fancy, the intellect could not naturally have any communication whatever with any real object, or any sensible power of cognition, and hence it would be totally insulated from all the proper objects of its action. The fancy, therefore, is for the intellect the *essential medium of communication* with the entire order of reality. As we are now constituted, the intellect cannot contemplate or even perceive any object, except as in some manner *embodied* and *reflected* in that *mirror*.*

The fancy can form no image every real component of which was not originally acquired by the actual observation

* "Corpus requiritur ad actionem intellectus, non sicut organum quo talis actio exerceatur, sed ratione objecti." (Div. Th. 1 p, qu. 75, a. 2, ad. 3.) "The body is required for the action of the intellect, not as an organ by which such action is exercised, but *on account of the object.*

of sensible things: a man blind from his birth can have in his fancy no real image of color; "quibus deficit unus sensus, deficit una scientia;" "they who never possessed any one sense, are destitute of one species of cognition."

WHAT, IN REGARD TO MENTAL THOUGHT, IS THE SPECIAL FUNCTION OR ACT OF THE IMAGINATION, WHOSE CONNATURAL OBJECT, AS ALREADY SHOWN, IS PER SE MATERIAL.

Imagination is generically the same in man and brute; in man it forms and presents images to the intellect, which the intellect contemplates, and by abstraction forms from them its intelligible concepts or ideas of things.* In the brute its images serve as objects for the faculty of sense, termed *potentia æstimativa*, or power of sensibly discerning objects as good or noxious for the animal: † called by what name soever, undeniable facts prove that brute animals possess this *faculty* of distinguishing such *uses* or *intentions* of sensible objects, no less than facts also prove demonstratively that they have no intellectual act.

That no brute faculty can apprehend the abstract or universal, or can judge, is strictly demonstrated by induction only; but this induction, it cannot be questioned, has long since actually been made by mankind, logically, over and over again, and in the most general manner; and each one's daily observation verifies the conclusion which is known, as a fact, to have been reached by mankind. Whence it logically suffices here merely to affirm the impossibility of any duly attested law or fact of brute action being adduced, which cannot be fully accounted for, by the operation of sensible or organic powers, as they are above described.

* With strange confusion, both of thought and of language, this action of the intellect is, by certain writers, called *imagination*. Wherefore, since this volume contains no treatise on the science of Psychology, it was judged advisable to explain more fully and explicitly in this place the specific and distinguishing acts of fancy and intellect, than is strictly pertinent to a work on Logic and General Metaphysics.

† "Ad apprehendendum intentiones quæ per sensum non accipiuntur ordinatur vis æstimativa." (Div. Th., 1 p., qu. 78, a. 4.) The *vis æstimativa*, or power of sensibly appreciating, is ordained for apprehending the uses or intentions which are not received through the external sense.

THE NATURE AND THE CONNATURAL OBJECT OF THE EXTERNAL SENSES; THEY DO NOT ERR PER SE, I. E., THEY CANNOT PHYSICALLY CAUSE ERROR.

The external senses are the five organs through which the mind becomes cognizant of various exterior* objects, by means of the properties of those objects. The organs are in themselves capable of being acted on, and of conveying to the mind the impressions received, but are indifferent as to their particular object; their action is determined in species by the connatural and singular object, which is duly present to them. The external senses are, sight, hearing, touch, taste, smell.

Sense† is an organic power of the soul, and is cognoscive only of those things that are *singular* and *material;* i. e., 1st, it is an *active* principle, whose subject is *man*, or the *compound of soul and body*, and not a part only of man, as is the case with the *intellect*, whose subject is the spiritual substance of the soul alone, not the compound; 2d, *sense* is termed *organic*, because it is *affixed to an organ*, which, as already observed, is a compound of soul and matter; and hence, under this respect, *sense* could also be denominated a *power of the body*, or a *corporeal power;* 3d, it perceives or apprehends only the *singular;* i. e., the concrete, determinate individual; while the intellect, on the contrary, has for its object the *universal;* 4th, it cannot attain in its action to every species of *singular thing;* v. g., it cannot perceive an *angel*, but its object is only the *singular* which is at the same time *material.*‡ The *sensible*, therefore, or *the object of sense*, may be defined to be "any material,

* "Sensus non apprehendit essentias rerum, sed exteriora accidentia tantum; similiter neque imaginatio." (Div. Thom. 1 P., Qu. 57, Art. 1, ad. 2.) Sense does not apprehend the essences of things, but only exterior accidents; likewise, the imagination does not apprehend the essences of things.

† "Sensus est facultas animæ organica, singularium materialium cognoscitiva." Sense is an organic power of the soul, capable of knowing singular material objects.

‡ "Omne sensibile est materiale." Whatever is sensible is material.

extended, and singular object or being, which is perfective of sense or organic power, by intimate conjunction with it."*

An object is *sensible*, either *per se*,† or *per accidens;* an object is *sensible per se* or *of itself*, which has, of its own nature, the power of perceptibly affecting, or producing an impression on the *sense;* v. g., *light* has of itself, and by its own nature, the power of physically producing such impression on the *eye; heat*, on the *touch*, etc.

An object is said to be *sensible per accidens*, when, without having any power in itself to act on the sense, yet it has conjoined with it some property or *accident* by means of which it does become known as present. In this case, while it does not itself physically act on the *sense*, yet it becomes known to the *sense* in some manner, by means of another thing in conjunction with it that does thus act; v. g., *Socrates* has *complexion*, animal *heat*, etc.; the *color* can be *seen per se*, the *heat* can be *felt per se;* but it is not *Socrates* the *person* that thus acts *per se* on the *senses*, for *sense* is *immediately* acted on, not by *substance*, but by *accidents* only; hence, *Socrates* is an object that is *sensible per accidens;* or, more generally, *substance*, as such, is *sensible* only *per accidens;* i. e., substance, as such, is not *properly* a sensible object at all.

For an object to become *sensible per accidens*, the following conditions must be fulfilled; 1st, it must be susceptible of a property or accident which is *per se*, or of itself, capable of acting on the sense, and also actually have such property or accident; 2d, it must be an object which can be known *per se* or in itself, either by the *intellect*, or by some *sense* or organic power; v. g, the *senses* perceive or know material *substance per accidens*, the intellect alone can know it *per se;* i. e., as its proper object; a *colored* object may be known *per accidens* by the *touch*, but it is known *per se*, or as its proper object only by

* "*Sensibile* est ens materiale extensum, singulare, perfectivum sensus per intimam cum eo conjunctionem." The *sensible* is a material being, extended, singular, and perfective of sense by intimate conjunction with it.

† "Sensus externus non fertur in præteritum nec futurum." External sense does not attain to that which is past, or future.

the *sight.* If both the foregoing conditions be not verified, an object cannot, indeed, be known by the senses at all.

The *sensible per se* is either *proper*, or *common;* the *proper** *sensible* is what can be perceived by one sense and only by one sense; v. g., *color*, as such, is the *proper* object of sight only, and therefore it cannot be perceived, as such, by any other sense.

The *common sensible*,† is what can be perceived by more senses than one, and it is on that account said to be *common* to them, or their *common* object. Under the name, *common sensible*, five classes of sensible objects are enumerated as including all things to which the term is applicable; viz.: "motion, rest, number, figure and size." These are all objects both of *sight* and *touch*, and they may, also, in certain cases, fall under the other senses, as a little reflection will show. All the qualities or accidents of material objects which can be perceived by more senses than one, can be reduced to one or other of the preceding five genera of *common sensibles. Size*, as perceived by the eye, is modified and corrected when perceived by the touch; and *vice versa. Distance* seen by the *eye*, and distance attested by the *touch*, serve to correct and perfect the judgment of it in the mind.

It may be said, then; 1st, that the *common sensible* modifies the *proper;* 2d, that the *sensible per accidens* is known only by means of the *proper*, but it does not in any manner *modify* the action of the *proper sensible*‡ on its own particular organ; 3d,

* "*Proprium* sensibile uno solo sensu sentitur: *commune*, pluribus." The *proper* sensible is apprehended by one sense only: the *common*, by more than one.

† "Communia non sunt sensibilia per accidens; quia hujusmodi sensibilia aliquam diversitatem faciunt in immutatione sensus" (alterius). (Div. Thom. 1 p., qu. 78, art. 4, ad. 2.) The *common* sensible is not sensible merely *per accidens;* for it *really causes* an effect on the sense.

‡ "*Sensibile per accidens* nullam vim habet ex se movendi vel immutandi sensum." The *sensibile per accidens* has no power, *of itself*, of moving or immediately affecting sense.

"*Proprium* est quod ita uno sensu percipitur, ut alio percipi non possit; et circa quod sensus errare non potest. *Commune* est, quod pluribus sensibus potest percipi, et circa quod sensus potest falli." The *proper sensible* is perceived by one sense only, and it cannot be apprehended by another: in regard to it, the sense cannot err. The *common sensible* can be perceived by more senses than one, and in respect to it, the sense can err.

in the *common sensible*, the same property may be perceived through different organs, but it is done by specifically different action in them.

The mind is invincibly impelled to refer the impressions received through the senses to the external objects acting on them, and thereby manifesting themselves to it as their cause; not, however, by blind impulse, but by the evidence. The mind thus refers the impressions received, even before any reflex judgment, because it thereby actually perceives through the senses the properties or objects that produce them. This inborn and resistless propensity to refer our sensations, or the impressions made on the senses, to corporeal or physically existing beings, as their actual cause; or, in other words, this sensation thus received and referred, is the testimony afforded by the senses.

Sensible objects act through their properties on the organs; these properties are, 1st, *primary* or *absolute* properties; that is, such as, in some manner, flow from their essence, and without which they cannot naturally exist; as, extension, figure, motion, or rest; 2d, *relative* or *secondary* properties; as, color, taste, particular size, etc. But as the senses do not of themselves judge, and are incapable of reflex action, it is only the mind that perceives the nature of objects, or that of their properties. It is true that there is an implicit or imitated judgment in every sensation as such, since it may be regarded as an *affirmation*, in a wide sense of the term; but, because the action of sense is in itself entirely subject to physical and natural law, this implicit or imitated judgment must be referred through the law of their nature, in obedience to which they act necessarily and truly, to the Creator of the senses.* Ex-

* "Veritas aliqua reperitur in simplici mentis conceptione, neque solum mentis, sed etiam sensuum . . constat quæ et qualis sit hæc veritas quæ in simplici mentis notitia reperitur: nihil enim aliud est quam veritas ipsa transcendentalis, his entibus accommodata." (Suarez Metaph., Disp. 8, Sect. 3.) There is a kind of truth found in the simple conception of the mind, and not only in the conceptions of the mind, but in those also of the senses. . . . It is clear of what nature this truth is, which is found in the simple knowledge of the mind: it is indeed nothing else than transcendental truth. accommodated to those things.

ternal objects, as remarked, act through their *properties* on the senses; the senses are, therefore, said to know *per accidens*, or *accidentally*, the *substance;* it being invariably conjoined with those properties. But, substance is *per se* known, i. e., can be said *formally* and *properly* to be *known* by the intellect only.

DOES THE MIND, THEN, ATTAIN TO THE CERTAIN KNOWLEDGE OF OUTWARD OR SENSIBLE OBJECTS BY MEANS OF THE SENSES?

The soul informs* each organ of sense; and on that account the soul is the *principle* through which the organ *feels*, or acts vitally; and hence, by some, consciousness, or the soul as conscious, is termed the basis of sensation. Yet, the soul being affixed to an organ, its natural action through that organ is subject to necessary law; i. e., the organs of sense, in actually perceiving the impressions from external objects, are governed by physical laws of nature which are immutable, except by miracle. When an organ is in its normal condition, the object and concurrent circumstances being the same, the organic action will always be the same; but a change in the normal state of the organ will, in obedience to physical law, modify the impression received from those objects, according to the nature and extent of that change.†

But it will help to the clearer intelligence of the matter, if we consider these sensible impressions: 1st, as they *affect* the organ, and are modifications of it; 2d, as *representative* of the objects from which they are received. These impressions, considered as modifications of the organ, are always true, whether the mind errs in its judgment or not; for, whether the organ be well or ill disposed, it conveys the impression just as it receives it. There is in it that necessary action which belongs to all agents, which operate in obedience to natural law; and, therefore, if the organ be disordered, the impression received

* "Forma est principium agendi in unoquoque." The *form* is the principle of action in every object.

† "Quidquid recipitur, secundum modum recipientis recipitur." Whatever is received, is received according to the nature of the recipient.

is modified by the disease, according to the nature and extent of the affection; but it still conveys what it receives, no more, no less. Therefore, the senses *per se*, or of themselves, do not deceive, since they act by the necessary laws of nature itself, and these laws are true and uniform; i. e., they always act in the same manner, under the same circumstances.

But when we consider sensible impressions as *representative* of the objects from which they are received, the senses, being ill-disposed, or right means not being employed to use them prudently in judging, may become the *occasion*, but not strictly the efficient *cause*, of error. Thus, when the palate is disordered, that may seem to the mind to taste bitter which is in itself sweet; to a diseased eye, that may seem yellow which is really white; but, in these cases, the qualities tasted and seen are not really, or *a parte rei*, the sweet or white in the objects; but these qualities as *modified* or *overpowered* by other causes. It is not the function of the sense to *judge*, or distinguish cause and effect; this is the function of the mind; the only proper office of the organ is to receive the impression as given and convey it to the mind as received. Hence, the senses, by accident, not *per se*, may be the cause, or rather the *occasion*, of erroneous judgment.

For the testimony of the senses to afford an infallible motive of certainty, the following conditions must be fulfilled: 1st, the object must be duly *present;* otherwise, a steeple, for example, that is square may be judged to be round; 2d, the organs of sensation must be in a healthy or *normal condition;* v. g., a jaundiced eye makes all objects appear with a yellow tinge; 3d, there must be agreement in the sensations received, both through the same organ, and different organs, according to the nature of the object; and they should be compared by the mind; in default of this condition, a staff that is partly in the water will be judged to be crooked, when in reality it is straight, the different refracting powers of air and water not being attended to by the mind.

Thus we have certainty as to external objects, because they afford the mind, through the organs of sense, the evidence of their existence, qualities, etc.; and, therefore, the mind is certain of their truth, because it sees that truth. From this it follows that the certainty which we have through the testimony of the senses is founded on *evidence*, the ultimate motive of all genuine certainty; for we see the essential connection between the testimony of the senses, and the reality of their objects, on the one hand; and on the other, the divine veracity; and this is evidence.

To affirm that the objects of sense can *per se* cause error; i. e., by their own real action *produce error*, is to compromise divine veracity; because the physical laws of nature depend for their force and whole efficacy on God; and natural *falsity*, either in them or in the objects subject to them, would be referable to God as its *cause*.

As the imagination, or power of forming and reproducing images of things, is *organic;* that is, the soul in intimate union by real composition with, and acting through, a material organ as its instrument; it is liable, as already remarked, to disease and disordered action, inasmuch as it is material. Hence, this organ, above all others, may interrupt or disturb the normal action of the mind; since the mind, as we are actually constituted, can have no normal action without it; in other words, the imagination truly co-operates in all thought, by presenting or exhibiting its images, or the objects of thought in which the intellect sees the intelligible. Whence it follows that the human mind, while in connection with the body on earth, cannot naturally have completely independent, or, in every respect, purely spiritual action; i. e., it requires the aid of the imagination.* Yet, this aid is merely extrinsic; for the acts of the understanding are immanent, and are elicited by the faculty alone, as their immediate or proximate principle. But, even in the concepts of objects the most abstract, the imagination co-operates with the action of the mind, by presenting terms and various related objects under their quasi images or their names. A striking proof of this necessary co-operation of

* Vide S. Th. 1 p., qu. 84, a. 7. "Principium nostrae cognitionis est a sensu." The beginning of our knowledge is from the senses.

the imagination in all our intellectual action, as noticed in another place, may be drawn from the facts learned by observation of insane minds. The mind, as such, or the soul, being immaterial and simple, is incapable of dissolution or decomposition, and, therefore, it cannot be diseased in its substance; but the imagination, being an organ, is material, and it is, therefore, susceptible of disease.

To recapitulate what has been said: The action of external objects on the sensible organs is modified by various causes, which may all, however, be reduced to two classes; 1st, the medium through which the object acts may be more or less changed by the agency of other mediums which intervene and combine or mingle with it; v. g., the appearance of an object seen at a distance is, in some instances, subject to many mutations of color, figure and size, arising from vapors, by which the refraction and transmission of light are changed. A second class of causes which affect the sensation as actually received, are such as influence the natural action of the organ itself; v. g., disease, excitement, diminished activity, etc. Although the external senses do not err *per se*, since they convey only the impressions which they actually receive from physical and real objects, even when these impressions happen to be modified either in the medium or in the organ; yet, it is conceded that they may err *per accidens*, or *accidentally*.* By this it is meant that, under special conditions, their impressions are *conjoined with error* in the cognition or judgment, which these impressions do not *physically produce*, but to which, however, they give *occasion*. This is an exceptional case, is accidental, and affords matter for exercising the intellectual virtues, *art* and *prudence*.†

While this contingent and occasional error does not destroy the essence of certainty in sensible cognitions, yet it cannot be

* "Qui occasione sensuum in errorem incidit, non ideo fallitur ob malum nuntium, sed quia ipse malus est judex." (S. Aug. de vera Relig., C. 33.) He that by occasion of the senses falls into error, is not therefore deceived because of a bad witness, but because he himself is a bad judge.

† "Ars et prudentia circa contingentia versantur." Art and prudence regard *contingent* things as their proper objects.

denied that it weakens the force of such certainty in its whole species.*

It should, perhaps, be said here, also, for the fuller explanation of the whole subject, that the *imagination*, when in an abnormal state, as it is in the demented, *errs per se*, or, truly *causes* error; for, in such condition of that organ, *true judgment is physically impossible*, at least in reference to some matter; or, in other words, error is then physically necessary. When the imagination is diseased, then by its own physical action, or *ex se*, it obtrudes images or *phantasmata* before the mind, which are *objectively false*, and which, nevertheless, the intellect *necessarily* apprehends as being really true. Hence, then, it may be argued thus: that organic power *per se* deceives, which physically necessitates error in the judgment or cognition; but the insane fancy does this; therefore, the insane fancy *per se* deceives. Hence it is that such agent becomes irresponsible.

But observe that, on the contrary, the image furnished by a disordered *external sense*, as a jaundiced eye, is not, in strict language, *objectively false*; for, its object is *real*, not *purely fictitious*, as are the phantasms of an insane imagination; and, moreover, in the event of abnormal sensations, correct knowledge and true judgment are still attainable, which is not the case in reference to the objects presented by the fancy when it is organically diseased, so as to be incapable of normal action.

ARTICLE III.

SIMPLE APPREHENSION, JUDGMENT AND REASONING, ALL FURNISH INFALLIBLE MOTIVES OF CERTAINTY, AS TO THEIR PROPER OBJECTS.

The understanding, or intellect, is an inorganic faculty; or,

* "Sensus fallitur circa proprium objectum; sed solum *per accidens*, et rarius: inde nihilominus naturalis cognitionis certitudinem minui, nemo negaverit." (Irenæus, De An., c. 2, sect. 2, §. 3.) The sense is deceived about its proper object, but only *per accidens*, or by accident, and very rarely; hence, nevertheless, no one will deny that the certainty of natural cognition is thereby somewhat impaired.

in other words, it is not affixed to any organ of the human compound; but its acts are proximately from itself, and are, in themselves, purely super-sensible; and it resides in the soul, as its only subject.

The formal, adequate and connatural object of the human intellect, i. e., the intellect of man, who *essentially* consists of soul and body united, *by substantial composition*, is the *quiddity*, or *essence*, of sensible things.* Its cognitions begin with the sensible; by means of the sensible it proceeds to the abstract or super-sensible, which it understands by comparing it to corporeal things, or the objects of sense.† The formal object of cognition should be proportioned to, or commensurate with, the power which knows; it, therefore, should possess a corresponding degree of immateriality with it. In other words, the object should be, in some proper sense of the terms, as far removed from matter as the power; for, as cognoscive power rises in perfection, so must its formal object rise also; and as the power approximates or recedes from matter, according to the greater or less degree of its perfection, so also must its object.

According to this principle, the uncreated essence of God, is the commensurate or adequate object of the divine intellect; spiritual or Angelic essence, i. e., created immaterial essence, is the proportioned object of Angelic intellect; the essence of the human soul, is the connatural and proportioned object of the cognoscive soul when existing separated from the body; the essence of sensible things, is the *primary* and *commensurate* object of the human intellect, when the soul is affixed to matter

* "Omnia quæ in præsenti statu intelligimus, cognoscuntur a nobis per comparationem ad res sensibiles et naturales." (Div. Thom., 1 p., qu. 87, art. 7.) All things which we understand in our present state, are known to us through comparison to things that are sensible and *natural*, (that act by necessary physical laws, or are sensible and physical agents.)

† "Intellectus humani, qui est conjunctus corpori, proprium objectum est quidditas, sive natura in materia corporali existens, et per hujusmodi naturas rerum visibilium, etiam in invisibilium rerum aliquam cognitionem ascendit." (Div. Thom., 1 p., qu. 84, art. 7 in C.) The object of the human intellect which is conjoined to the body, is the essence or nature existing in corporeal matter; and by means of such *natures* of visible things, it also ascends to some knowledge of invisible things.

by union with the body; the singular concrete, and material, as having color, taste, smell, or as affecting the living organ, is the proper object of sensible or organic power.* Hence, it will be readily seen why man is often termed, "the link that binds together the material and spiritual orders."†

It would be an error, however, to infer from the preceding doctrine that the human intellect is organic; for it by no means follows that because its primary and adequate formal object is the essence of the sensible, the intellect is therefore the subject of sensible and organic mutations, or that it has organic action.

But it does logically follow that man's intellect knows God, and other superior substances of the spiritual order, only by comparison with what he immediately knows in the sensible order; and that he rises by reflexion on sensible things, and by abstraction, to the conception of those substances which are of another order.‡

It would be equally erroneous to infer from what is above stated, that the human intellect knows only the sensible and material; for it also reasons of God and angels.§ The mean-

* "Sensus non fertur *per se* nisi in singularia et accidentia materialia." Sense *per se*, i. e., of its own action, attains only to singular objects and material accidents.

† "Natura humana rationalis ab Angelica degenerat, quod sit ordinata ad informandum corpus, cui propterea alligatur; attamen cum Angelica convenit, quod sit spiritualis; et in eo sensitivam superat cum qua similiter convenit, quod sit materialis; unde homo dicitur a nonnullis *fibula* spiritualis et materialis ordinis, eo quod inter utrumque medius, utrumque in se copulat." Rational human nature falls below the angelic nature in that it is ordained to inform a body, to which it is, therefore, bound; however, it agrees with the angelic nature, in that it is spiritual. In this respect, also, it rises above sensitive nature, though it agrees with it in that it is material. Whence man is called by some the *link* between the spiritual and material orders, for he stands between both, and unites both in himself.

‡ "Invisibilia Dei per ea quæ facta sunt, intellecta conspiciuntur." (Rom. i. 20.) The invisible things of God are clearly seen, being understood by the things that are made.

§ "Mens seipsam *per se* novit, quia tandem in suiipsius cognitionem pervenit, licet per suum actum." (Sum. 1 p., qu. 87, art. 1, ad. 1.) The mind knows itself *by itself*, because it does come to the knowledge of itself, although by its own act. The soul knows itself only by its acts: it does not immediately or intuitively perceive its own *real essence*.

"Quamdiu anima est corpori unita, intelligit convertendo se ad phantasmata. Sed cum fuerit a corpore separata, intelligit, non convertendo se ad phantasmata, sed ad ea quæ sunt *secundum se* intelligibilia: unde seipsam *per seipsam* intelligit. Est autem commune omni substantiæ separatæ, quod intelligat id

ing which is intended to be conveyed in defining the adequate or commensurate object of man's intellect is, that the human understanding *primarily* and *formaliy* knows as its first and proper object, material essence; and that all its knowledge of higher things it acquires by aid of the material or sensible, through which it apprehends what transcends the senses, and, by comparison and abstraction, forms for itself concepts or notions of superior essences.

The intellect of man first conceives God, angels, spirits, under imaginary corporeal forms; which imperfect ideas of super-sensible substances, it corrects by reasoning; v. g., not unlike what takes place when we observe the staff which is partly in the water; it may be first conceived to be really bent, but by reflexion and further knowledge of truths not immediately presented in what the senses manifest, we come to know that the staff is not bent, but is really straight.

Similarly, due proportion being allowed for intellects that know by *simple intelligence*, and not by the less perfect way of *reason*, in order for the angels of one order, or hierarchy, to conceive those of another, they must compare and measure them by the primary and formal object of their own intellect, which is their own essence;* for, as every sense has its own adequate or commensurate object to which it is limited; v. g., the *eye* has figure and color, the *ear* has sound for its proper

quod est supra se per modum suæ substantiæ. Sic enim intelligitur aliquid secundum quod est in intelligente. Est autem aliquid in altero per modum ejus in quo est." (1 p., qu. 89, art. 2 in C.) So long as the soul is united to the body, it understands by converting itself to the images in the fancy. But when it is separated from the body, it understands without converting itself to the images of the fancy, but it converts itself to those things which are *in themselves* intelligible; hence, it then understands itself *by itself*. It is likewise common to every substance separated from matter, to understand that which is above itself, by means of its own substance. For, a thing is understood, according to the manner in which it is in the one understanding it; and a thing is in another, according to the nature of that other in which it is.

* "Modus intelligendi est proportionatus modo essendi: seu modus cognoscendi non sequitur modum rei cognitæ, sed modum essendi potentiæ cognoscitivæ." The mode of understanding is proportioned to the mode of being: or, the mode of knowing does not follow the mode of the thing known, but the mode of being which is in the cognoscive power.

"Sensus est singularium; intellectus universalium." The sense is of singulars; the intellect, of universals.

object; so must every created intellect have its connatural and determinate object, beyond which, or apart from which, it cannot operate; that of the divine intellect must be the uncreated and infinite.

The adequate or commensurate object of the human intellect should be so stated and understood as to be clearly distinguished from that of sense, and from the respective objects of the purely spiritual or angelic, and the Divine intellect. For this end, it should be observed that every agent must act or operate according to its essential mode of existing;* or, it must act according to its nature. Nor can its action ever exceed its essence;† for, powers are the appendices of essence, and are measured and limited by it; as no accidents can exceed their subject, so no properties or essential attributes can exceed the essence from which they flow or result. It is manifest, also, that powers must have objects of their action which are proportioned to them, and which, therefore, must be *proportioned in perfection* to the essence which is the subject of those powers, since the power follows the essence, and is limited by it.

In man, the soul is bound to the body, with which it is united by substantial composition; in that condition it is dependent on the external and internal senses for its intelligent action, though the coöperation of these organic powers is only *objective;* i. e., they efficiently coöperate in so much as they present the object, whose intelligible essence the intellect comes to know from the sensible impressions, by means of abstraction; and, in fact, man, as he is now actually constituted, cannot immediately perceive any other being than one which is, in some respect, material. Hence, the primary and proper object of man's intellect must be the *essence* of sensible

* "Uunumquodque operatur ad modum sui esse." Every thing acts, according to the mode of its existence.

† "Unaquæque potentia in operando limitatur per essentiam cujus est potentia." Every power is limited in its operation, by the essence of which it is a power.

"Corpus reqiritur ad actionem intellectus, non sicut organum quo talis actio exerceatur, sed ratione objecti." (Div. Thom., 1 p., qu. 75, art. 2, ad. 3.) The body is required for the action of the intellect, not as an organ by which such action is exercised, but on account of the object.

and material things; and it is only by reasoning upon sensible things that he rises to notions of immaterial or spiritual beings. Careful reflexion upon the facts of one's own experience and intellectual operations, strikingly confirms the truth of the foregoing statements.

The three principal acts or operations of the understanding in cognition are, Simple Apprehension, Judgment, and Reasoning or Ratiocination. A judgment consists of concepts or ideas that are compared; and reasoning consists of judgments compared to each other. The principal and characteristic function, or act of the understanding, is, to perceive truth, to distinguish the true and false; the good and evil, as true and false. In the ideas or concepts of things, by means of abstraction or remotion, it perceives the universal and the intelligible essence of the objects presented to it by the organs of sensation. These it compares, and, by means of analysis and synthesis, it forms a multitude of new concepts and judgments.

Simple Apprehension is the mere perception of the object, without any explicit affirmation or negation. The apprehension, to repeat here briefly an explanation already given, when the term is used to express the concrete result or product of the act of apprehending, is also called an *idea*, a *concept*, a *notion*. The word *idea* is more generally used; and it was selected because the mind, by the act of apprehending, forms a sort of *similitude* of the object perceived; and the term *idea* means a *visible appearance*, or a *likeness*. This *idea*, by means of which the mind *expresses* the object of its cognition, is also termed the *mental word*, *verbum mentis*, since the mind is conceived to *speak* it, as it were. But this *mental word*, or *idea*, in the mind perceiving, must not be confounded, as already remarked, with *sensation*, or with the *image*, in the imagination; both of which present only sensible qualities, and are effects of organic action, which are common to us and the brutes. Of the concept whose object is entirely abstract, as the infinite, the imagination forms no image; but, when we think of such objects, it strives to form its image of them, and it always presents, at least, the *terms* for them.

The object which the mind perceives, considered in itself with its *marks* or *determinations*, by which it is what it is, and nothing else, is the *material object* of perception; but the object, as actually manifested to the mind, is the *formal* object of perception.

The distinction between an apprehension, a judgment and reasoning, may be aptly illustrated by an example. If we conceive an idea of *world*, the mere act of perceiving or seeing that idea of *world* without affirming or denying any predicate, is a simple *apprehension;* but in uttering the proposition, "*the world is a contingent being*," there is a *judgment* formed; since it affirms the agreement of a predicate and subject. If we compare several judgments, and deduce from them another, or new judgment, on account of its *nexus* with them, this operation of the mind is *reasoning;* v, g., "The world is a contingent being; therefore, its cause is a free being; but this cause being *free*, is also *intelligent*, since *freedom* and intelligence connote each other." This is reasoning, or deducing one judgment from others.

All these acts of the intellect are *immanent;* that is, they *remain in* the mind; or do not, as such, pass out of it to an exterior term, or object of efficient action.

Immediate or *simple judgments* are those that are formed by the mind seeing directly and *immediately* the agreement of the subject and predicate, without any reasoning. The material object of this *immediate judgment* may be either ideas or facts; and these *facts* may be either *internal* or *external.* We form a judgment of *ideas*, when we consider their objects in their essence, apart from their actual existence. We judge of *facts* when we think of objects in the *concrete*, and actual order of physical existence, and make any affirmation concerning them; whether they be *facts* of *internal* consciousness, or of *external* objects.

The objects of thought may be divided: 1st, into those that pertain to the *order of reason*, or to *necessary matter;* 2d, into those that belong to the *experimental* or *empirical order*. Judgments whose objects are wholly of the sphere or *order of reason*, are *necessary* and *universal;* for their objects are not limited to the *particular*, as are, *these trees*, *these men*.

But when the objects of the judgment are in the *order of experience* or of the *experimental order* the judgment is *particular* and *contingent;* because its objects are *particular* and *contingent*. But in the judgments formed upon both these classes of objects, the *evidence* is *immediate;* in the sense that it is not derived from a comparison of other judgments, but is furnished by the simple comparative apprehension of the ideas, which are affirmed to agree or disagree.

Mediate judgments are such as are formed by discursive reasoning; i. e., by comparing several judgments, and perceiving that the *nexus* of the premises and conclusion is such that we cannot assent to the premises without assenting to the conclusion; in other words, it is by the *medium* of *reasoning* that such judgments are formed.

Reasoning which proceeds from certain and evident principles, is termed *demonstrative*, or *apodictic*. This reasoning which is termed *demonstrative*, or *apodictic*, is of four kinds: 1st, *reasoning a priori;* as when we conclude from the *cause* to the *effect*, or from the *principle* to its *application;* v. g., "that which has life has motion; an animal has life; therefore, an animal has motion;" 2d, *reasoning a posteriori;* as, when we deduce the *cause* from the *effect;* e. g., "order exists in all the works of the universe; therefore, all the works of the universe have an *intelligent* cause;" or, as in the proverb, "ex pede Herculem," from the footprints, I conclude it was Hercules; 3d, the reasoning is *direct*, when from one notion of the subject we infer another; e. g., "man is free; therefore, he is intelligent;" 4th, reasoning is *indirect* or *apagogic*, when we show that its contradictory or contrary leads to an absurdity, called, also, *reductio ad absurdum;* e. g., "If God is not eternal, then He had a beginning; if He had a beginning, He had a cause; and if He had a cause, then He is not *God* at all; which is absurd."

Of these forms of demonstration, the one *a priori* excels the rest; that is, it is the most satisfactory to the mind; for in it the mind reposes at ease, with no desire to know more of the conclusion thus demonstrated to it, or made evident in its causes; in the others, the certainty is perfect in species, since all doubt is excluded; but the mind's repose is not so complete, it may desire more, and, when the nature of the matter permits, it will strive to know *a priori* the truth which it thus attains by reasoning *a posteriori*.

Knowledge acquired by reasoning *a posteriori*, in itself is not *scientific knowledge;* as will be shown in a subsequent article.

Reasoning is also divided into *pure*, *empirical* and *mixed*. The *pure* is that in which the premises are both *necessary*, or are of the *order of reason;* v. g., "None but a straight line is the shortest distance between any two points; a curved line is not straight; therefore, a curved line is not the shortest distance between two given points."

The *empirical* argument has both premises *experimental* truths; "the rose bush that is set out in May will grow; this rose bush was set out in May; therefore, it will grow." The *mixed* reasoning is that in which one premise is absolute truth, and the other empirical; v. g., "a *contingent* being cannot exist unless there is a *necessary* being; but there exist *contingent* beings; therefore, there is a *necessary being*."

In all these species of ratiocination, the conclusion has the nature of the premises in some mode, and it follows the less worthy premise in quality and quantity.

The intellect, by its *perceptions* or in forming concepts, passes from the particular to the *universal;* but, in *reasoning*, this process is reversed; and the progress is from what is more general to that which is less so; for the middle term is always general, in respect to the conclusion. Under this point of view, reasoning is *synthetical*.

The conclusion is implicitly in the premises; it is first explicitly seen, as such, only when the middle term is found; the *nexus* with the premises then becomes evident. This truth solves the objections against the syllogism, whether it be considered as a means of discovering or of proving truth.

By means of these acts of cognition, namely, *simple appre-*

hension, *judgment* and *reasoning*, the mind acquires genuine certainty of their objects; for, there is truth in all of them. As already shown, truth is the conformity of the mind knowing to the object known; and, in apprehensions and judgments, there is this conformity in different degrees, to be sure; but each is perfect, according to its kind.

The specific perfection of every cognition, is the truth that is in it. In a simple apprehension, an object is perceived, though no explicit judgment is formed; this is conformity of the mind to the object, perfect in its species and degree. In judgment, and reasoning, this conformity is more perfect in degree, because they affirm explicitly; and while in apprehensions there is only that implicit affirmation, or transcendental truth participated in by them, and referable ultimately to the first truth; in our judgments, truth is explicitly affirmed by the mind, giving to reason and intelligence their specific nature, and their highest value.

If the judgment faithfully affirms only what the ideas are immediately seen to include, or exclude, it is clear that no erroneous judgment can be assented to. All our cognoscive powers are determined to their acts of cognition by the *evidence* in their objects; and when truth is seen to be such, it is known to be such; and their acts are as true, as they are necessary, *partaking of the truth of their first cause.*

This doctrine cannot be denied, unless by that systematic scepticism, in which the human mind is *morally* false to itself, and is, therefore, perverse in its own enunciations. For the ailment of those minds that can *sincerely doubt* evident first principles, *philosophy* can furnish no remedy.

ARTICLE IV.

OBJECTIVE REALITY OF IDEAS.

The ideas here meant are those that express or represent in the mind the essences or natures of objects, and which the intellect forms by reflecting on its concepts, and abstracting or removing from them the conditions of individuality, i. e., the concrete accidents. They are not the same then as the ideas which the mind acquires immediately, by simple apprehension and by the senses, whose objective truth was sufficiently evinced in the preceding articles.

The ideas whose objective truth is here to be shown, are those reflex ideas, or notions, that are general, or, that include many objects; v. g., *substance*, *cause*, *effect*, *the possible*, etc. The question is, then, do such ideas really and truly express or represent the objects for which they stand, or is there through them a conformity of the mind to the *objects* of its cognitions? Have these ideas any *objective* value, or have they true agreement with their objects outside of the mind, as perceiving or knowing them? or, are they merely certain subjective and innate *forms*, or *types* in the intellect, according to which the mind *forms* for itself its *objects* which it calls *substance*, *cause*, *effect*, etc.? Is that which is expressed in these general and primary ideas, in any respect, *in the objects* for which the ideas stand; or is it merely subjective? Is the conclusion from the idea to its object, valid illation, as the conclusion from the photograph likeness to the person represented by it, is valid illation? Has, for example, that which is called *substance*, really in itself what the mind attributes to it in its idea of it; or, does it exist only in the idea or *form* in the mind, the idea having no extrinsic object truly corresponding to it?

In the foregoing interrogatories the same thing is variously expressed, the same notion is presented under different phases, purposely in order that the real state of the question may be more clearly apprehended by the youthful inquirer.

It is affirmed, then, that ideas are truly and really the representatives, and exponents of their objects, as they are; that the objects of cognition are truly expressed in the mind, by those ideas or final and general mental words. This is no more, indeed, than affirming that the mind is capable of acquiring true ideas of the objects which it perceives.

That which is understood in the mind is the same as what is in the object; but in the one it exists in concrete, while in the other it is in the abstract, yet, the relation between them is that of truth, or it is the mind conformable to its object of cognition. We must assign to objects actually perceived concurrent causality, direct or indirect, in the formation of all our ideas,* of every kind. In other words, we find a verification of all that we know or can positively conceive even as possible, in what we have actually perceived in the order of reality. The idea in the mind then must truly represent the object, so far as that object efficiently concurred in its production, else it would be an effect that has no real resemblance to its cause.

The objective verity of our ideas, is one of those truths that cannot be formally demonstrated, nor does it require such proof. Nor can it be denied, either, without implicitly affirming what is in question. For he that denies it, i. e., that ideas are truly representative of their extrinsic objects, thereby assumes that his idea *of an idea* is truly conformable to, and representative of, its object, for logical truth is the conformity of the mind to its object; otherwise, he asserts nothing. Therefore, to deny the objective truth of ideas, is an explicit assumption of the truth that is in question.

It is evident that if the ideas by which the mind expresses the objects of cognition, do not truly present those objects; then, the mind is not capable of attaining truth, or of conforming itself to objects known. But, just as it must be admitted that the mind can and does know, through the medium of the senses, the existence and distinction of singular and concrete objects truly as they are; so, it is equally evident, that its farther notions of their essence and nature, formed by abstraction and generalization, by reflexion and right reasoning, are really verified in those objects. He that can doubt the objective value of his ideas, and the share that their objects have in efficiently helping to their origin and formation, should also doubt all first principles, and even internal facts themselves; nay, he would be incapable of forming a certain judgment, and, consequently, incapable of any reasoning. For

* "Ex objecto et potentia oritur notitia." Knowledge proceeds from the object and the power.

the evidence is not more clear for the certainty of first principles, internal facts, or for any judgment, than that which the mind has for the agreement of its ideas with their objects; in other words, for the objective truth of its own notions or ideas. They are all evident, and, therefore, all true.

Hence, the doctrine that the general or common ideas in the mind do not express or declare real objective truth, but are only a kind of *subjective forms* by which the intellect is directed in thinking; is purely an assumption, directly against what we see and know by the facts of experience; is destructive of all certainty, and has no argument in its favor, except those purely fanciful analogies which are the only basis of every merely arbitrary *hypothesis*. This hypothesis does not explain or account for the evident facts of experience, for instead of being founded on those facts, or being itself a conclusion deduced from them as premises, these facts must be distorted and our concept of their nature be changed, in order that they may be adapted to explain and prove the theory.

The manner in which our general or universal ideas are formed, and the mode in which they are verified in their objects, will be rendered more clear by the fuller explanation of the whole subject, which is given in the following article.

ARTICLE V.

UNIVERSALS; THEIR OBJECTS; UNIVERSAL IDEAS, HOW FORMED.

There was long a dispute in the schools as to the nature and object of what are termed *universals;* the disputants were divided into three celebrated parties: the *nominalists*, *exaggerated realists* and *moderate realists.*

The *nominalists* maintained that *universals* are mere *names*, that express *indefinitely* and *confusedly* a collection of individuals; some thinking they neither existed in objects nor in concepts; while others of the same school contended that they exist in the concept, but have no real relation to the objects included. The *exaggerated realists* contended that the *universal* is in the concept, and in the object outside of the mind, *in the same manner* that it is conceived in the mind; that there is, in objects of the same species, one and the same real essence, really common to all the individuals included in it. By their theory, individuals of the same species, being essentially identical, differ only in their accidents; there is one common *human essence* which is actually in all men, as there is one common *entity* in all beings. For example, the *human nature* which actually exists in Peter, is really identical with the *human nature* that is affirmed of *man* in general; and, therefore, Peter is both *universal* and *particular*, as regards his *human nature* or actual *essence*.

It is clear that this doctrine does not differ materially from the theory of Pantheism, or the system which identifies every real being with God.

The *moderate realists* taught that there is in objects of the same class a *nature* or *essence* which is apprehended by the mind in a universal idea; but it does not exist in the mind and in the object, or *a parte rei*, in the same manner; it is *concrete*, in the one; and *abstract*, in the other.

Now, as a fact, there are in our minds *universal* ideas, and there are *names* or *terms* in language that stand as signs for them.

General or universal truths constitute the elements of all the sciences; nearly all the names, or *nouns*, of language, except the proper names of individuals, are *common* or *universal* for their classes of objects. *Genus*, *species*, *difference*, *attribute*, *accident*, express real generalizations in the mind, and, when actually applied to objects, are by no means vague, indefinite names, expressing nothing but mere concepts which are really unfounded in objects outside of the ideas.

Common or *universal* names do not stand for a collection of particular individuals; as a *family*, a *people*, a *thousand;* for, these terms or names cannot be affirmed of each individual of the collection singly: but are applied to many *copulatively*. But, on the contrary, the common names, *animal*, *spirit*, *vege-*

table, are predicated of many taken *singly*, but not of many taken *copulatively*.

The perception of similarity in individuals gives rise to universal ideas in the mind; and even the idea of a mere *collection* of particular individuals, presupposes the *universal* idea.

Common terms, then, express a concept which presents to the intellect something that is found equally in many individuals; and, therefore, these terms express real ideas in the mind, as even the faculty of consciousness directly testifies.

There is nothing in the objects outside of the intellect which, of itself and anterior to any operation of the mind, is universal.

For, what is universal cannot become singular, since the *universal* and the *singular* are opposites; and opposites cannot become identical; v. g., *one* and *many*, *white* and *black*, *communicable* and *incommunicable*, cannot as such become identical. No real object, i. e., *no actual nature*, can of itself be universal; so as to be the same in the many really, that it is in the individual. If it were universal, would its *specific*, or its *generic* nature be universal, or both? Clearly, the *universal*, as such, does not exist, *a parte rei*.

Every universal, as such, is formed by the intellect; but it is *truly founded* in the realities which it includes.

Two things are verified in a universal; or it has two constituents: 1st, that which it expresses, is *one;* 2d, it is *communicable* to *many;* i. e., it is really *multiplied* in many individuals, so that they are numbered, as individuals are numbered.

If a *universal* be not *one*, then the individuals in which it is multiplied would form only a *collection* of different things; and at the same time, if it were not *communicable* to *many*, it would not be *universal*, but *singular*. The *universal* is, therefore, *logically verified* in objects, though not really or *a parte rei* existing in them as *one*, and *many*.

A *collection*, as already observed, is constituted by many singular things, which are considered as *one;* the term *collection*, and *universal*, both include the idea of *many*, but the *universal* is affirmed of that many, so that it is applied both to the whole, and is *distributively* applied to its *inferiors* or *subjects;*

while *collection* is affirmed only of the *whole number* of its *inferiors* or *subjects;* and its individuals are only parts of it, of which *collection* cannot be affirmed.

A thing, while an object of sensation, is singular; when an object of intelligence, it is, in some manner, universal; or, as the old axiom has it, "singulare dum sentitur, universale dum intelligitur;" it is singular, as it is in the sense; it is universal, as it is in the intellect.

This subject will be more easily understood, if we analyse the operation by which the intellect passes from the *singular*, in the simple apprehension, to the *universal idea*. The operation of the intellect, in forming the *universal idea*, is *precisive* and *comparative;* i. e., it perfects the *universal* by the acts of *prescinding*, or *abstracting;* and by *comparing* the inferiors or subjects of the ideas thus formed. When an individual object is presented by means of sensation to the intellect, it abstracts or educes the essence from the sensible representation; and thereby forms the concept in which that essence is separated from all individual conditions, or concrete accidents.

This is a *precisive* cognition, and is the proper and characteristic act of the intellect; and it furnishes the *comprehension* of the universal, and common terms. This *precisive* cognition of the essence thus known, may be called a *direct universal;* because it is formed by a *direct cognition;* yet, it does not explicitly affirm *universality*, until, by *comparison*, its relation to all actual or possible *inferiors* or *subjects* is perceived and affirmed by the intellect.

Thus, by this *precisive* act of the mind, and by *comparison*, the intellect forms the idea of *unity* of *nature*, from the individual objects presented to it; a *unity*, that is not *real*, but *logical*. The essence which is thus *one*, becomes the *species* and *genus*, and is called the *reflex universal*. It is by thus operating, then, that the mind forms the concept of the universal nature or essence.

The basis on which all universals are founded, or the *matter* of them, is the similar nature that is in the things that constitute its *inferiors* or *subjects;* the generalized idea of that nature constitutes the *formal universal*, or the *universal* properly so-called. By abstraction the mind can generalize the *nature* known in one thing, so as to extend it to all possible things of the kind.

Hence, then, to state still more precisely, and sum up the preceding doctrine, the specific and distinguishing properties of the *reflex universal*, are, 1st, its unity, or it is *one*; 2d, its *aptitude or adaptability*, to be predicated of *many*, or exist in *many*, whether as essence, property, or accident. In this wide sense of the word, all *common* terms stand for *universals*. The five *universals*, or *universal predicables*, namely, genus, species, difference, property or attribute, and accident, are the only *universals* that can be predicated *univocally* of all the ten categories, or highest genera. Other *common* terms do not apply to all the categories, but are confined to special ones; also, the *transcendental predicables*, as "being,* something, one, true, good, etc.," cannot be applied in any *univocal sense* to all the ten categories, but yet they are applied *analogically* to all the categories. When, therefore, it is said by logicians that there are *five universals and only five*, the meaning is that there are just five universals that can be predicated *univocally*, through all the *ten categories or ultimate genera.*

That the five universals, genus, species, difference, property or attribute, and accident, include all that is univocally predicable of the ten categories may be thus shown: *genus*,† which includes species under it, is not whole or entire *essence*, as essence exists in the *individuals* of a *species*; but it may be regarded as the *matter* of *whole essence*. The *specific difference* is the *forma*, or *formal principle*, which, by uniting with the *matter*, constitutes the *quasi compound*, *species*, which expresses

* "Sex transcendentalia sunt: res, ens, verum, bonum, aliquid, unum; quæ barbara voce amplexa sunt per initiales litteras *reubau*." There are six transcendentals: thing, being, true, good, something, one. To assist the memory, the initials of the corresponding Latin words are formed into the barbarous word, *reubau*.

† "Genus est quod prædicatur de pluribus specie differentibus *in quid incompletum*, seu *in quid tanquam pars materialis*." Genus is what is predicated as *something incomplete*, or as a *material part*, of many things differing in their species.

whole or perfect essence; i. e., *essence* as it actually is in individuals. Also, this essence as in individuals has properties that are *per se* connected with it, i. e., properties that *necessarily belong to it*, resulting necessarily from the essence as it is in itself intrinsically; and again, the individuals of the species may have accidents that are *purely contingent*, i. e., which may be *present*, or *absent*, without affecting the *essence* in any manner.

Now, whatever can be predicated at all of any object, must be either *within* the essence of that object, or *outside* of its essence; if it be *within* the essence, it must be either its *material* principle, in which case it will be *genus* that is *predicated;* or, it must be its *formal* principle, in which case it will be the *difference* that is predicated; or, finally, it must be the union or compound of the two, and in this case, it will be *species* that is predicated. Again, if that which is predicated be something that is outside of the essence, either it is something that *necessarily* belongs to the object, then it will be property or attribute; or, it is something that *contingently* belongs to it, and then it will be accident. There is no univocal predicable applying to all the ten categories that cannot be referred to one or other of these five.

The five universals which Logicians enumerate as the only ones that are strictly or univocally such, are, then, as already observed, *genus*, *species*, *difference*, *attribute*, and *accident*, and they differ essentially from each other.

Species and genera differ among themselves *essentially*;* that is *essential* without which a thing cannot exist. Things may have some essential attributes common to them, and yet differ by other essential constituents which determine them to wholly diverse natures. For example, *brute* and *man*, have in common all that is included in the generical concept, *animal;* but man has, in addition, intellect that judges, reasons, knows the universal or the super-sensible. This is an *essential difference*

* "Omne quod de pluribus univoce prædicatur vel est genus, vel est species; vel differentia, vel proprium, vel accidens." Whatever is predicated univocally of many things, is either a genus, or a species, or a difference, or a property, or an accident.

by which man is constituted of a wholly different *species* from brute.

In the *direct universal*, which the mind has whenever it forms its first concept of any intelligible essence or nature, the intellect does not positively refer the intelligible essence conceived by it to its *inferiors;* for, when the concept of any essence becomes actually related* in the mind to its inferiors, it is then the *reflex universal.*

Hence, the direct concept of an essence makes it only *negatively* or *inadequately universal;*† but the *reflex and comparative*, which presents the essence as actually referred to *many*, is *positively* and *adequately universal.* We may, therefore, consider the *essence or nature* in different states: 1st, as it is in singular or concrete individual objects, in which, while it is truly and formally *singular*, yet it is materially and remotely *universal*, in as much as it is capable of founding the universal; 2d, the essence may be considered in abstract, as first conceived by the mind, but not actually referred to many; 3d, it may be considered as *one*, and yet positively referred to many; this last is the *universal*, properly so called.‡

When it is said, "the more universal knowledge is, the more *imperfect* it is;" and that, "philosophy treats of the highest and *most universal* causes of all things;" the term *universal* is employed in two different senses: in the first case, it is the *direct universal*, which is always more or less *vague*, and *indeterminate;* in the second, it is the *reflex*, which refers to its inferiors *positively*, and *determinately;* and it constitutes man's most perfect mode of knowing.

* "Universale secundum quod accipitur cum intentione universalitatis." (Div. Thom. I p., qu. 85, art. 5, ad. 4.) Universal, according as it is taken with the intention of universality.

† "Cum enim universale sit ens rationis cujus totum esse est, ut cognoscatur: haud dubie, non est *universale* quod ut tale non cognoscitur." For since the universal is an *ens rationis*, a creation of the mind, whose whole essence is that it should be known; there is no doubt that what is not known as such is not a *universal*.

‡ "Natura non dicitur *adæquate universalis*, priusquam concipitur uti *una apta inesse multis.*" A nature is not said to be adequately universal before it is conceived as "one fit to be in many."

Hence, it must be evident that the *universal* proceeds both from *things*, and from the *intellect.* The nature actually exists in the material basis of the universal, individual and *real*, in each singular thing; while, in the mind, it possesses only an *ideal* existence, and is acquired by *reflex* and *comparative* cognition.

As the mind, by means of the idea, is conformed to its object; and because the idea is formed by the combined agency of the object and mind, the *idea* expresses the relation between the mind and object; therefore, the *idea* is *objectively* true, i. e., it is truly *representative* of the object.

When we say, " the mind as knowing is conformable to the object known," we affirm a *relation* between the *mind* and the *object* of its cognition; and this *relation* is *logical truth*, strictly so called. Now, a *universal* idea expresses an actual relation of mind and object; for the idea proceeds from both. Though the *universal nature* does not exist *really*, but only *logically*, yet it is founded in *realities*, and is verified in those *realities*; as the *rule* or *measure* is verified, as such, in the objects conformable to which it is made, and to which it is applied.

The *universal*, then, as referred both to the *object* and the *idea*, does not possess a *real unity* and *identity*; but it is *logical unity* only; for that which is *really common* to many, is not *universal*, but *singular.*

The conclusion follows, then, that every *universal*, as such, is constituted by the intellect; but it is truly founded in the realities which it includes as its *inferiors* or *subjects.*

It may not be far amiss to observe in this place, that, as to the theory that one *species* of substance may be developed by natural agencies into another one; and which its defenders carry so far as to assert that man even was actually developed from rude matter, through various intermediate *species* of plant, animal, to the ape, and finally to man; the following propositions should be carefully considered:

First: As a fact, there appears to be no instance really known of a new species of organism *being developed*, either from purely inorganic matter, or from another organism of a totally different species.

Second: All the reasoning employed in favor of this so-called "genesis of species," is based upon remote analogies, which, of course, cannot afford demonstration; for no mere indeterminate analogy can ever found a real demonstration.

Third: So far as facts are known, they all, without exception, go to prove that there is no development by nature of any organic being except from a germ, or from a principle which is the equivalent of a germ.

Fourth: It is repugnant to reason to affirm that a being can, in its action, go beyond the limits of its own essence or nature,* or that it can transcend its own species, so as to produce, of its own efficiency, an object not only of an essentially different species, but which *is intrinsically superior* to it.

Fifth: As a fact, also, there are many species of substances actually existing; each of these species having its own essential constituents, by which it is identical with each individual of its species, and by which it differs, intrinsically and essentially, from the individuals of every other species.

Sixth: To affirm *that all* material and spiritual *substance is only force*, or a collection of co-related forces, is to assert a mere hypothesis, for which no real proof is adduced, or can be adduced.

Force presupposes an agent or substantial principle from which it proceeds; and it is as intelligible to say that every thing is *motion* or *time*, as it is to say that every thing is *force;* for we can as easily conceive motion apart from some-

* "Effectus non superat causam." An effect is not above its cause.

"Modus agendi sequitur modum essendi." Manner of acting must agree with the manner of existing.

"Materia non potest producere effectum immaterialem. (Vide Div. Thom. 1 p., qu. 118.) Matter cannot produce an immaterial effect.

"Forma est principium speciei; et ab una forma non proveniunt diversæ species. (Sum. 1 p., qu. 76, art. 5.) The form determines a thing in its *species* or *essence;* and from this form, other forms of different essence or species cannot proceed.

thing moving, as we can conceive force without some agent exerting it.*

"But," it may be said, "*force* is here the same thing that *act* is when it is understood as the *formal principle* in every thing that *actually exists*."

God is called in true philosophy, *actus purissimus*, or the *absolutely pure act*. In this sense of the word, to *exist substantially*, is *act* (*actus*), and *actus purissimus* includes not only existing *substantially*, but existing in a manner that implies infinite perfection, and absolute independence of a cause. By the terms, "actus purissimus," besides the positive perfection affirmed, there is excluded from the concept of God all *potentiality*; i. e., all *perfectibility* in him by any sort of *mutation*, from non-action into action. *Created act* perfects the creature; for, by action, it acquires what it had not before. The human soul, and, likewise, all other created *substantial forms*, are also said to be *acts*; i. e., are *substantial and active principles*; but they are perfected by *successive action*; or, their existence or their action is not simultaneous; i. e., their existence is by successive acts of existing; but infinite and eternal act is simultaneous; i. e., free from all succession, or all successive action.

It is evident, then, that the concept of *pure act*, and the concept which we have of a *substantial principle* which is *in potentia* first, and then becomes *actual*, exclude each other as completely as do those of the *finite* and the *Infinite*. These things being true, it may be affirmed that, any theory which resolves all actual things into *co-related forces*, so as to ignore or deny the preceding distinctions, must be false; for, it must, in some sense, identify beings which are totally and absolutely distinct, or make no distinction between beings which have nothing that is, in any *univocal* sense, *common* to them, and which are, therefore, totally distinct.

The ambiguity of the term *force*, which is used one while to

* "Prius est esse quam agere." "Nulla substantia creata potest fieri immediate operativa." Existence is presupposed to operation. No created substance is immediately operative; i. e., it must possess *powers*.

express the *degree of power exercised;* another while for the *concrete agent* itself; and then for what is purely *phenomenal*, gives rise to much equivocal and fallacious reasoning.

Not a few recent writers on philosophical subjects confound, and even identify, certain organic effects which precede or accompany *intellectual thought*, with the action of the intellect itself; thus they perplex and darken for their readers some truths that are in themselves clear, with language that is in reality either superficial or eccentric. Such authors will speak of the acts of fancy, or even those of the external senses, as if they were really *intellectual* operations.

ARTICLE VI.

MEMORY.

Memory* is the power of recalling to the mind, recognizing and distinguishing things formerly known.

The *memory*, therefore, performs four principal functions: namely, *retention* of the object or idea; its *reproduction*, with the help of the fancy; its *recognition*, and the *distinction of its time*.

There is a *sensile* or *organic* memory; and there is the *intellectual memory*. The *sensile* or *organic memory* recalls to the imagination† objects of the senses formerly known through them, and recognizes them by means of the *sensible* conditions or properties with which they are invested. This memory, being purely organic, is possessed even by brutes; v. g., the dog recognizes his master; the cattle return at the same time and to the same place for food; and numberless other facts will readily occur, which put the the truth beyond a doubt.

* "Memoria præteritorum est: Seu est ipsa *ratio præteriti* quam attendit memoria." (S. Thom. 1 p., qu. 78, art. 4.) Memory is of past things; or, it is precisely the *past as such* that memory regards.

† "Imaginatio est quasi thesaurus formarum per sensum acceptorum. (Sum. 1 p., qu. 78, art. 4.) The imagination is, as it were, a treasury of images acquired through sensible power.

Since the *sensile memory* is *organic*, it is subject to all the contingencies of disease and decay, which, in the present order of Providence, are common to all living organs.

The *sensile* or *organic* memory, therefore, has for its object *sensible facts*, reproduced with some of their *sensible* conditions, and distinguished by their *intentions*, i. e., as *pleasing*, *hurtful*, etc.; and known as past.*

The action of the *intellectual memory* has a higher order of cognition in it; this faculty may be defined: the power of reproducing, and recognizing *concepts* or *ideas* and *judgments* formerly had. Memory may act *spontaneously;* or it may be made by the will to *exert* itself, and, along with the understanding, or rather by means of it, to pass through intermediate or associated ideas to ideas more remote.

This exercise of the memory, in which the understanding is applied to various reproduced ideas in order to recall forgotten things by means of comparison and reasoning on their relation to something which is remembered, is called *reminiscence.*† Such mode of remembering is proper only to *rational* beings.

Why is it that among the ideas with which we are perpetually occupied, some are remembered; and others entirely vanish from the memory? In memories which are in a normal state, the difference depends, in a great degree, upon the *attention;* and on the *association of ideas.*

The *attention* is the direction of the mind to an object to which it adheres for a time. The attention, in such case, is either *spontaneous*, or *voluntary* and *reflex*. There is *spontaneous* attention in all thought; even when the mind takes no reflex notice of its own operations. It is violently arrested, and long kept, by objects that are strange or marvelous; and often returns to them.

* "*Sensus (hominis) est deficiens quædam participatio intellectus.*" (Sum. 1 p., qu. 77, art. 7.) Sensible power is a certain imperfect participation of intellect.

† "Reminiscentia est inquisitio alicujus, quod a memoria excidit; seu, memoriæ amissæ instauratio ex aliquo interno principio, quod oblivione deletum non est." Reminiscence is seeking for something which has escaped from memory; or, is the bringing back of a forgotten object, by means of some internal principle which is not lost in oblivion.

Attention is *voluntary*, when the will directs the mind to an object to which it adheres for a time; and this it does either by one, or many repeated acts. These repeated acts of the attention, by which the powers of the mind are often directed to an object, constitute *meditation.**

A good memory is *susceptible*, *retentive* and *ready*. Its *susceptibility* much depends upon a happy constitution of mind and body. *Retentiveness* and *readiness*, depend in part upon the same cause; but also upon that degree of attention which enables the understanding to form clear and distinct ideas of its objects. Prudent exercise of the memory greatly improves it in all these perfections. Habitual moral truth and the virtue of temperance are requisites for perfecting in it healthful and vigorous action.

The *association of ideas* is also a great aid both for *retentiveness* and *readiness* of *memory*. Ideas may be associated, or united, with other ideas which are distinctly remembered, by any circumstances of time, place, number, mode, quality, analogy, resemblance; or even by any arbitrary law. But it is advisable, when it can be done, to associate truths in the memory by some principle of logical connexion. In any of these cases, when one idea occurs to the mind, it readily recalls those that are associated with it.

The correctness of intellectual acts, much depends on the fidelity of memory: and even the greater or less capacity of the intellect, indirectly proceeds, in no small degree, from greater or less perfection in the organic powers, sensile memory and imagination,† owing to its peculiar dependence on these organs.

The memory, though naturally it is so susceptible of direct

* "Pluribus intentus, minor est ad singula sensus." If the mind be intent on many objects, its attention is less to single ones.

"*Meditatio* est frequens et iterata mentis attentio objecto voluntarie adhibita." Meditation is the exercise of frequent and repeated acts of attention in the mind, voluntarily directed to an object.

† "Illi in quibus virtus imaginativa, memorativa, et cogitativa est melius disposita, sunt melius dispositi ad intelligendum." (Div. Thom.) They in whom the internal senses, imagination, memory, and the cogitative power are best disposed, are best fitted to understand.

improvement, is often debilitated by disease, is impaired by indolence and sensuality, and it grows dull and feeble in old age. But, *in its ordinary and normal state*, it may be affirmed,

First. *That memory never deceives per se, i. e., of itself*, or by its own efficient action.

Second. *It affords certainty as to the objects which it recalls amd distinctly recognizes.*

The memory never deceives *per se;* for, either we distinctly remember the past thing, or we do not; if we do not distinctly remember it, no error is committed, provided we do not judge it to be different from what it is remembered to be; and we judge it only as it is remembered. It follows, then, that the memory, of itself, does not deceive, but that error in its case, as in all others, proceeds from the will urging the understanding to affirm precipitately or imprudently more or less than the mind sees. But if we distinctly remember the past thing, we are perfectly sure of it, and are not deceived.

This perfect and unerring certainty of memory is implied in all the important affairs of individual life and civil society; it is implied also in all our reasoning; for, without memory, there could be no process of reasoning. Hence, it is false to affirm that memory can afford the mind only *probability;* it gives *perfect certainty*, as to the most important things. Who can doubt that he often heard of London, Paris, Rome, and that he remembers with perfect certainty numberless past things? Nay, we are as certain as to the objects of that faculty, as we are of those of external sense, or any other power, through which the understanding comes to know truth.* Memory will seldom prove to be even an *occasion* of error, provided we affirm precisely, and only what the memory recognizes in its comparative apprehension, and *as* it recognizes it.

* "Unusquisque judicat prout affectus est." "One judges according as he is affected." Feeling and passion greatly influence the judgment, and they are frequently the cause of error.

ARTICLE VII.

TESTIMONY;* DOTH IT AFFORD A MEANS OF PHILOSOPHICAL CERTAINTY IN SOME IMPORTANT MATTERS.

Philosophical certainty is the *reflex* certainty which is derived from a critical examination or scrutiny of the motives and the principles that afford ordinary direct certainty, whether it rest on the evidence of the object, or on authority.

Our senses enable us to know by *experience* only present objects that express themselves in our minds through the organs. But objects not known through our own senses, and which are distant in time or place, we can know only through witnesses, or by faith in testimony.

A *witness* is one who assures another of a fact or truth which he either knows of his own knowledge, or on due authority. An *immediate*, or *eye-witness*, is one who testifies to a fact or object which he perceived in its own evidence to him; a *mediate*, or, an *ear-witness*, is one who gives testimony of a fact

*In the phraseology of the Legal Profession, or in our civil jurisprudence, the consistent testimony of a sufficient number of competent witnesses, is said to *furnish evidence* to the court or jury, or to *constitute evidence*, of the fact to be proved; and in some connexions, the terms *evidence* and *testimony*, are employed by jurists as synonymous; v. g., "the witness gives evidence," and "the witness gives testimony," are expressions which are frequently used by them, indiscriminately or as being identical in meaning.

It is perfectly legitimate for lawyers, in order to secure simplicity, clearness and precision, to restrict or extend the application of terms employed by them in a technical, and, therefore, an arbitrary sense. But it would be erroneous, and not scholarly, to found a philosophical explanation of *evidence* and *testimony* as motives of certainty, on this confined and special view of the subject, and this particular use of those terms in civil courts of justice; this is actually done, however, in some books of Logic. It is manifest that to treat the motives of certainty philosophically, greater scope must be given to their explanation. It should be based, it would also seem, on that signification of those terms which is attributed to them by prevailing use among the learned in general.

The object or truth which is *evident* to us, we *see;* that which we know only by *testimony*, we *believe*, but do not *see;* for that which is *seen*, is *evident*, and, *vice versa*, that which is *evident*, is *seen*. This exemplifies the proper meaning of the words, according to approved general usage; as the observant reader will, doubtless, have noticed for himself.

In fact, there is seldom a case actually occurring, in which the testimony elicited before a civil court possesses all the requisites to constitute it a motive that furnishes philosophical certainty; or, in other words, the certainty which there suffices, because the best which is practically attainable in juridical matters, can rarely fulfill the requirements of philosophical certainty, which excludes even the *possibility of error*.

which he heard from others; whether these others were themselves immediate, or *mediate* witnesses.

Proposition: The testimony of witnesses can furnish infallible certainty in regard to sensible facts or events.

The testimony of the witnesses for its credibility depends, first, upon their knowledge of the fact or event to which they testify; and, second, upon their veracity. Now, if we suppose the witnesses to be numerous; of different interests, habits, education, age, character, etc.; and that they unanimously and constantly testify to the same substantial statement of the fact, such, v. g., as is the case with regard to the existence of such cities as Paris, London, Rome, etc., or any other public and notorious fact, to which many bear testimony. It is perfectly evident that many persons, under the conditions thus described, can neither *conspire* to deceive in regard to a *sensible* fact, nor could they themselves be deceived.*

In regard to the *facts or events* in question, we should suppose that they are *public*, *sensible*, and *striking or important.*

When the testimony of witnesses has all the preceding conditions verified, it is *physically impossible* for them to be deceived; and it is *morally impossible* for them to deceive; or, assuming the *physical* and *moral* laws in the case supposed, it is *metaphysically impossible* for their testimony to be false; i. e., it affords *philosophical* certainty.

If error or falsehood could originate from such testimony, it must be either because the witnesses are deceived themselves, or because they are not truthful, and deceive us; but neither can happen in a case such as that above supposed. For, we cannot even conceive the possibility of error or deception under such conditions without referring it to the Author of the physical and moral laws by which human nature is governed in its operations, and thereby compromising Divine wisdom

* "Conditiones quæ necessariæ sunt ut testimonium præbeat certitudinem, sunt præcipue hæ tres: 1. Ut sit circa factum possibile et sensibile; 2. Ut testes communiter sint plures; 3. Ut evidenter appareat testes non esse in collusione." (Philos. passim.) The conditions requisite for the testimony of witnesses to furnish certainty are chiefly these three: 1st, that it regard a fact which is possible, and sensible; 2d, that the witnesses ordinarily be numerous; 3d, that the witnesses be evidently not in collusion.

and Providence. Hence, it is *evident* on every side, that the testimony of witnesses can, and does, furnish unerring certainty as to many sensible facts or events.

Against the truth thus proved it is sometimes objected, as in the following specious argument: "The testimony of one witness to an extraordinary object affords only probability of its truth; therefore, the testimony of many witnesses gives only a sum of probabilities; but no number of probabilities can produce certainty, which is of a different species." Answer: the testimony of one witness, *in se*, or *in itself*, is often both *physically* and *morally certain as to the witness himself;* but, in case of a solitary witness to a fact, owing to special contingencies, which have no existence when the witnesses are many, his testimony to the certainty which he has himself cannot be accepted as such by us. These extrinsic and special reasons or contingencies which afford cause for doubt or fear, are: 1st, he *may* have deceived himself by haste, imprudence, or other cause; 2d, he *may* intend to deceive us purposely. But these special grounds for apprehending deception are entirely removed when the witnesses, besides being *numerous*, have the other conditions above specified; for, the fulfillment of all these conditions entirely removes any and every *possibility of deception*.

Hence, the testimony of many concurrent witnesses is not a *sum of probabilities*, in the case supposed; there is the sum, if you choose, of as many *physical* and *moral certainties*, as there are witnesses; but without any one of the special reasons for doubt, which we have when there is but a single witness. Yet, the *truth*, as such, in its objective entity, is as perfectly such in one eye-witness as it is in all; for the objective truth in such case is really *one*, though seen by many. The fact that many see an eclipse of the sun at the same time does not multiply the truth in itself that there was an eclipse of the sun; the multiplicity and the diversity of the witnesses may and do take away *extrinsic reasons* for doubt, as regards persons who learn that fact on their authority.

The *assent* which the mind yields to the testimony of witnesses is *faith* or *belief*.

The *dogmatic* or *doctrinal* teachings of scientific men,* philosophers, etc., which depend upon the light of natural reason for their evidence, are worth no more than are the reasons or proofs which can be adduced for them. Hence, such authority of itself, or *per se*, does not always afford certainty, properly so-called.

The judgments of mankind which are based upon good common sense, and which regard evident and practical matters, are true; v. g., when those judgments regard first principles, or the immediate deductions from them. These judgments, when constant and general, are a certain argument for truth; but they are by no means the general criterion of truth, as some authors have erroneously maintained; nor are they an *ultimate motive for certainty.*

It is obviously in accordance with the preceding doctrine that the documents and monuments of authentic history, under proper conditions, afford complete certainty as to the substance of important facts of past times.

ARTICLE VIII.

SCIENTIFIC KNOWLEDGE; IN WHAT IT CONSISTS; THE SCIENCES; THEIR SPECIES, WITH THEIR CO-ORDINATION AND PRINCIPLE OF UNITY.

Knowledge, in its general acceptation, includes every species of cognition, how perfect or imperfect soever it may be. But *scientific knowledge*, or science, *is the evident and certain knowledge of a necessary thing* by its *proximate and real cause.* The object of *scientific knowledge* is a *necessary* thing in the sense,

* "Alii sancti hoc tradiderunt, non quasi asserentes, sed sicut, utentes his quæ in philosophia didicerunt; unde non sunt majoris auctoritatis quam dicta philosophorum quos sequuntur, nisi in hoc quod sint ab omni infidelitatis suspicione separati." (Div. Thom. in 2 sent. disp. 14, art. 2, ad. 1.) Other holy authors taught this, not as asserting it positively, but as using what they learned in philosophy; hence, they have no more authority than the sayings of the philosophers whom they follow, unless in this that they are free from all suspicion of infidelity.

that it is a conclusion which necessarily follows from its premises, or an effect which proceeds necessarily from its cause. We truly know a thing only when we know it in its principles, or cause; not the cause as a *fact* only; but the cause as *producing* it or giving to it its being or existence as an effect.

Science has for its object, then, the *ontological* causes of things, their *causæ essendi.*

A demonstration* is a legitimate argument that gives an evident truth which *necessarily* follows from evident premises: such conclusion is, therefore, *scientific knowledge*, since it is an effect known to follow *necessarily* and *immediately* from the premises by which it is produced.

But distinguish between the *ontological* order, and the *logical* order; or, the order in which effects are produced by their causes, and the order in which reason knows them, or learns them. In *a priori* arguments, we reason from cause to effect; that is, the argument proceeds in the *ontological* order; and in this case, the logical order agrees with the ontological order. In *a posteriori* reasoning, the ontological order is inverted, since we argue from effect to cause. When we conclude from effect to cause, and then reflexly see the effect as truly and necessarily produced by its cause, such knowledge of that effect is *scientific;* for it is the knowledge of an effect as produced by its proximate and true cause, i. e., its *ontological cause*, (*causa essendi.*)

When we say an effect *necessarily* follows from its cause, the *necessity* referred to is either that which arises absolutely from the essence of things; or that which is *consequent upon supposing* physical or moral laws, according to the nature of the matter which furnishes the premises and conclusion.

The *proximate* cause is that *nearest* cause which *directly* and *immediately* produces the effect; it is *real*, because it is distinguished from an *apparent*, or *accidental* cause.

* "Demonstratio ea est ratiocinatio quæ scientiam efficit: et scientia est *demonstrationis conclusio* seu *effectus.*" Demonstration is reasoning which produces scientific knowledge; the scientific knowledge, then, is the *conclusion or the effect of demonstration.*

"*Scientia* est syllogismus *faciens scire.*"

A reasoning mind does not rest quiet in the mere facts of experience, or in causes which are known merely as facts, or in remote causes; but it seeks to know why the thing is so, why it exists as seen: this it finally learns in its *causa essendi*, its dependence on its *ontological* or *real* and *immediate* cause;* and this the inquiring mind seeks for in all the objects of cognition.

Here it might be objected that a *cause* is *extrinsic* to its effect; whereas, perfect knowledge should represent the *intrinsic* or *essential* constituents of a thing; and, therefore, the knowledge of a thing by its *cause*, is not rightly called *scientific* knowledge.

Before answering this objection it is proper to observe that by *cause* we mean a principle on which a being depends for its existence.

Also, it must be borne in mind that all causes are reduced to four principal kinds; namely, the *final*, *efficient*, *formal* and *material*. The *final cause* and *efficient cause* are really extrinsic to the effect; the *formal* and *material* causes are intrinsic to the effect, and by their union constitute the effect.

The *efficient* cause is that which *produces* the effect; v. g., the builder who *makes* a house, is its *efficient* cause; the *final* cause is that *end*, or purpose, on account of which the efficient cause produces its effect, or operates: v. g., the house, *for the sake* of a *home*; or, as regards the builder, *for the price*; the *material* cause, is that thing out of which the effect is made; v. g., the stone, brick, wood and other *material*, out of which the house is made; the *formal* cause is that by which the essence or particular nature of the effect is determined to be what it is; as, v. g., the *plan*, *design*, or *form* of the house is that which determines or constitutes the material, a house, in the example supposed. The marble is the *material* cause; and the *shape* the *formal* cause, of the statue or bust.

Now, for knowledge to be perfect and adequate, all the

* "Cognitio rei perfecta in causis est nobilior quam cognitio in effectu. Ordo causarum est nobilior quam ordo effectuum." The perfect knowledge of a thing in its causes, is nobler than the knowledge of it in its effect; for the order of causes is more noble than the order of effects.

causes on which an effect depends should be known; which, however, it is not possible for man to know, with completeness at least; yet, though our knowledge be not adequate, we may approximate perfect knowledge within degrees which satisfy rational longing. For this object, any one of the four causes may suffice, according to the nature of the effect contemplated.

The *definition** which gives the *formal* and *material* cause of an object is usually selected, when possible, to enunciate *scientific* truth; as the *scientific* definition aims to assign the formal and material causes of the object defined, whenever the nature of the matter permits it.

A *definition* which assigns the matter and form is preferable, when it is possible; because they are the intrinsic constituents of an object: *genus* and *specific* difference, assign the quasi *matter* and *form*.

We may define by all the four causes, either all given, or some only. Their proper order is: 1st, by the *matter;* 2d, by the *form*,† which is the principal, as the *form* determines and perfects the *matter;* 3d, the *efficient* cause, or agent; 4th, the *final* cause, which though *last* in the *execution*, is the *first* in the *intention*. The *final* cause *is not* demonstrable *a priori;* because it is first, there is none *prior* to it, and it is the cause of the other causes. The *form*, is the cause why the *matter* is perfect; the *agent* or *efficient* cause, is the cause why the *form* perfects the *matter;* and the *finis*, or *end*, is the cause why the *agent* produces the *form* in the *matter;* no further cause can be assigned why the *finis*, or *end*,‡ moves the agent or *efficient cause*.

A collection or system of *demonstrated* or *scientific* conclusions, regarding many objects of the same species, constitutes a *science;* v. g., the body of demonstrated conclusions in regard

* "Definitio est oratio explicans rei naturam." The definition is a discourse which explains the nature of a thing.

† "Forma est principium agendi in unoquoque. Seu unumquodque agens agit per suam forman." The *form* is the principle of action in everything, or, every agent acts by virtue of its *form*.

‡ "Finis est prima et altissima causarum." The end is the first and the highest of causes.

to the heavenly bodies, constitutes the *science of Astronomy;* and similarly for other classes of scientific objects.

It is evident that the sciences have their species determined, and are to be classified, according to their objects; or, it is their objects that specify them.

But it would serve the uses of philosophy to coördinate them according to some clear law or principle of unity.

Philosophers in all ages regarded the reducing of all sciences to unity as a matter of importance; though, in striving to accomplish this object, they did not agree upon a principle of unification. Some sought for this principle of unity in the genera of objects; others looked for it in the powers of cognition; but they discovered no principle by which they could unify the sciences, without d stroying their specific differences; they failed to make them *one*, and yet preserve their *species*.

Some make a general classification of the sciences, according to the degree of abstraction which the intellect employs when contemplating and determining the objects of those sciences. There are three principal degrees of this abstraction: 1st, we may know *sensible* objects, as such; as trees, crystals, animals, etc.; 2d, we may prescind from all sensible qualities, except quantity; *continuous* quantity, as lines, surfaces, etc.; or *discrete* quantity, as numbers; 3d, we may abstract from all sensible conditions, and go to the super-sensible; v. g., to the essential prototypes of objects, to spirits, to God.

These grades of abstraction correspond to physics, mathematics and metaphysics. The principle of unity is abstraction; and the sciences are divided into classes by the different *degrees* of abstraction required to know *scientifically* the different classes of objects about which each *science* is conversant.

The general principles on which this theory rests are these: 1st, sensible things taken as singular and in concrete are the objects of the senses; their essence is the object of the intellect, and this object it attains by means of abstraction; 2d, *science* has for its object *universals;* the singular belongs to history, to the testimony of the senses; history is not a science, because its subject matter is contingent truth, or facts; it pertains to *science*, however, to assign the proximate and necessary causes of facts, when this is possible; 3d, *universals* are the work or product of abstraction; and the more perfect this abstraction, the higher is the science.

In the sciences which depend merely upon the natural light of reason, metaphysics is supreme, or it rules all other sciences; for it furnishes the ultimate principles by which they are finally judged, and from which they receive their last decisive proof. Therefore all mere human science is *subject* to metaphysics.

"No science proves* its own first principles." For, as science is from demonstration, either those first principles are known *per se*, i. e., are self-evident, in which case they cannot be demonstrated; or they are *demonstrated conclusions* from another science;† in which case their *demonstration* pertains to the science in which they are conclusions from first principles; so in either case they are assumed.

It suffices for scientific demonstration that the *medium* be *analogical unity* only. The *medium* of demonstration for the existence of God, i. e., *creatures*, *as effects*, has only analogical unity; for God and creatures, when included under the general concepts, *cause*, *being*, etc., *agree only by analogy*. If this unity of analogy did not suffice for demonstration, then the existence of God could not be demonstrated *a posteriori*.

It will not be out of place here to distinguish between the different species of intellectual cognition, or the perfections in the understanding, usually termed, *intelligence*, *science*, i. e., scientific knowledge, and *wisdom*, or philosophical knowledge; they are also called, *intellectual virtues*. These different species of cognition in the understanding have *speculative* matter only for their object; or, in other words, they do not directly regard the merely contingent and *practical* at all, as such, but they directly consider truth only as it *necessarily* is in itself, apart from its *practical* application to the *feasible*, and to *moral ends*. *Art* and *prudence* have for their object the *practical*, not

*"Nulla scientia sua probat principia." No science proves its own first principles.

†"Ad scientiam sufficit unitas analogica." (Div. Thom. 4 met.; lect. 1.) Analogical unity suffices for scientific knowledge.

the *speculative*. *Art* enables its possessor to accomplish what is *feasible*, or physically capable of being effected; *prudence* enables one to choose that which is morally best, in respect both to means and end; or, as it is briefly said in an axiom, "*ars, est factibilium; prudentia, agibilium.*" Art is of that which can be done physically; prudence, of what can be done morally.

Intelligence is not the intellect itself, but it is a perfection of this faculty, by which it is strengthened, and directed in assenting to the *true*, and dissenting from the *false*. It is sometimes termed *lumen intellectuale*, the light of the understanding; it was called by the old philosophers, *a habit*, "intellectus est *habitus* primorum principiorum." The understanding, as thus empowered by the *habit* or perfection termed *intelligence*, has for its object only *self-evident truth*, "verum per se notum;" or, intelligence has for its object, *evident first principles*. *Science*, or scientific knowledge, as already explained, has for its object the necessary conclusions derived from evident first principles, "verum per aliud notum;" or, it has for its object, *demonstrated conclusions from evident first principles*. It is manifest, then, that scientific knowledge is essentially the product or fruit of *reason*, since it attains its object, not immediately, but through the medium of demonstration.

But principles may be *first* either in a particular genus of cognitions only, as v. g., the *first principles* of Geometry, of Astronomy, of Logic, of Physiology, etc.; or, they may be *first* in respect to the *whole sphere* of man's knowledge. Now, the principles that are *first* in the particular genera of man's cognitions classified according to their objects, together with the necessary conclusions deduced from them, constitute the objects of the *sciences*,* and the *knowledge* of them is *science* or scientific knowledge. But the knowledge of particular genera of first principles as compared among themselves, and also their conclusions, all as tested and judged by the *highest principles* of man's knowledge, is *philosophical knowledge*, or *wis-*

* "Secundum diversa genera scibilium, sunt diversi habitus scientiarum; sapientia non est nisi una."

*dom.** Hence, *wisdom* considers both all scientific knowledge, and its principles; and, therefore, its conclusions are the highest and most universal of all that *reason* can attain to. Although its principles are the *last* which the mind comes to know, they are absolutely *first;* or are objectively first.†

Hence, *philosophical knowledge*, or *wisdom*, has for its object the highest and most universal causes. They possess the greatest of all objective certainty, "necessitatem essendi:" they are not only necessary and immutable, but they are presupposed objectively to all scientific truth, though they are the last learned by human reason, which attains to them only by rising from that which is lower.

Philosophical knowledge, or wisdom, is at the same time *scientific knowledge*, in as much as it demonstrates conclusions by their principles; but it has this in addition to *mere science*, and peculiar to itself, that it judges of all, not only the conclusions, but the principles also; and this is the respect in which it goes higher than *science* does, *strictly as such.* Hence, it may be said that philosophy begins where the sciences end; and it is, therefore, justly styled the science of the sciences whose principles are furnished by natural reason.

An example will help to make the preceding distinctions clear to the mind; the *axioms* of geometry may be regarded as *first principles;* for, they are self-evident; they are, therefore, an object of *intelligence.*

The following thesis, "the solid contents or geometrical *quantity* of any cube is equal to the product of its three dimen-

* "Sapientia est habitus intellectualis circa altissima occupata." Wisdom is a habit of the intellect which is concerned about the highest things.

† "Ea quæ sunt posterius nota quoad nos, sunt priora et magis nota secundum naturam; ideo, id quod est ultimum respectu totius cognitionis humanæ, est id quod est primum et maxime cognoscibile secundum naturam; circa hujusmodi est sapientia, quæ considerat altissimas causas." (Div. Thom. 1, 2, p., qu. 57., art. 2.) Those things that are last known as regards us, are according to their nature first, and they possess most of what makes knowledge, or most to be known; therefore, what is last in respect to the whole of human knowledge, is what is first and greatly the most capable of causing knowledge, according to its nature: wisdom, which considers the highest causes, regards such objects. That which is in itself the highest and greatest truth, is the last known to us, because the medium of knowing is extrinsic to it, and obscure.

sions," is a *demonstrated conclusion*, and is, on that account, an object of *scientific knowledge*.* The question, "is *quantity*, as extended in space, absolutely separable from material substance?" proposes *philosophical matter.* For a determinate answer to this question, we must consider *quantity* as geometrical, *quantity* as material, and also the *essential and metaphysical conditions* which are prerequisite for matter to exist at all: the conclusion which logically follows, is *philosophical truth*, or, is an object of that virtue in the intellect which we termed, *wisdom.*

It may be affirmed, then, that *Philosophy*, which embodies and explains the teachings of *wisdom*, is entitled to the rank assigned it, as "Queen and Moderatrix of the Sciences." The name, *Philosophy*, is directly and appropriately due to *Metaphysics* alone, since Metaphysics alone has for its *proper object* the most universal truths and principles.

* "The terms *science* and *philosophy*, are employed by many popular writers in a vague and indeterminate sense, for whatever pertains to any species of superior learning. Even with not a few well educated authors, these words seem to have no fixed or precise signification, but are made to include a number of undefined and undistinguished generalities; by them, the terms appear to be used indiscriminately, so that all philosophy is science, and conversely, all science is philosophy.

But the discerning student of philosophy will quickly discover for himself the fact that, among exact writers on these subjects, the distinction between *science* and *philosophy*, which is based on their wholly distinct objects, is clearly made and is strictly maintained. As defined by their proper objects, *philosophy* seeks for the highest and the most universal causes of things; *science* has for its object, the necessary and proximate or immediate causes of things. Their objects are, therefore, determinate, and it is clear that they are specifically distinct kinds of knowledge.

Hence, it is an inept use of language, and a confusion of things that should be kept distinct, to give the name *philosophy* to *physics*, or the collective branches of physical science which explain the causes of natural phenomena. The *philosophical* study of physical and material nature, is properly, and in accordance with long established usage, named *cosmology*, in a course of philosophy.

It was believed that these remarks should be here made, in the interests of learners: since precision of language, correctness of cognitions, and accuracy of judgment, mutually aid each other in the work of mental discipline.

APPENDIX.

DISPUTATION; OR PRACTICAL EXERCISE IN REASONING.

In many colleges and higher institutions of learning, the students of Logic and Metaphysics, or the class of Philosophy, have regularly some practical exercises in argumentation, lasting for half an hour at a time, or longer, and occurring two or three times a week, and even oftener, when the class is sufficiently numerous. These disputations usually begin soon after the class has reached the second part of Logic, or Logic Applied. So important is this practice judged to be by many instructors of youth, that, in a large number of well-couducted institutions of learning it is never dispensed with.

The *form* or *manner* of conducting this useful exercise, which, in familiar language, is usually styled the "Circle," is here briefly described, for the information of those readers who are unacquainted with it.

A day or more in advance of the exercise, one proposition, or even two propositions, the proofs of which may be gathered from what was already seen in the text book, or was explained in class, are assigned to a student, to be proved and defended in class by him. In some cases several propositions are divided for this purpose between two students; and occasionally the disputation takes place in presence of a select audience of educated persons, in addition to the class. Also, two or three other students are selected beforehand to prepare objections to be brought by them against the assigned theses. These objections are required to be brief, and in correct *logical form;* for, an objection which is *not in logical form*, is not regarded as legitimate in the "circle," and, therefore, care should be taken never to offer in argument a syllogism *which is not in form.*

On the appointed day the exercise begins by one of the objectors or opponents denying the proposition which he intends to assail, which is equivalent to asking for the proofs of it. The defender then enunciates the thesis or proposition, distinctly, and somewhat deliberately. He may begin either by explaining briefly the precise meaning and scope of his thesis, or, if that be judged unnecessary for it, by stating his principal argument in the form of a syllogism, or in any of the legitimate forms of argument which are recognized in Logic; though the simple categorical syllogism is generally preferable. In such case, his further proofs and explanations, in which he should have some latitude to dispense with strict syllogistic forms, will generally regard the minor or second premise. In order not to perplex the attention with matters of only secondary importance, it is a sufficiently approved practice always to call the *first* premise of a regular syllogism the *major*, and the *second* the *minor* premise, without regard to its technical propriety.

After the brief proof, or proofs by which the truth of his thesis is demonstrated, the objections against it immediately begin. In answering them he should suppress excitement or anxiety, avoid precipitancy, and strive to avail himself of the advice given to him who defends the truth, by the well-known axioms of the "circle;" "raro affirma, sæpe nega, semper distingue;" rarely affirm, often deny, always distinguish. A plausible objection to the truth, besides being in *logical form*, will generally contain both something that is true, and something that is false.

The defender always begins his answer by repeating the argument of the adversary, just as it was stated by him; it is then repeated a second time, the answer being given to each proposition as soon as it is enunciated. In the solution of the objection, either some one, or more *terms*, will be distinguished, so as to grant what is true, and to deny what is falsely affirmed by them; or else one or both *premises* will be denied. The objector, in his next argument, having in his preparation beforehand anticipated the answer given to his first objection, will be ready to bring an argument to prove what is denied; and thus the contest may be continued at pleasure. Practice will speedily render the disputants skillful in finding arguments, extemporaneously, or "at the spur of the moment."

Either the teacher, or some one else who is competent for the task, presides as moderator at these exercises, and sees both that the objections are rightly put, and that they are accurately and satisfactorily solved; it is also his duty to see that the whole exercise is conducted with decorum, and that the disputation be not uselessly or unduly protracted.

When both parties prepare diligently beforehand for their contest, it is found by experience that the "circle" always proves to be both a highly interesting exercise for advanced students, and a profitable one.

An example will help to render the *form* of conducting this exercise more clear to the mind: suppose the thesis to be defended is the following; "The external senses furnish to the mind an unerring motive of certainty, as to their proper objects."

The defender might here first explain the scope and meaning of the thesis; v. g., 1st, that it supposes the senses to be in a healthful or normal state; 2d, he might mention some conditions to be complied with for prudently using the senses; 3d, he might distinguish between inducing error, *per se*, i. e., *causing*, or *physically effecting* error; and erring *accidentally*, in which latter case, error happens through precipitancy in judging, etc. He may then state in form one of his principal arguments; v. g., "No agent that acts only by natural or necessary physical law, can be false; but the external senses act only by natural or necessary physical law; therefore, the external senses cannot be false." In explaining and proving the premises, he may employ the syllogism, the enthymeme, the sorites, or any legitimate form of argument, that may occur to him; and it would be appropriate to the argument, as above given, to show how *false action* in natural or physical agents, if conceived to be at all possible, would be referable to God, etc. His proofs may proceed till finished; or they may be suspended, at the discretion of the moderator, in order that the objections may be given.

The objector, when the proofs are finished, begins at once; v. g., "Those organs cannot be said to furnish unerring certainty, which mislead the judgment; but the external senses mislead the judgment; therefore, the external senses do not furnish the mind unerring certainty."

The objection having been repeated, in order to prevent misunderstanding as to its precise meaning, is then answered by parts; v. g., "Those organs cannot be said to furnish certainty which *per se* mislead the judgment, or by their own action necessitate error in the mind, I grant; but that their accidental connexion with error, really and properly *causes* that error, I deny; similarly I distinguish the minor, and, therefore, I deny the consequence and consequent—or, I deny the conclusion."

Objector insists, "To *cause* error even accidentally, is really and truly to *cause* error; but, as you admit, the senses cause error *accidentally;* therefore, the senses really and truly cause error."

Answer, after repeating the objection; "I distinguish; that to cause error *per se*, that is, physically and efficiently to cause it, is really and truly to cause it, I grant; that to cause error *accidentally*, is really and properly to cause error, I deny, and, therefore, I deny the conclusion."

Objector insists, "Whatever has the nature of a *cause*, has its own proper *effect*, which it brings about; the accidental cause has the nature of a cause; therefore, it has its own proper effect which proceeds from it."

Answer, after repeating the objection, "That the cause *per se*, or cause that really and positively influences action, has its own proper effect, which it positively brings about, I grant; that the *accidental* cause really and positively influences in the production of any effect, I deny;" etc.

Here the defender might be required to explain more precisely what this *accidental cause* is, and under what respect it is termed a *cause* at all.

The foregoing example is by no means offered as a model of argumentation; but, though imperfect, it may serve to illustrate by something visible, the *form* or *manner* of conducting logical and metaphysical disputations in the class-room, or the college hall. It is hoped that even this outline description of the exercise will suggest reasons to prove its importance and value for cultivating the reasoning power, and as a means of acquiring precise notions and judgments. When a proposition stands either as a premise or the conclusion of a well conceived syllogism, to which, by the nature of its matter, it belongs, its full meaning and value are then distinctly appreciated.

It was said above that in the regular disputation, no objection was regarded as valid or legitimate, unless it be in *logical form:* the reason for thus absolutely excluding these vicious or spurious arguments, is manifest. For, if the disputation were permitted to turn merely upon fallacies in the form of argument, it would thereby become degraded to the rank of *sophistry;* which, considered as an exercise of reason, possesses little more value or dignity than the trivial practice of punning.

Logic, which is the means of ascertaining and imparting truth by discourse of reason, would thus be rendered practically aimless; for its natural tendency as a study would then rather be to make the mind astute and disingenuous, than to develop and cultivate in the understanding healthful and normal habits of thought, or give it facility in demonstrating and maintaining truth by its reasons.

It would be erroneous, however, to infer from what is said, that all exercises in the fallacies or sophistical methods of reasoning, which are adapted to give readiness in detecting and refuting errors in the form of arguments, are to be condemned, or are intended thereby to be censured. The "circle," which may be considered an exercise that is, under some respect, public, is designed to represent the contest for truth, so far as practicable, just as it is conducted by sincere and upright opponents. Hence, the objections offered to the proposed thesis, which thesis may perchance happen to be really untrue, should by no means be limited to feigned difficulties against the doctrine defended: but if valid arguments can be adduced which refute it, they are not to be withheld; for truth should prevail, even if the defender of the assigned proposition be discomfited.

But the practice of giving exaggerated, and even exclusive attention to the mere forms of argument, or of making all exercise in Logic consist in the various transformations or conversions which are possible in these forms, employing for the purpose only abstract, algebraic formulæ, or the related parts of certain diagrams, is, perhaps, as much a mechanical, as it is an intellectual operation; and while the limited use of such methods is not without its advantage, yet excessive attention to these extrinsic devices has not a beneficial effect upon the mind. The rules of correct argument are, for the mind that is loyal to truth, few and simple. It is the ignoble office of persistent error to employ subterfuge, obscurity, equivocation, and all the vices of false reasoning.

It cannot be justly doubted that the direct proofs of truth, and its positive criteria, as explained in Applied Logic, and the principles of General and Special Metaphysics, furnish the most profitable subject matter, for exercising the young mind in Practical Logic.

END OF LOGIC.

ONTOLOGY

OR,

GENERAL METAPHYSICS.

ONTOLOGY;

OR,

GENERAL METAPHYSICS.

The *metaphysical** transcends the conditions of material and sensible existence, as the term *metaphysical*, i. e., *beyond the physical*, implies. It considers truths and principles in the prototypes of things; or, as they are contained or implied in the essential concepts of things, abstractedly from the existence of those things, or, also, as verified in their existence. Hence, it has for its object the most universal attributes of beings; and the laws and axioms of all the sciences are subject to it, and are tested by its principles; since error is refuted, and truth demonstrated, only by means of principles that are known *per se*, i. e., are *self-evident*, *necessary* and *immutable*. In a more special sense, it also includes whatever is immaterial, as spirits, God; since we naturally know spirit only by metaphysical principles and reasoning.

As ontology or general metaphysics, which is the science of

* "Metaphysicus considerat rerum essentias et modos essendi; Logicus considerat prædicationes seu modos prædicandi." The Metaphysician considers the essence of things, and their necessary modes of existing; the Logician considers predicables, or modes of predicating.

"Metaphysica in objecto suo includit ens universalissimum et ejus attributa essentialia." Metaphysics includes for its object, being as most universal, and its essential attributes or properties.

being in the most general sense of the term *being*,* furnishes to the mind the fundamental and ultimate principles on which all philosophy rests, and by which all science must be finally tested, its importance is very great. Its neglect cannot but prove disastrous to all sound method of philosophizing, and thus result in vague hypotheses and dark theories, instead of certain and genuine science. By a careful study of it, the educated mind comes finally to rest quiet in its conclusions; for it sees them as they flow from their first and necessary principles.

* "Metaphysica speculatur universalia entis attributa; quæ videlicet enti per se insunt, et quæcunque spectant ad eadem illa, sive per oppositionem sive per connexionem: Ex. gr. in ente, *unum, verum, bonum, essentiam, existentiam,*" etc. Metaphysics regards the most universal attributes of being; namely, whatever is essentially in being, or pertains to its essential attributes, whether by opposition or connexion; v. g., its unity, truth, goodness, essence, existence, etc.

CHAPTER I.

ARTICLE I.

WHAT THE NOTION BEING IN ITS GENERAL SENSE INCLUDES; ESSENCE OF THINGS; EXISTENCE; UNITY; IDENTITY; DISTINCTION.

Being, in its most general sense, includes in its concept what actually exists, and what has any sort of entity, whether it be substance or accident, Creator or creature. *Being*, thus understood, is the *material object* of ontology. *Being*, in this general sense, is not *generical* in its meaning when applied to different objects, v. g., *mineral*, *animal*, *substance*, *accident;* here its signification is not *univocal*, but *analogical.* For, genus requires the term which stands for its essence to be *univocally* applied to its inferiors or subjects; v. g., "the horse is *animal;* the lion is *animal;* man is *animal.*" In these examples, *animal* expresses precisely the same concept in all the objects termed *animal.* But in the examples, "accident is *being*, substance is *being*, matter is *being*, spirit is *being;*" the word *being* has not the same, univocal significance in its application to these objects; for, accident as compared to substance, or matter to spirit, is *being*, only by analogy, since they are in their real entity generically different, therefore essentially and wholly different, and we cannot say that the one is the other, except by some relation of analogy.

The word *being*, which stands for the simplest and most universal of our ideas, cannot be defined, nor does it require a definition. It cannot be defined, for, *genus* and *specific difference* are both *being*, and even every synonym of the term is also *being;* hence, *being*, when thus understood, cannot be subjected to definition.

The general concept of being (*entis*), does not expressly say for its object, either substance or accident, Creator or creature; but all of them, as in some manner *one*, i. e., as *being;* of course, they are *one*, or *are being* only by a sort of analogy. As observes Suarez, "To the formal concept* of *being*, corresponds one *objective* concept, adequate and immediate, which does not expressly say either substance or accident, either God or creature, but says them all as one: namely, as being similar in some respect, and as agreeing in this, that they are all *beings*."†

Hence, it may be inferred that *being* is not predicated *equivocally* of God and creature, for then nothing could be demonstrated concerning God from creature, since the *medium*, or middle term, would be *equivocal;* it is neither predicated *univocally*, for in this case God and creature would be of the same species; it is predicated of them only *analogically*, owing to a certain similarity by which they are, in some sense, *united* in the same concept of being.

The word *nothing*, taken absolutely, expresses the exclusion of all being or entity; yet the mind can make of *nothing* a *quasi object*, by its relation to *something*, which it excludes. But, considered as an *object*, it is merely a creature of the mind, *ens rationis*, whose only foundation in reality is the relation referred to.

When, by a reflexive judgment, the mind affirms, "whatever exists, is; what does not exist, is not," it thereby employs the *principle of identity*, for the purpose of giving more reflex certainty to the proposition.

When, for the same purpose, we affirm that "it is impossible for the same thing to exist, and not exist at the same time;" we thereby employ the *principle of contradiction*. When we

* See Article I, Log., I Part, p. 16.

† "Conceptui formali entis, respondet unus conceptus objectivus, adæquatus et immediatus, qui expresse non dicit substantiam neque accidens, neque Deum neque creaturam; sed hæc omnia per modum unius; viz., quatenus sunt inter se aliquo modo similia, et conveniunt in essendo." (Metaphys. Disp. 2, Sect. 2.)

put the affirmation under this disjunctive form, namely, "either the thing is, or it is not," it is called the *principle* of the *excluded middle;* since no *medium* is possible between *being*, and *not being;* or, as applied under the same respect, and to the same thing, all middle or *medium* is *excluded*, in a complete disjunction.

The *essence* of a thing includes all *that by which the thing is what it is, and without which it could not possibly exist at all;* v. g., a *triangle* is constituted such by having three angles, and three sides. Its constituent elements are the *three angles*, and *three sides*, and if any one of these essential constituents be wanting, its *essence* is thereby destroyed, and it ceases to be a triangle, for they are all and each necessary for the very concept of it. The *essence*, therefore, is that without which a thing can neither exist, nor be conceived, and which makes it what it is, when it exists. Essence of a thing, is the real answer to the question: "What is it?"

When the essence* of a thing is considered as *active*, or as a principle, capable either of eliciting or putting *acts*, it is in that sense the same as the *nature* of that thing; the *essence constitutes* the being what it is; its *nature* is the *essence* viewed in reference to its operations, or as *empowered* to *act*. That which constitutes a being *immediately* operative or able to act, may be considered as the *complement* of essence.† This *complement* of essence consists of all the powers, or active and passive virtues, that belong to that essence.

Hence, since the *nature* ‡ of a thing is its *essence* as empowered

* "Essentia est in ordine ad esse, natura, principium agendi." What is *essence*, in respect to existence, is *nature*, when regarded as a principle of action.

† "Nulla substantia creata est immediate operativa." No created substance is immediately operative.

‡ "Potentia definitur per actum." Power is defined by its act.

"Definitio est oratio explicans rei naturam." Definition is a discourse explaining the nature of a thing.

"Actus specificantur ab objectis." Acts are specified by their objects.

"Substantia rei cognoscitur ex operatione; operatio vero ex objecto circa quod versatur." (Lessius opuscul. de immort. animæ,, Lib. 2, No. 55.) The substance of a thing is known by its operation; the operation is known by the object which it regards.

"Præterea nulla forma materiæ immersa in essendo et operando, potest re-to *act;* and, also, since *powers*, i. e., *nature* as *operative*, are *defined* by their *acts*, and *acts* are *specified* by their connatural objects, it follows that we know the species of any thing from knowing the species of its *acts*, and this we know from the connatural objects of these acts; when, therefore, two acts are specifically different, the *powers* or *natures* that put these acts are also specifically different.

The following demonstrative argument exemplifies both the force and the application of this undeniable principle, namely, that by knowing the species of the *acts*, we thereby know the species or kind of the *nature* that puts those acts: "the human intellect has for the connatural objects of its acts the *true*, the *universal*, the *abstract*, the *super-sensible;* but these objects of its acts are absolutely *immaterial;* therefore, the intellect or *intelligent nature* which by its acts attains to them, is *absolutely immaterial* also." Or, in fewer words, that is *immaterial*, the connatural objects of whose action are immaterial.

The *essence* may be considered as *physical*, or *metaphysical.* The *genus* and *specific difference*, assign the *metaphysical* essence of an object; as v. g., *material and inorganic substance.* These terms, *substance*, *material*, *inorganic*, give the *metaphysical* constituents of the object. The *physical essence* includes the constituent attributes, or elements, as they are *actually* and *concretely*, in the object.

The human mind may understand and quite clearly comprehend the essence which it constitutes for itself out of *genus* and *specific difference*, which it founds on the realities of objects as known to it; but the *physical essence* of objects, as they are actually existing, it can know, not immediately and intimately; but only *mediately* or through their extrinsic action and effects.

This is evident, when we reflect that we depend for our

flectere supra suam operationem; v. g., oculus non videt suam visionem, etc., anima autem rationalis reflectit supra propriam operationem. Ergo anima rationalis est superior omni materiæ in essendo et operando." (Philosophi. passim.) No form which is dependent on matter, both in existing and in operating, can reflect on its own act; v. g., the eye cannot see itself seeing, etc.; but the rational soul can reflect on its own act. Therefore, the rational soul is superior to matter, both in its essence and its action.

"Actus et potentia sunt ejusdem generis." Act and the power are of the same genus.

knowledge of the objects around us, upon the senses, which are acted on by those objects through their qualities; and, therefore, the mind does not perceive their essence immediately, but by experience, comparison, reflexion and abstraction, it forms its concept of that *essence*, as the *nature* of the object. But, on the other hand, it is very erroneous to assert, as Locke does, that we know *nothing* of the *physical* essence of things; for we do know physical essences, at least so far as they manifest themselves in their properties and operations.

The essence of an actual being is *true* because it is conformable to the type of that being, as it exists in the Divine Mind. The essential prototypes, or essences of things, as in the Divine Mind, are eternal, indivisible, and immutable. For if they could be divided, or diminished, and thus changed, they would thereby become something else; some other essence, or cease to be what they are, which, in reality, would be to conceive other essences, not to change these. (Vide page 61 et seq. and *note* page 63.)

IN WHAT REAL MUTATION CONSISTS.

It will help towards a fuller comprehension of this whole matter, if we distinguish the different senses in which the expressions "mutation," and "change of one thing into another," are understood by philosophers; v. g., as, *conversion*, *transubstantiation*, *alteration*, *annihilation* and *creation*, all of which operations imply some sort of *change* in the terms, or objects of them.

For the *conversion* of one thing into another, the fulfillment of the following rules and conditions is essential:

First: There must be two terms, both of which are *positive;* i. e., not mere *privations* or *negations*, but some positive and real substance. The first one of these terms is called the *terminus a quo*, or *conversus;* i. e., the term, object or thing that is changed; the other term of the conversion is called the *terminus ad quem*, or *convertens;* i. e., the term or thing into which the first one is changed, or which, in some manner, replaces the first one.

Second: There must be a *subject* either *in* which, or *in respect* to which, the change is made, this subject in itself remaining unchanged; i. e., what is intrinsical to one term is changed into what is intrinsically of another term, something receiving that change as a subject, or at least as a *quasi* subject, this subject thereby passing from the one to the other without being itself otherwise changed.

Third: The *terminus a quo* must cease to exist in the subject, and be succeeded by the *terminus ad quem*, the cessation of the one and the succession of the other having some relation of dependence on each other; this ceasing of the one term and beginning of the other can be effected only by some real physical action.

Fourth: Hence, there must be a double mutation: one by which the *terminus a quo* passes from existence to non-existence; and the other, by which the *terminus ad quem* passes from non-existence to existence, a subject receiving the one, after giving up the other; this subject is the *matter*, or *quasi matter.*

An example, though it does not perfectly embody these conditions, yet may help to illustrate for the young mind what is thus far said: suppose an orange and an apple be placed near to each other on the table. Now, if all that specifically or essentially constitutes the orange what it is, were caused to pass into the apple, in such a manner as to force all that specifically or essentially constitutes the apple to give way, or cease to remain in the matter in which it dwelt, and thus be succeeded therein by the corresponding constituents of the orange, thereby making that which was an apple become an orange, such change would be the *conversion* of one thing into another, and, in this instance, it would be the conversion of an apple into an orange. The apple would be the *terminus a quo*, and the orange would be the *terminus ad quem.* The *matter* in which the essence of the apple ceased to be, and into which the essence or specific nature of the orange subsequently came, is the *subject* of the conversion.

As to whether there is any conversion, as thus described, of one material substance into another, by natural laws and agency, is a question which, in the opinion of some great minds, is not yet demonstratively and definitively settled by philosophers and physicists.

The misfortune of the *Alchemists* was the assuming as a general principle, such conversion of material substance to be naturally possible; and hence their many futile and disastrous attempts actually to *convert* base metals into gold. But all agree that absolutely and intrinsically the conversion of one substance supposed to consist of a dual principle, as implied in the idea of conversion, into another, is not impossible to Infinite Power; still more evidently is there no repugnance when that change of one thing into another is a *transubstantiation.*

In this case it is not alone the formal, or specific principle of the dual constituents of material substance that is converted into another, the material principle remaining in itself unchanged as the subject of two successive substantial forms; but in *transubstantiation* the whole substance, both as to matter and substantial form, ceases, and a complete new substance succeeds it, the accidents which are *sensible*, or the sensible species alone remaining unchanged, except as to their relation to the substance.

In the case of Eucharistic transubstantiation, the sensible species exist without a subject of inhesion. This transubstantiation is not effected by natural, but by supernatural agency. There seems to be no proof, however, that such transubstantiation can be effected by any merely natural agency.

Alteration expresses change of one quality into another; the *terminus ad quem*, in *alteration*, is quality; in *conversion*, the *terminus ad quem*, is *substance*, as already said.

There is *alteration* in the most strict sense, only when some quality of a given substance is changed into a contrary; v. g., when *black* is changed into *white*, they being conceived as contraries. In this case, the whole substance, which is the subject of *alteration*, passes from a positive quality which ceases, to a new and contrary quality, which succeeds it. Accidents that *perfect* their subject, are not said to *alter* it, since it is not consistent to say that a thing is *altered*, or becomes, in any proper sense, *another*,* by being perfected.

In *creation*, a thing is produced from nothing; i. e., it is not educed in any sense from a preëxisting subject, but derives its whole being from a *purely* efficient cause. By *annihilation*, a being is totally reduced to non-existence, so that nothing of it that is either substantial or accidental, is remaining.

Since the *essence* of a thing includes precisely those constituents that are necessary to make it what it is individually, and which, at the same time, render it conformable to its archetype in the divine mind, it is *per se* evident that neither this type of it in the divine mind, nor the truthful copy of it in the actual being, can be intrinsically changed.

The mutations above described as *conversion*, *alteration*, etc., include all real changes in a being that are possible, or conceivable; but in no one of them is there change of *intrinsic essence*. Even *existence*, and *non-existence*, are only different states or conditions of a being or essence, which include no intrinsic change of *essence in itself*. Hence, all mutation is limited to the existence or non-existence, and to the real relations, of its terms; and, therefore, essences are intrinsically immutable.

Essence is eternal: Essence, in the possible or intelligible order, could have had no beginning; for it was always true that if a thing of a given or determinate essence ever existed afterwards, it must have such or such essential constituents; since this eternal possibility depends on God, who is eternal, is the cause of truth, and knows in His own essence the *essential prototype* of every possible creature, from eternity; therefore, essence, regarded as a concept of the divine intellect, must be eternal.

Existence is affirmed of those essences that are actual, or that have passed from possibility into the order of real things; and they are then said to *exist*. It is manifest that existence

* "*Conversio* terminatur ad *aliud; alteratio* ad *alterum*." The term of *conversion* is another substance; that of alteration, another quality.

cannot be strictly defined; and yet nothing is more clear to the mind than it is.

Essence, as possible, being logically presupposed to its actual existence in the real order of things, metaphysicians amuse themselves with the subtle question, "Is *actually existing essence* truly different from its *real existence?*" Though the question is not practically important, and perhaps turns partly on an equivocal use of terms, it may, however, exercise mental acumen in the inquisitive student of philosophy, to state it briefly in this place.

One side, interpreting in their favor the expressions often employed by the "Angel of the Schools," St. Thomas of Aquin, v. g., "essentia entis perfectissimi, absoluti, necessarii, etc., est suum esse;" the essence of absolutely perfect being includes its existence; "essentia entis contingentis non est suum esse;" the essence of contingent being does not postulate in its concept actual existence; "in creatis, est compositio inter essentiam et esse;" in created things, there is composition between essence and existence, etc., argue that the two are different; that is, that real essence and its actual existence are different objectively. They hold that the *term* of every creative act must be *actually received by a subject*, since all created essence is *participated* or *derived.* Hence, in this theory, *existence* is the *actuality*, and *essence* is the *subject* that receives it; some saying that the existence is a substantial form *educed* from the essence; others, that it is *modal* only. It thence follows, therefore, that essence and its existence constitute a *dual* principle, like to that of *matter* and *form*, in corporeal substance, the *essence* being the *potentia*, or *quasi matter*, and existence being the *form.*

The other side, who maintain that it is a distinction without a difference, answer that this theory, thus applied, presents a less simple and perfect concept both of the *creative act*, and the *nature* of uncompounded or simple substance; that, for the existence of corporeal substance, it necessitates the admission of a *double dual principle;* namely, *matter* and *form*, *essence* and *existence.* They argue, moreover, that their adversaries' theory being true, namely, that all *actual* being must be *received*, no sufficient reason can be given why the series of dual principles should be limited at all; that this hypothesis is obscure, and difficult to be comprehended; that it is susceptible of no *positive* or conclusive proof; that it is a *multiplication of entia*, which rather perplexes than simplifies philosophic thought, and that it, therefore, is introduced without logical necessity.*

From this imperfect outline of a few arguments adduced by each side, some idea may be formed, at least, of the *point* on which the dispute turns.

Possibility: Whatever creature exists is capable of existing, and was capable of existing before it existed at all. A thing is *intrinsically possible*, when its essential constituents have no repugnance or contradiction among themselves; as v. g., it is possible to construct a locomotive that is impelled at a given velocity by steam. *Extrinsic possibility*, besides presupposing the intrinsic possibility, implies also that there is a sufficient cause that can actually produce the effect; v. g., the *builders*, *material*, etc., of the locomotive, in the example supposed.

Possibility, taken simply or *adequately*, includes both the *extrinsic* and the *intrinsic possibility*.

Corresponding to this double respect of possibility there is a twofold *impossibility; intrinsic* and *extrinsic impossibility*. All things that are *intrinsically possible*, are, in respect to the power of God, also *extrinsically possible*. In respect to the power of creatures, many things which are intrinsically, and, therefore, extrinsically possible to God, are for them *physically impossible;* v. g., it is *physically* impossible for men to stop the motion of the earth, and still more is it *physically impossible* for a creature to *create* from nothing. A thing is *morally impossible* which, considering the moral nature of man, cannot be done by him; v. g., all parents cannot hate their offspring; all men cannot unite in a lie.

Intrinsic possibility does not primarily proceed either from

* This question is argued acutely and at great length by Suarez (Metaphysics, Disput., 31); where he defends the latter opinion, and denies that there is any real difference between *actual essence* and *its existence*.

the power or the will of God; but from the essences of things as seen by the Divine Intelligence; or, in other words, they have their origin in the Divine Essence itself.

It is obvious that both power and will presuppose the *possibility* of the thing to be done or effected, since intelligence must logically precede both volition* and the power that follows, or obeys volition. Otherwise, one might say, "God can make a circle that is not round, if its *possibility* depends formally on his *will*, or his *power;*" whereas, the supposition is absurd; for contradictions mutually destroy themselves, and, in the case supposed, leave no term of action. It would be the same as saying, God can make a circle and not make a circle at the same time and under the same respect; which is actually saying nothing at all, as an object of thought or real term of action.

Hence, it is easily seen that, as before stated, *intrinsic possibilities*, or, what is virtually the same, the essences of things, are *immutable*, and are, therefore, incapable either of increase or diminution.

Every being is one. Unity is the negation of division in a being.† For, every being is either simple, or it is compound; if it is simple, it is indivisible; if it is compound, it ceases to be a being when divided, and becomes not a being, but beings. Yet, a thing may be *one* in some respect, and *many* in another respect; v. g., the essence of a thing is *one;* but its integral parts may be *many*. The universal is actually *one*, but capable of becoming *many*, under a certain respect.‡

Identity§ is founded on unity, and signifies the agreement of

* "Nihil volitum nisi præcognitum." That which is wished must have been previously known; or, more litterally, nothing is wished unless what is foreknown.

† "Omne principium est unum." Every principle is one.
"Ab uno non nisi unum."

‡ "Universale, *unum* est actu; *multa* in potentia." The universal is one actually, but many, potentially.

§ "*Unum* in substantia facit *idem; unum* in qualitate facit *simile; unum* in qantitate facit *æquale*, seu æqualitas fundatur in unitate quantitatis, servata distinctione extremorum." To be *one* in substance, makes *identity; one* in quality, makes *similarity; one* in quantity, makes *equality;* or, equality is founded on unity of quantity, keeping the distinction of the extremes.

a thing with itself. Identity may be *generic*, as, *animal*, in man and brute; or *specific*, as *man*, when applied to different men; or numerical, as a *man* compared with himself.

*Similarity** is connected with identity and unity, since it is founded on unity or identity under some respect.

Similarity is an agreement of *distinct things*. This agreement is in some quality or perfection, and it may exist in objects of different species; "the child resembles its mother; the color of the evening sky is like to that of gold;" "vices in the evening of life, *like* shadows at the decline of day, *grow great and monstrous*." The resemblance between the objects in the last example is properly that of analogy, though the comparison be termed *simile*. Agreement in all respects is peculiar to objects of the same species, as, Peter is like Paul; this is *specific identity*.

Leibnitz and Clark disputed as to whether two objects of the same species could be so completely alike as to differ only numerically; Leibnitz denied the possibility of it; Clark maintained it to be *intrinsically possible;* and in this he was correct.

Distinguish between similarity and analogy; similarity is founded on the specific identity of some one or more qualities or properties in objects which are otherwise different, and which are, therefore, predicated of the objects univocally. These objects, or the subjects of the like qualities, may be either of the same or different species. Analogy, on the contrary, properly supposes its objects or the terms of it, to be of different species.

Analogy is not founded on *specifically identical quality* in its objects or terms; but on a certain *proportion* between its objects, or their proper effects, by which the one becomes *related* in the mind to the other.

This proportion is not that which is in *parity*, which is reducible to mathematical quantity, and which, being of the same species, is predicated univocally of its terms; but the proportion which makes analogy is not reducible to mathematical

* "Ut duo dicantur perfecte similia, debent habere secundum eamdem rationem id in quo conveniunt." For two things to be called perfectly similar, they must possess that in which they agree, in the same manner.

quantity; it is a relation or agreement which has no proper unit of measure, is neither univocally nor equivocally predicated of its objects or terms, and yet they have that basis of somewhat indeterminate resemblance which founds for the mind a relation of the one to the other.

Both similarity and analogy, therefore, are founded on likeness of objects, and hence, they may be considered as agreeing generically, though they differ specifically.

*Distinction** is opposed to *identity*. *Real* distinction is either *substantial* or *accidental;* the distinction between an apple and a pebble is *substantial;* also, that between the *body* and *soul* in man, though constituents of the same compound. The distinction between *substance* and its *accidents*, or among the accidents themselves, is, under different respects, either *accidental distinction*, or substantial distinction.

The *distinction of reason* † is so called, because it is made by the *reason*, and exists only in the *reasoning* which the mind employs in its efforts to comprehend or explain certain difficult objects in which, being unable to use the real, it helps itself by this artificial distinction.

This *distinction of reason* is two-fold; it is either *virtually founded in the object;* or, it is *purely mental.* The distinction of the attributes in God, as all-wise, all-powerful, free, merciful, just, etc., since his absolute perfection contains in a certain pre-eminent manner what we thus denominate, is a *distinction of reason founded* in its object; though God and his attributes are *really identical.*

The distinction between *man and rational animal*, or *Cicero and Tully*, is purely mental, or of *reason;* one being the other differently expressed. The mind employs these distinctions of reason in its operations that regard objects, whose unity and simplicity, or greatness, it is unable to express by one direct and adequate concept of those objects.

* "Distinctio est carentia identitatis." Distinction is a want of identity.

† "Distinctio rationis est duplex: distinctio rationis ratiocinatæ, quæ fit cum fundamento in re; et distinctio rationis ratiocinantis, quæ est sine fundamento in re." The distinction of reason is twofold: the one is founded in the object; the other is not founded in the object.

To this head we may likewise refer various mere figments of the imagination: "ens imaginabile latius ampliat quam ens possibile;" the fancy extends its action even beyond the possible object, to the impossible or absurd.

ARTICLE II.

TRUTH.

*Truth** is a predicate of every being; and is, therefore, enumerated among the *transcendentals*, or the *transcendental* predicables: it consists in this, that every being agrees with the essential type, or concept of itself. Truth, thus understood, is now more commonly called, *metaphysical truth.*

All truth, as already declared in speaking of logical truth, is a relation of agreement between intellect and object.† When Leibnitz defines it to be, *order* in the constituents of *being*, his definition pertains rather to the goodness or perfection of being.

Absolutely speaking, things are true because they agree with the intellect that constitutes them; that is, when they agree with the archetypes, or essential ideas according to whose exemplar they are made. Thus all actual things agree with their exemplars in the Divine Mind; and, similarly, artificial things made by man are true, as agreeing with the preconceived idea of them in the mind of him who devises and makes them. Hence, it is easily seen that *falsity*‡ in beings, or real things, is *nothing;* but falsity, or *not being*, is predicated of them by a concept *of reason*, which attributes to them what is really in the judgment, or in the mind only.

A statue is said to be *false*, which fails to express the intended likeness; a deceiver is called a *false* friend; objects are called *false*, which give occasion for false judgment, as "fools' gold," etc. But *falsity*, formally taken, is the negation of truth, and

* "Omne ens est verum." Every being is true.

† "Veritas est adæquatio intellectus et rei." Truth is the equation of intellect and object.

‡ "Falsitas in rebus nihil est." There is no falsity in real things.

in its primary or radical sense, is to be referred to *will and judgment*, or, to finite cognition, but not to things or beings, as positive.

After a little attention to the preceding considerations, the following propositions will be readily admitted:

First: There is truth in all real things, and that independently of our knowledge of them. For they are conformable to their archetypes in the Divine Intellect; and this relation of agreement is *metaphysical truth.* Also things are principally or primarily true by their relation to the Divine Intelligence, to which must be referred the origin of all essences.

Second: No object is false, in respect to the Divine Intellect. For God is infinite in intelligence in which they originate, and freedom which wills to create, and power which actually effects them, or gives them their real being; therefore, all things that exist must agree with their essential exemplars, as they are in His intelligence: this is truth in those things; since they must be what they are *seen*, *willed* and *made* to be, by Him.

Third: Every being is true: (*omne ens est verum.*) For so far as any thing is being at all, so far forth is it true; since we can predicate *not true* only of that *which is not.*

Fourth: In respect to the Divine Intellect, created things are as the measured to the measure; but in respect to the human intellect, on the contrary, *creatures are as the measure to the measured.* That is, Divine Intelligence is the *cause* of created things; but these created things are the cause of the human intellect knowing them; for, as objects, they *specify* the acts of human knowledge which they cause; and without their active concurrence, the human intellect could not know them.

ARTICLE III.

GOOD AND EVIL.

Every thing that exists may be conceived as having for its object a certain good which is connatural to it, and to which it tends, therefore, by the law of its nature. This propensity or positive tendency to that *good* which is an end for each being, is often called, under different respects, its *appetite*, or its power of *appetition.*

Appetite, then, is the propensity or positive tendency of a being to its connatural good. *Elicited* appetition is this propensity or tendency to a *known good;* and since *knowledge* may be either *sensible* or *rational,* it is obvious that *appetite* may also be either *sensible* or *rational. Rational appetite,* which is the *will,* tends to a good which is apprehended by the intellect, as the *sensible appetite* tends to good which is known through the organs of sense.

An act is *elicited* by a power when it proceeds immediately and physically from that power; or, when that power is the active principle that gives origin to it. Thus, the *will* elicits its own acts, or they are immediately and physically from the will. Owing to the authority of the will over our faculties and members, their acts which are put, in obedience to the will, are *commanded* or ordered *acts.* Objects which have not a *vital* principle of action in them do not *elicit* acts; but are moved to action only by an efficient and extrinsic cause.

IN WHAT THE LIBERTY OR FREEDOM OF THE RATIONAL APPETITE, OR THE HUMAN WILL, CONSISTS.

That power is free, which, all things being put which are required for its action, can either act, or not act.* Hence, when the objects which are subject to the will's free choice are actually presented to it by the intellect, it is truly *indifferent* in respect to them; i. e., its election or choice is not determined by the objects proposed to it, but is determined by the will itself, by its own proper act.

* "Potentia libera illa est, quæ, positis omnibus requisitis ad operandum, potest operari et non operari."

"Omnia bonum appetunt; malum est præter intentionem." All things desire their good; evil is beside intention.

"Voluntas est appetitus intellectus, seu est inclinatio ad bonum per intellectum apprehensum."

"Appetitus boni cum ratione."

The will is the appetite of the intellect, or it is inclination to good which is apprehended by the intellect; it is the appetite of good with reason.

As there are two distinct classes of objects which the action of the will regards, the liberty or freedom of the will may be considered under two corresponding respects: 1st, it may be considered as exempt from *force*, or forced action, but not exempt from *necessity*, or *necessitated* action; 2d, the action of the will may be considered as exempt, both from *force* and *necessity*. It is liberty or freedom of action in this second sense alone, that is specified in the preceding definition of liberty. In this case, therefore, even all things being supposed which are required for its action, the will can either act, or not act, the final choice being strictly its own act.

Distinguish, therefore, between the will's action as thus free, and its necessitated action. Beings that see God intuitively are *necessitated* by that vision of *perfect good*, to love God supremely; but they are not *forced* to do so, since force implies violent and compulsory action. For, it is manifest that *force*, or *forced* action, comes from an extrinsic principle, and the subject which is compelled by it is entirely *passive*, and, therefore, does not positively or efficiently contribute to the forced action.

It is essential to the very concept of appetite, or power of appetition, and above all to a *rational* appetite, that it tend by its natural action only to what is apprehended as the *good* of its subject; and that it avert from evil, when it is apprehended precisely as such. For, if the appetite could tend to evil, *as evil*, it would itself be physically and essentially evil, for, in such supposition, it would tend to evil as its connatural object, and, therefore, its evil action would be in obedience to the necessary physical law of its nature. The appetite would, in such case, be intrinsically evil, as is evident; but this would dishonor God. Therefore, an appetite must, of its very nature, tend to what is, at least in some respect, the good of its subject.

Hence, it must follow that the will can, by its natural action, tend to no object which is not apprehended as, under some respect, *good* for its subject. And this is, at the same time, as a little observation and reflexion will verify, an obvious fact of experience, as regards the operation of all those agents which have natural to them these principles of action termed appetites, or powers of appetition.

The will, when considered as exempt from force or compulsory action, but yet as *necessarily* tending, in all its action, to *good*, is often termed a *natural agent;* in the sense that, like all physical and second causes, its action is *spontaneous*, i. e., springs from itself, or its own nature as operative: its action is still *voluntary*, or of the will, but it is not *free*.

The term *spontaneous*, is used in several distinct senses: 1st, the action even of inanimate beings, as minerals, stones, etc., is said to be *spontaneous*, in the sense that their action is their *own*, or really proceeds from them, as a principle that puts or produces it; 2d, that species of *choice*, in a wide and analogical sense of the term, which irrational animals make by virtue of sensible power in them, among the objects of their appetites, is often termed *spontaneous* action in them: 3d, the action of the will as necessitated to desire good, is termed *spontaneous* action; and, in the same sense, it is often called *voluntary* action, as opposed to *free* action, inasmuch as the *will* is its principle, or it is elicited by the will; 4th, the *free* action of the will is also termed *spontaneous*, as opposed both to forced and necessitated action.

Hence, *spontaneous* action, in the primary sense of the word from which its other meanings are derived, is opposed to *forced* action; or, *spontaneous* action is that action which is not *forced*, but is put by the agent as its principle.

The will is properly termed free, as already observed, only when it is exempt both from force and necessity or necessitated action. As subject only to *necessity*, it is still the formal principle of its own action, or it *elicits* its volitions: but it does so, in obedience to physical and necessary law. Every agent, truly such; the intellect, the senses, irrational animals, inanimate substances, can all act, and do act, with some sort of *spontaneity*, or without being *forced* to operate, as above explained; but yet, they are never exempt from *necessity;* or, all their actions are necessitated, for they are *determined* by their objects. The intellect in its three principal acts of simple apprehension, judgment of composition, and judgment of illation, and every other cognoscive power, all depend for action on the objects, for the objects must *determine* them to act; and when their objects actually influence them, they must necessarily act.

But no object, in regard to which the will is free, ever determines its action; it determines its own free action for itself. Over its election between those objects which are subject to its choice, it has complete empire; but no other power ever has any such control over its own action.

In respect to the relation which the will may have to the different objects which are subject to its choice, its liberty or freedom is distinguished into that of *contrariety* or specification, and that of *contradiction* or exercise.

Liberty of *contrariety* or *specification* implies capability in the will of selecting between *species* of objects which are subject to its choice; v. g., if the matter or objects which are proposed to it be, "will I write a letter now, or go into the grove, or visit my friends?" The actual choice between these objects may be considered the exercise of liberty as to the *contrariety* or *specification* of its action. But when the terms are employed more strictly and precisely; liberty of *contrariety* regards objects which are *contrary*, as *good* or *bad;* liberty of *specification*, regards merely the *species* of the objects.

But if the question be, "will I answer the letter, or not answer it?" This is to determine between acting, and not acting; which is exercising liberty of *contradiction.* In virtue of its liberty of contradiction or exercise, then, the will can either positively choose, or not choose, a certain good object proposed to it.

Liberty thus to choose between species of acts, and between acting and not acting, or liberty of *exercise*, necessarily requires *indifference* in the will; i. e., that it be *undetermined* to one side or another, whether by the object proposed, or by any other principle which is extrinsic to itself, thus leaving it so disposed that the choice actually made will come from itself.

The powers which act only when determined by their objects, are *not indifferent to action*, nor to the *species* of their acts; but when the objects are sufficiently presented to them, and actually influence them, their action is necessitated, and, at the same time, their acts are specified by those objects.

THE WILL, WHEN FREELY CHOOSING, IS NOT DETERMINED BY THE GREATEST MOTIVE.

It must not be supposed that the will, in choosing among objects that are subject to election, is *determined* by the *greatest motive*, as some authors erroneously affirm. In such a supposition, the will would really not be free at all; for, in that case, its action would be *necessitated* by the motive or object, just as it always happens in respect to the powers of cognition. Hence, the theory which teaches that among the objects which fall under election, the one which furnishes the *greatest motive* to the will is thereby *predominant* and *necessarily determines* the will to choose it, is repugnant to the very concept of liberty and destroys its essential character. In truth, the will can, in such cases, yield to the less motive; nay, it can abstain from any positive action at all in respect to the proffered objects.

THE FREEDOM OF THE WILL IS KNOWN TO ALL, AS AN EVIDENT FACT.

The freedom of the will is known to be a fact, in its own immediate or objective evidence, to every rational man, on the direct testimony of his own consciousness, just as every sane man knows that he perceives, reasons, remembers, etc. The liberty of the will is, therefore, a primitive fact, in the same sense in which the direct acts of cognition, of consciousness, of judgment, of sensation, etc., are primitive facts.

Facts are not inaptly denominated "stubborn things;" for they are independent of man's trustless words, they overturn his most specious theories, and they defy his keenest sophistry.

Any difficulty of reconciling the evident fact of man's freedom with other truths, which are sometimes artfully made to *appear* as contradicting it, can proceed only from ignorance of those other truths, or else from failure to detect a logical fallacy. But a full treatise on the will, properly pertains to Psychology.

As figure and color constitute the object of vision, sound that of hearing, truth the object of the understanding, so, *the good** forms the object of the will. As man has many appetites by which he is drawn to various objects presented to him under the form or respect of good, *sub ratione boni;* in a similar manner, his highest appetite, that is, his rational appetite, or will, loves the good which is of a corresponding and superior order; and, in one respect or another, his will *tends necessarily to that good.*

The *goodness* of a thing is founded on that required and befitting perfection which renders that thing desirable to the power of appetition, whose connatural object it is. *Sensible good* is the connatural object of *sensible appetite*, and is perfect in its species when the sensible appetite is satisfied by it, and rests quiet in its enjoyment. A similar proportion exists between the superior or rational appetite, the *will*, and its connatural objects.

The good is presupposed to the appetition of it, and it acts on the mind by way of a final cause. When good is thus understood; that is, absolutely, as the *formal* and *essential* object of the will or rational appetite, without which it cannot act at all, under this respect it is not subject to choice or election; but the will tends to it necessarily, as to its *only end.* The *means* to that end, however, does fall under the election or choice of the will. The will cannot love *evil as evil*, (*malum sub ratione mali*)*;* its only object, therefore, *is good.*

When all objects are regarded as subordinate to this end; that is, as giving connatural exercise to the powers of appetition, the good that is in those objects may be divided, relatively to that end, into the *becoming*, the *useful*, the *pleasant.* The *good* that is *becoming, or fit, is good* that is in accordance with

* "Bonitas est prior natura quam appetibilitas; agit per modum causæ finalis." "Finis non cadit sub electione; quia electio versatur circa media, non autem circa ipsum finem." Goodness is by nature prior to appetibility; it acts by way of final cause. The end does not fall under election; for election regards the means, not the end itself.

right reason, and it includes, therefore, *moral good; good* as *pleasant* supposes cognition and power of fruition; the *useful,* which is loved, not for itself, but for something ulterior to it, is a means to that end. As to what constitutes the *summum bonum,** or *chief good* which is the ultimate end of man as a rational being, it pertains to another treatise to investigate.

Hence, it follows, that *good* is *absolute,* or *relative; physical* or *moral. Every being is good; both in itself and in respect to other being than itself.*† *Good is diffusive of itself,* for its *end* is to be possessed and loved. *All good is from God.*‡

Evil is the privation of good; or, it is *the want of some due perfection in a being.* Evil is *physical* or *moral;* or, it is the absence of some due physical or moral perfection.

Physical evil is the privation of some natural good; as sickness, blindness, ignorance, etc.

Moral evil is the privation of moral good, and, as is manifest, can be found only in agents that are *intelligent* and *free.* It consists in a *defection* of the *free will* from what is morally right or good.

According to Leibnitz, there is also *metaphysical* evil; which is *finiteness,* or *limitation* of perfection. But this is not properly an evil; for, when a created being is perfect in its species, it possesses all *due* perfection; and it is confusion of language to say that *finiteness,* or not being identical with God, is *evil,* when viewed under such a respect.

There is no evil, except in a subject that is good; and, as already seen, every being, as such, is good. Since evil consists in privation of good, what has no being, can have no evil; that is, it must be *nothing;* which, properly, is neither good nor evil. The efficient cause of evil is good,§ as a being; and no will can wish evil purely as such, or purely for itself; but it may wish evil which is presented to it as good; v. g., as gain or pleasure.

* Vide Div. Th. I P., Qu. 5, Art. 6.

† "Bonum est diffusivum sui." Good is diffusive of itself.

‡ "Deus est omnis boni bonum." God is the good of every good.

§ "Malum non agit nisi virtute boni." Evil does not act except in virtue of good.

ARTICLE IV.

BEAUTY.

As the *goodness* of an object depends on its having all the perfections of its species or essence, together with all the qualities that complete and adorn it; so, the *beauty* of that object depends on the same conditions. The object of *love*, and *contemplation*, therefore, is the same, though it respects different powers of the soul; *good* being the object of appetition, and *beauty* that of contemplative, or cognoscive power.*

Beauty is *intellectual*, *moral* and *sensible*. Philosophers have found it difficult to give a definition of *beauty*, which clearly and satisfactorily includes all its species. Some have defined it to be, "unity with multitude and variety." But we can conceive an object to possess "unity with multitude and variety," which is yet misshapen or deformed.

Unity, multitude and variety may be necessary conditions of beauty in most cases; but they are not its only constituents. Nor are "order and utility" its specific characteristics, as some allege; since "order and utility" refer to *perfection* and *goodness*.†

Sir Joshua Reynolds, in his admirable lecture before the Royal Academy, December 14, 1770, said, that in each of the various species of God's works, there is a perfect "*central form* which nature most frequently produces, and always seems to intend in her productions; and from it, every deviation is deformity." This central form is more or less beautiful, according to the perfection of its species.

His observation is acute and suggestive of happy thoughts as to the nature of beauty. But the question may be asked, what constitutes the beauty of this *central form?* In accordance with his theory, his answer should be, *its perfection is its beauty*.

*"Pulchrum ad visum, bonum ad appetitum spectatur; seu quæ visa placent." Beauty pertains to vision, the good to appetite; what is seen gives pleasure.

† "Pulchrum et bonum in subjecto sunt idem; quia super eamdam rem fundantur, viz.: super *formam*." (Summa 1 p., qu. 5, art. 4.) The beautiful and the good, in the subject, are the same thing; for they are founded upon the same thing, namely, the *form*.

Beauty does suppose perfection in its object, and hence, it is obvious that different species of objects have, in themselves considered, greater or less beauty, according to their degrees of essential and accidental perfection; v. g., man has more specific beauty, and that, too, of a higher order, than the brute has; and similarly for animals in comparison with inferior forms in material nature.

Since *beauty* pertains to *cognoscive power*, and, therefore, to contemplation, and not, as such, to appetition, we may, perhaps, with some appropriateness, define beauty to be "*proportion, that is perceived;*" i. e., proportion and light.

Proportion, in its proper concept, includes unity, together with the order and variety of parts, appropriate to each particular object, and its light or evidence makes it an object of contemplation; since a thing is perceived by its light or evidence.

Moreover, since deformity and incompleteness in an object are incompatible with perfect proportion; and since *beauty* has that clearness or brightness which is essential to it, when the proportion from which it emanates is evident; it follows that the pleasing effect which we attribute to the beauty of an object, proceeds immediately from the contemplation of its *light*, and *proportion*.

Intellectual beauty exists in objects of the intelligible order.

Plato defines beauty to be the "splendor of truth;" "*splendor veri;*" or, as Boileau interprets it, "*the beautiful is the true.*"

Truth, as a relation or proportion between mind and object, and between object and its essential prototype, is beautiful. Truth also in its similitude and proportion to another truth is beautiful; this proportion of truth to another truth is expressed in metaphors and similes, and it attributes to them their exquisite beauty; there is still higher beauty also, *in the more exact proportions* of the necessary and universal truths to which the sciences and philosophy lead the mind.

If the decision made by authority, in matters of taste, forbids the denial of the æsthetic principle, according to which obscurity may become an element of genuine beauty in painting, music, poetry, and other works of fancy; it must, however, be borne in mind that the concurrence of obscurity in the production of the beautiful is *merely negative;* i. e., it terminates or limits, and thereby diversifies the shades or the proportion of light and color as to quantity and intensity. But it would be wholly absurd to apply this principle to *truth*, in which any obscurity which lessens certainty, is essentially, or by its very nature, imperfection, and is, therefore, deformity.

Beauty, in the works of art, as such, depends upon their *verisimilitude;* that is, *their truth to nature*, which they *imitate or reproduce*.

Sensible beauty,* as *visible*, has for its matter, *figure and color;* their proportion made clear to the vision, which renders the object to which they belong, beautiful. In this proportion, are included *symmetry*, *unity*, *variety*.

Proportion in *melody* and *harmony* constitutes the *beautiful in music*. A particular note or sound has its pitch, quality, and intensity; and when in a certain proportion, they cause even that single sound or note to be musical in its undulations or vibrations; a succession of such notes, of various pitch, intensity, quality and motion, all of which preserve a certain proportion to the *key note* or *tonica*, forms a beautiful melody; *beautiful harmony* is added to the melody by accompanying notes, whose differences of pitch, quality, etc., are always according to some determined proportion which they bear to the melody. Hence, beauty in music consists in proportion of sounds which have various pitch, quality, and intensity.

The other senses being farther removed from intelligence, or being less perfectly cognoscive, their objects are not said to be beautiful; a *beautiful taste*, *beautiful smell*, *beautiful feeling*, are expressions that are not used. Sensible impressions which are so gross, are less fitted to furnish the mind suitable objects of contemplative knowledge, than are the impressions received through the sight and hearing.

* "Sensus est quædam ratio; cognoscit ordinata, quæ visa placent." (Sum. 1 p., qu. 5, a. 4.) The sense is a sort of reason; it knows ordered things, which being seen, please.

Moral beauty is in *virtue*, or moral goodness. The law commanding some things, and forbidding others; the great difficulties to be surmounted; the noble soul, the heroic will, the pure intention, are all harmonized in the acts of persevering virtue, and constitute an object justly considered to be of the highest order of finite beauty which can be contemplated in this world.

The eloquent and philosophic Cicero, pronounced the heroic acts of the noble virtues to be *divine*, in their beauty and grandeur: "Animum vincere, iracundiam cohibere, victoriam temperare, adversarium nobilitate, ingenio, virtute præstantem non modo extollere jacentem, sed etiam amplificare ejus pristinam dignitatem, hæc qui facit, non ego eum cum summis viris comparo, sed simillimum deo judico." (Oration for Marcus Marcellus.) "The man who conquers his own soul, who suppresses resentment, who is moderate in victory, who not only raises from a fallen estate an adversary illustrious for his birth, his talent and his bravery, but even amplifies his former dignity: I do not compare the man who does these things to the greatest of human beings, but I judge him to be most like to a god."

The science of the beautiful is termed *æsthetics;* and the power of rightly discriminating and appreciating *beauty*, is called *taste*, from its analogy to the palate in distinguishing objects as *sweet*, *bitter*, etc.

The *sublime* is akin to the *beautiful*; the objects that possess it are *grand*, or such as, by their greatness and power, which it exceeds the capacity of the mind to comprehend, excite the strongest emotions; for instance, wonder, astonishment or awe.

Obscurity, in objects which are fancied to be great, mighty or awful, helps to intensify the strong feelings naturally caused by what is thus conceived to be grand, wonderful or terrible; *ignotum pro magnifico;* "the unknown is *magnified*." But observe, however, that emotions which arise merely from obscurity in the object, or ignorance of its nature, are ignoble in their species, and, therefore, it is only evident grandeur of the object, at least as manifested in the effects, or action of the object, that constitutes sublimity, properly so-called.

Here it might be asked, what definitively constitutes *that proportion* which renders an object *beautiful?* It is, perhaps, not possible to assign more precisely, in a general proposition, the degrees and relations that constitute it, than is done by the term as above explained; for its combinations are too numerous and various. But the proportion in which beauty consists, is that which supposes a high degree of perfection in the beautiful object; and yet, variation in that degree of perfection may make the same object, under different respects, better fitted to the capacity of different tastes. Perfect proportion requires unity, variety, order and fitness, which are according to the nature or species of the object.

No definition of *the beautiful* has yet been given, which reduces its constituents to unity; or, in other words, no generalization of its properties has ever been made, which enables us to define its essence by one distinctive mark or attribute. Some great minds have concluded that such generalization is, therefore, not possible. But the proof of this conclusion is negative only; and hence, it is perhaps too much to affirm absolutely that a specific definition of beauty is simply impossible, or is a work, the ultimate accomplishment of which, has been demonstratively proved to transcend the natural power of human reason.

CHAPTER II.

ARTICLE I.

SUBSTANCE; ACCIDENTS; SUBSTANCE AS OPPOSED TO ACCIDENT.

Substance is a being that exists *per se*, i. e., *by itself*, or *alone*, without inhering in another being as a subject that sustains it. *Sub-stans*, here expresses that which *stands under* all the qualities or accidents which the mind perceives through the different powers of cognition, in various concrete beings, and which is constant, though its accidents are mutable. The notion of substance, which is acquired by experience, is first learned at the dawn of reason. A child in its earliest exercise of judgment can practically and truly distinguish between substance and accidents, in familiar objects; v. g., that apples of different sizes, taste, smell, ripeness, are still apples.

The concrete nouns, and adjectives, which are essential to the framework of human language, show how universal and invincible this judgment is, that accidents exist dependently upon their subject, and that substance, as it were, *stands alone*,* or does not depend on a subject to support it. The testimony of

* "Substantia est ens quod *per se* est, seu quod non indiget alio ente tanquam subjecto cui inhæreat." *Per se*, has four distinct senses; but when applied to existence, or when it defines a *mode of existing*, it means *alone;* or, *without a companion*.

"Res est *per* se, quæ *sedet solitarie;* id est; quæ non eget alterius consortio, cui inexistat. *Per se*, in aliis modis *perseitatis*, respicit modum prædicandi, vel causandi; sed *per se* in hoc casu, respicit modum existendi."

To exist *a se*, means to exist independently of all *cause:* this, of course, is verified only in Infinite Being, in God; hence distinguish between existence *per se*, and existence *a se*. To exist *per se* is to exist without inhering in a subject; to exist *a se*, is to exist independently of any *cause*.

consciousness affords us complete certainty that the mutations which occur in ourselves, i. e., of thoughts, feelings, different states of the body, etc., are extrinsic to essence, and are accidental; and that they depend for their existence on something, as a subject, which exists independently of them, and is in itself immutable or constant under them. Nay, the line of distinction between substance and accident is clearly traced by the mind, and it does not confound one with the other. As we are now constituted, the mind does not immediately perceive any substance at all, but sees it only through its operations or accidents. Yet, the mind perceives that this substance is essentially distinct from its accidents, and is presupposed to them. Locke errs when he says, that, in our idea, substance is a mere "congeries of qualities perceived by the senses, the mode of their existence being entirely unknown to us." The distinctions between substance and accident are the clearest cognitions which the mind has of singular and sensible objects.

Substance is *simple* or *compound; complete* or *incomplete. Simple* substance does not consist of parts annexed to parts, and is, therefore, indivisible and unextended.

The *compound* substance consists of parts joined to parts, which, by their union, form a whole; and, as each part is in itself a whole, the *compound* can be resolved or divided into its component parts.

A *complete* substance is one whose nature does not require union with another substance, but contains all in itself which is necessary for its natural action; as tree, man, angel.

Incomplete substance is one which connotes, and requires another substance in order to complete it for natural existence and normal action; v. g., the members of the body; the branches of the tree; the soul and the body in man.

It is evident that it is not naturally possible for the sensible qualities or accidents of material substance to exist apart from their subject, which is the substance in which they physically inhere. But, is their separate existence intrinsically impossible, so that even Divine Omnipotence could not effect it?

It is by no means impossible for God to preserve accidents,

at least such as are in themselves positive *realities*, in existence separate from the substance to which they belong. Because, what a second and dependent cause can do, for a still greater reason can the first cause effect; if substance, which depends both for its existence and for its efficiency on God, can sustain the accidents, it is still more obvious that God can do it by a direct and immediate exercise of his power. To deny this reasoning in respect to that class of accidents that have a specific *reality* of their own, would be absurd.

With regard to those accidents that are purely *modal*, and, therefore, have no positive and distinct entity, as *rest*, *relation*, *motion;* as also those attributes or properties that flow immediately from the essence, as their principle; v. g., vital power, intellect, etc., there is no question; they cannot exist apart from the subject on which they intrinsically depend, and they, therefore, have no real entity apart from the subject to which they belong. The positive effects, or actual impressions and immutation, produced upon the senses, by corporeal substance, are proximately from real and distinct accidents, or, such as have distinct and positive reality; v. g., color, taste, smell, quantity, etc. These properties, at least with the exception of quantity, have a peculiar activity, which affords proof conclusive that they have real and distinct entity, apart from the substance in which they naturally inhere; and that they are, therefore, really added to substance.

It may be said, consequently, that there are two classes of accidents which are distinguishable in reference to the preceding questions: 1st, there are certain accidents which have no entity apart from a subject—" sunt entitates adeo debiles "—and cannot exist, therefore, unless in a substance, or in another accident as *quasi* subject; v. g., motion, union, relation, etc. Also, vital powers and other essential attributes are inseparably affixed to their subject, and could have no existence or entity apart from it. 2d, Those accidents which naturally inhere, but which, by infinite power, can exist apart from their subject: quantity, qualities such as color, taste, smell, etc.

From the preceding observations it is manifest that substance and accident differ essentially or specifically. Therefore, *being* cannot be predicated of them *univocally;* but only *analogically;* v. g., as *being* is predicated only by *analogy* of *spirit* and *matter.*

PROPERTY IS AN ACCIDENT; BUT IT DIFFERS FROM COMMON ACCIDENT.

Property is an *accident* that is *proper;* or, it *belongs* to its subject; hence its name, *property.* It differs from accident that is *common,* in this: *property* belongs to the *species* of the object; i. e., agrees with an object on account of its *specific nature* or *form;* the *common accident* agrees with an object or individual in virtue of its *matter,* or *quasi matter;* v. g., "*Man limps,* because *Peter is lame;* Peter *laughs,* because man is a *laughing being.*" *Lameness* is an accident that is *common* to individuals of many species of animals that walk; *laughter,* strictly so-called, is peculiar or *proper* only to man.

Property is said to *flow from the essence* or form; as do the powers of intelligence, sensation, volition; in this, it differs from *common accident,* which *accedes from without* or extrinsically, and is common to many species on account of their *matter;* v. g., *quantity,* in man, wood, mineral, etc.

Since *property* necessarily flows from the essence of its subject, wherever the *essence* is, *there* is the property; "convenit omni, soli, semper." It is, on that account, regarded as convertible with essence, and may be employed to define *essence or species.*

Property, thus explained, is found only in the *proximate* or *lowest* species of things; for, only in the individuals of a species is found the *form* or *specific principle* which really constitutes *substantial and actual essence;* yet, by a certain analogy, higher genera are said to have properties; v. g., *one, true, good,* are termed *properties* of *being.**

* "Juxta aliquam analogiam, unum, bonum, verum, dicuntur entis proprietates; suscipere contraria, est substantiæ proprium; progressio, animalis perfecti: motus ab intrinseco, viventis; quantitas, corporis," etc. By a certain analogy, one, good, true, are termed properties of being; to receive contraries is a property of substance; progressive motion, a property of the perfect animal; quantity is a property of bodies, etc.

Though, in strictness, *property* stands for an attribute that is always found in every individual of the whole species, yet the term is often applied to one that is more purely *accidental;* v. g., to be an *orator,* in respect to *man,* which is *proper* to *man,* but not to *all men;* to be *biped,* which is proper not only to all men, but to some other animals, etc.

But the *proper* and the *common* accidents agree in this, that they are both *extrinsic to essence;* "sunt extra essentiam rei;" hence it is that they both agree in being *accidents.*

Although *property* or the *proper accident* is sometimes made convertible with *essence,* is necessarily and intimately connected with it, and defines it; yet it is only *adjacent* to essence, not its *constituent.*

The *common accident* can never define an object, from the fact that it is *common* to many species of things on account of their *matter.*

Properties, which, as already observed, flow from, or result immediately, from the essence of objects, are the same in fact as the *specific difference** of those objects; they most intimately inhere in their objects, and are inseparable from them. Hence, *properties* are said to be *predicated per se* of their subjects; i. e., they *necessarily,* or *of their nature,* inhere in their subjects, and are not in them *per accidens,* or accidentally, as happens in the *common accident,* which is a predicate of this or that subject, not *per se,* as *flowing from its essence,* but *per accidens,* or *accidentally.*

COMMON ACCIDENT THE SAME AS THE FIFTH UNIVERSAL PREDICABLE, CALLED ACCIDENT; ACCIDENT AS OPPOSED TO SUBSTANCE, IS PREDICAMENTAL ACCIDENT.

The word *accident* is used not only as expressing one of the *five universals,* in which sense it means *common accident,* and is distinguished from *property* or *proper accident;* but it is employed also to express all that is not *substance,* or as opposed to *substance.* In this sense, it not only includes all *property,*

* "Differentia essentiæ et proprietas, sunt idem re." (S. Thom. Metaph. 61, lect. 2, lit. c.) Essential difference, and property or attribute, are really the same thing.

but it likewise comprehends *nine* out of the *ten categories*, or *ultimate genera*, *substance* alone being excepted.*

Therefore substance and accident, as thus opposed to each other, reduce all the ten categories or predicaments, i. e., all real things, to two categories; namely, to *substance*, and the category or predicament *accident*, which in this division includes under it, as just said, nine out of the ten categories or ultimate genera.†

Actual inhering in a subject is essential to the existence of *properties* which are *predicated per se*, and which are, therefore, convertible with *specific difference;* but *aptitude for inhering* in a subject is all that is absolutely essential for other *accidents*, as such; for they can absolutely be sustained in existence without their actually inhering in their subject, at least such of them as have positive entity or reality of their own; i. e., those *accidents* that are not purely *modal.*

In further elucidation of this doctrine it may be said, that the *subject* of properties is for them really a *principle;* from it they result, or take their origin; on it they depend for beginning, and continuing to exist.

But, since the *common accidents accede extrinsically to* their subject, the *subject* is not, in the same sense, their *principle;* and hence their connexion with it, and dependence on it, are not *intrinsic*, but *extrinsic*, and they are, therefore, more purely *contingent;* i. e., they are more immediately and completely dependent on the free cause of their subject.

* "*Accidens* est vel *prædicabile*, vel *prædicamentale;* accidens prædicabile pertinet ad *omne prædicamentum;* accidens prædicamentale, pertinet ad unum aliumve novem prædicamentorum."

† When it is said, "substantia categorica est *univoca*, respectu inferiorum;" "accidens est *analogum;*" "substance is *univocal* throughout its category; accident is *analogical;*" this holds of *accident* as distinguished from substance, or as *predicamental*, not of accident as one of the five *universals*, or as a *predicable*, for as the *universal* it is predicated *univocally* of its inferiors.

ARTICLE II.

QUANTITY; QUALITY.

All the ten categories, or predicaments, except *substance*, have only *accidents* as their inferiors; for every real being that is not *substance*, is *accident*.

Quantity, as extended, consists of parts adjoined to parts, in which case it is called *continuous quantity*, or extension. The *parts* are either *actually* such, or *potentially* such; i. e., parts into which the object having quantity can, absolutely, be divided.

The old philosophers maintained that *quantity** is the nearest or most adjacent accident to *matter;* that it is, in some sense, presupposed to the other accidents, which pertain to its *form*, or that which perfects the matter in its species, and determines its nature.

EXTENSION.

Perfect extension consists of length, breadth, and thickness, or has three dimensions; but length, or length and breadth, also form quantity. The termini, or limits of continuous quantity, are not *positive*, but *privative* being. Extension in space, is a property of matter, but it is not so essential to it, that the separation of material substance from it in existence is *intrinsically impossible.*

In other words, it is not repugnant to reason that material substance should exist in a more simple and perfect species of relation to space, than bodies possess, as they now actually exist, subject to our senses. But the full explanation of this subject belongs to another treatise.

Extension is of two species, *circumscriptive* and *definitive;* in the *circumscriptive extension* the extended object occupies the whole place included within its boundary, and each part of the object fills a proportionate part of the whole place; v. g., a

* "In materialibus, *quantitas* sequitur materiam; *qualitas* sequitur formam." "In viventibus *quantitas* sequitur *formam*, saltem quoad terminum magnitudinis seu parvitatis." (Suarez Metaph.; Disp. 42, sect. 1.) In material things *quantity* follows the matter, *quality* follows the form. In living things *quantity* follows the form, at least as to the limit of its size, as great or small.

cubic block of marble occupies a cubic space of the same size or extension, and a fourth part of it fills a fourth part of that extent, a half occupies a half, etc.

In *definitive extension*, the substance is complete in the whole, and is whole in each part of its extension; v. g., the soul is whole in the entire body, and whole in each part of it.

Quantity is either *continuous*, as above defined, or it is *discrete;* if extension be divided into parts, the number which expresses or includes the whole collection of those parts, is *discrete quantity.* But *abstract* number, or that which does not express actual parts of a divided quantity numerically, does not belong to the category or predicament that is called *quantity;* but is *transcendental*, i. e., may enter any of the *categories*, express their units, or unities, or be applied to any beings.

To say with Zeno of old, that lines consist of indivisible points; surfaces are formed by lines, and solids by surfaces, would be erroneous; *continuous* extension cannot be thus generated.

IS QUANTITY INFINITELY DIVISIBLE?

Quantity is infinitely divisible *in potentia*, or potentially. To this proposition the objection will at once occur: "what is infinitely divisible, can be thus divided actually, at least by infinite power; and thereby it can be resolved into an infinite number of parts."

But if its divisibility were thus *exhausted*, then it was not *infinitely divisible* by hypothesis; since that which is *finished* is not *infinite* potentially. Similarly, quantity may be increased *infinitely in potentia* or *potentially*, by addition or multiplication; but yet infinite extension, or infinite number, cannot be actually generated by successive increments; for that which *begins* and *ends*, is not actually infinite, but may receive further increase.

Hence, to conclude from the *potential infinite*, to the *actual infinite*, is not valid illation; for the infinite *in potentia* cannot pass to the infinite *in actu*, and thus become completed; as that would destroy the hypothesis; i. e., the supposition that it may be increased *sine fine*, or *without end of increase.**

The actual infinite is *all*, without the possibility of *more;* or, as the axiom expresses it, *tot ut non plura;* the potential infinite does not *actually* contain *all*, without the possibility of more; it is *non tot quin plura.*

QUALITY.

Qualities are accidents which are superadded to created substance in order to perfect it, both in its existence, and its action; or, qualities intrinsically ornament and perfect actually existing substance. *Quantity* pertains rather to the *matter*, as such; *quality* follows the *specific essence*† of the matter, *its form.* It is the specific essence of a *rose* which makes it different from a *pink*, as it is also the specific essence of the *pink* that makes it what it is, and not some other form of matter.

It may be said, then, that qualities follow the *species* of substantial objects. It is on this account that substances are often defined by their qualities, which is legitimate, when the *genus* and specific difference are not known, or cannot be assigned.

Figure‡ pertains to *quality* when it is considered as determining an object as to its proper and specific *form*, or shape; but considered as *extended*, it is *quantity*. Material objects depend much for their specific nature, on their *figure* or shape; it beautifies them, and perfects them also in action as well as in strength. Hence, *figure* or *shape* is intimately connected with

* "Ab infinito *syncategorimatice*, seu in potentia, ad infinitum *categorimatice*, seu actu, non valet illatio." "Infinitum actu est, *tot ut non plura;* infinitum in potentia est, *non tot quin plura.*" From the infinite syncategorimatically, or the potential infinite, to the infinite categorimatically, or the actual infinite, illation is not valid. The actual infinite is *all without more*; the potential infinite, is *not all without more.*

† "Qualitas sequitur formam, quia forma complet et perficit essentiam rei et confert principalem vim agendi." (Suarez Met., Disp. 42.) Quality follows the form, because the form completes and perfects the essence of a thing, and confers on it its principal power of action.

‡ "Figura, quatenus materialiter extensa, pertinet ad quantitatem; sed quatenus ornamentum substantiæ, et quatenus deserviens ad actiones et naturales motus, pertinet ad formam." (Suarez Met. Disp. 42, sect. 1.) Figure, as materially extended, pertains to quantity; but as ornament of substance, and assisting action and natural motion, it pertains to form; i. e., to the formal principle of the substance.

specific nature, and results from that specific nature, as one of its distinctive qualities; v. g., organic beings, also crystals, all have their peculiar and determinate figures or shapes.

Sensible qualities are either permanent or transient; the ruddy hue of the cheeks, when lasting, is ordinarily a sign of health, and is, in that case, a *permanent* quality; a *blush*, from sudden emotion, is *transient*. A happy combination of the sensible qualities, figure and color, makes *visible beauty*.

NATURAL POWERS OF SUBSTANCE; THEIR ACTS.

Natural powers are qualities that perfect a substance for action. *Power* is either *active*, or *passive;* as *active*, it can cause a mutation in another object, as when you move your book. As *passive*, the power *receives* an action; v. g., the *senses*, which, under different respects, are both *active* and *passive*, *receive* the impressions which external objects make on them.*

Immanent acts, are such as *remain in*, and *perfect* their subject; v. g., acts of the understanding, as perceiving, judging, reasoning; these acts do not, as such, *pass out* of the mind, but physically they *remain in* the powers that *elicit* them. None but *living* agents are capable of *immanent* action; the action of *lifeless* objects is *transient;* i. e., it *passes from* them to the extrinsic object which is its term; and they must be *moved to action* by an efficient cause which is really distinct from them; for, having no *immanent* action, they are *absolutely inert*, or, are incapable of self-motion.

Hence, it may be said: all *immanent* action is *vital*, and all *vital* action is *immanent;* or, the distinctive characteristic of *vital* action is that it is *immanent*. But observe that the term, *life*,† is

* "Actio aliquando dicta effectus, quatenus est ab agente, tamen magis proprie, est via ad effectum." Action is sometimes termed an effect, inasmuch as it is from an agent; yet, more properly, it is the way to the effect.

† "Vita aut sumitur in actu secundo, et sic dicit operationem; aut in actu primo principali et radicali, et sic est ipsa natura seu substantia rei viventis. Nos non aliter possumus intelligere rem viventem, nisi in ordine ad efficientiam, quatenus scilicet potest sese movere aut agere aliquo modo; et censemus rem aliquam antea viventem amisse vitam, quando omnem intrinsecam motionem amisit." (Suarez Metaph. disp. 30, sect. 34.) Life is either taken as something actual, and thus it says operation; or, it is taken as something primary and radical, and in this sense it is the nature or substance of the living

understood in two senses: 1st, as expressing the living substance itself; 2d, as expressing vital act or operation. We usually conceive life as the *living act*, and when we actually form a concept of it as a substance, it is always by the relation of that substance to its *living operation* or action. Life, therefore, which is directly known to us *only as action*, pertains exclusively to those agents that can *move themselves;** and capability of being moved only by an *extrinsic efficient cause*, is peculiar to non-living agents. *Motion* is here used in its widest sense, and includes all *immanent* operation of any principle which is intrinsically active, i. e., which can proximately or immediately *move itself to act.*†

The principal acts of life‡ are, 1st, self-movement; 2d, *nutrition* by the intus-susception of food; 3d, sensation; 4th, intellection. The first named may be regarded as generic, and, therefore, as including all vital action; vegetable life is limited in its sphere of operation to nutrition, growth by assimilation of food received, and reproduction; animal life, in addition to these operations, is capable of acts of sensation; man, besides all these operations, has acts of *intelligence*, which absolutely transcend the sphere of *sensible* or *organic* action, as is proved in Article I of the preceding chapter.

It may be said, therefore, 1st, power of action is common to all substance; 2d, *vital* or *immanent* action is common to all *living* substance, and is limited to the powers of *living agents;* 3d, the *immanent or vital action* merely sufficient for knowing

thing. We understand a living thing only, by its having order to efficiency: namely, as capable of moving or actuating itself in some manner; and we judge a thing that once lived, to have lost life, when it has lost intrinsic motion.

* "Illa proprie sunt viventia quæ seipsa, secundum aliquam speciem motus, movent." (Div. Thom. I p., qu. 18, art. 3.) Those things are properly living things, which, according to some species of motion, move themselves.

† "Vivens efficit suam operationem per veram causalitatem et motionem, qua seipsum movet." (Suarez Disp. 30, sect. 14.) A living thing effects its own operation by a true causality and motion, for it moves itself.

‡ "Vita dicitur et substantia vitalis, ut est anima, et natura angelica; et *operatio vitalis*, quæ nimirum *in operante*, a quo emanat, manet; qualis est intelligere, amare, sentire, etc." (Lessius de Perfect. Divin.) Life means both vital substance, as the soul, angelic nature; and also *vital operation*; namely that operation that remains in the agent which elicits it; as, to understand, love, feel, etc.

singular, concrete and material things is proper, as such, to animals only; 4th, the power which elicits the *immanent* acts of knowing *universal* or *abstract truth*, distinguishes intellectual substances from all the rest.

The power of action which is common to *lifeless substance*, is *pure potentiality;* i. e., it has no power of motion except that which is implied in a mere *capability* of being efficiently *determined* or *moved to act* by an *extrinsic cause*, the state of *rest*, or *inaction*, being *connatural* to it. On the contrary, in respect to *living beings*, *actuality*, or immanent action positively going on, and which, therefore, excludes complete rest or non-action, is essential to their life, so that its total absence is evidence of death. Power is defined by its act; the act is known by means of its object.

HABIT.

Habit, in its general sense, pertains to *operative* nature,* and it gives facility of action to the power in which it resides. In its species, it is a quality which is *stable*, or which cannot be removed from its subject without difficulty.† Because all created substance acts only through the powers of that substance, it is justly inferred that the proper subjects of all *operative habit* are only the powers of substance.‡

* "Aliæ qualitates, v. g., sanitas, pulchritudo, etc., disponunt subjectum ad bene esse; sed virtutes animi seu habitus operativi disponunt ad bene operari." (Gotti. tom. vii.) Other qualities, v. g., health, beauty, etc., dispose their subject for existing well; but the virtues of the soul or the operative habits, dispose it for operating well.

† *Disposition*, in its general signification, imports order in objects which, in some respect or other, consist of parts. When active power is its subject, it also gives facility of action. But it differs from *habit* in this, that it is easily removed from its subject, for it is *per se*, or in itself, unstable, or, it is never firmly radicated in a power. In the acquisition of a habit by repeated acts, it may be said that the first acts, with the accompanying preparation, *dispose* the subject for the subsequent permanent effect; i. e., for the *habit*. (Div. Thom., 1, 2, qu. 49.)

‡ "Subjectum habitus operativi, est potentia operativa." (Philos. passim.) "In ipsa essentia animæ immediate nullus est habitus ad naturam naturaliter ordinatus, quia substantia non est immediate operativa; sed tamen est in ea habitus supernaturalis, nempe gratia sanctificans." (Div. Thom.) The subject of operative habit, is operative power. There is no habit naturally designed for nature which is immediately in the essence itself of the soul, because substance is not immediately operative; but yet there is in the essence of the soul a supernatural habit; namely, sanctifying grace.

The powers which are most susceptible of the superadded perfections termed *habits*, are the *understanding*, the *will*, and, in an inferior degree, the *imagination*, the *sensile memory*, and also the senses in general, at least for that action in them which is under the direct control of reason.

Habits are either *infused*, or *acquired*. The knowledge which Adam received immediately after his creation, was *infused* into his mind; Christian Faith, Hope and Charity are *infused habits*.

Intelligence, regarded as a natural ability in the understanding to see clearly and promptly the truths that are known *per se*, or are *self-evident*, was termed by the old philosophers, a *natural habit;* a much higher degree of which may be *acquired* by prudent exercise of the intellect. But this is less properly termed habit; for the capability of immediate action pertains to the very essence and entity of a natural power.*

Yet, on the other hand, the intellect is capable of receiving superadded perfection which gives it increased facility of action, and this increased facility of action has the nature of the virtue which is termed *habit*, whether it be acquired by exercise, or be in itself the gift of nature.

Acquired habits are permanent effects usually produced in a power by repeated acts or continued exercise of that power.

* "Omnis naturalis propensio et inclinatio potentiæ ad actum, est per ipsammet naturam et entitatem potentiæ: et non per habitum distinctum, et illi a natura inditum." (Suarez Met., Disp. 44, sect. 13.) All natural propensity and inclination of a power to action, is of the very nature and entity of the power, and not by a distinct habit which is given to it by nature.

"Intelligentia (seu intellectus) est habitus primorum principiorum." Intelligence (or intellect) is the habit of first principles.

"Prudentia et ars sunt in operativa parte animæ, et circa contingens aliter se habent; sapientia, scientia et intellectus sunt habitus speculativi, et considerant necessaria quæ impossibile est aliter se habere." (Div. Thom., I, 2, qu. 57.) Prudence and art pertain to the operative part of the soul, and they have for their object the *contingent*, which they consider under different respects; wisdom, scientific knowledge, and intelligence, are speculative habits, and they consider necessary things, or those which cannot be otherwise than they are.

"Prudentia, magistra virtutum, est agibilium; ars, factibilium." Prudence, the ruler of virtues, concerns those things which can be done, morally; art, what can be done, physically.

"Habitus alii dant simpliciter posse, alii dant facilius posse." Some habits are essential for acting at all; others, give facility of action.

"Intuitio primorum principiorum est intellectus." Intelligence is the intuition of first principles. Intuition is the actual exercise of intelligence.

In the understanding, *intelligence*, *knowledge*, *wisdom*, which are *speculative; prudence* and *art*, which are *practical* in their objects, are all *habits* or intellectual virtues which may be acquired in a greater or less degree of perfection. In the will, all the *moral virtues*, and also their opposite *vices*, may exist as *acquired habits*, but not simultaneously; for, moral virtue and vice are opposites, or are contraries, and, therefore, the one excludes the other.

Habit, on account of its stability, or the difficulty of eradicating it from its subject, is sometimes called "a second nature." The capability of the natural powers of cognition, and superior appetite, to acquire these habits, or superadded qualities by exercise, is one of the peculiar perfections of those powers as they exist in *rational natures*.

Though brutes are not capable of habits, in the sense in which habits are conceived to pertain necessarily to rational powers, or, at least, to powers which are immediately subject to the empire of reason, as expressed by the old philosophical axiom, "habitus est quo utimur cum volumus," "habit is something which we use at will;" yet, the perfect brute animals, or such as have memory, and are capable of learning some things by experience, can be made, at least when under the tuition and control of man, to acquire what seems to possess the physical requisites of *habit*.

The axiom in respect to habits, "habitus quo utimur cum volumus," appears, as Suarez remarks, to regard rather the moral character which habits may have, than to express their physical nature. (Metaphysics, disp. 44, sect. 3.)

It will be useful for better understanding the nature and function of habits, to distinguish more precisely between the subjects capable of them, and those which are not susceptible of habit at all.

God cannot receive habit; for, being infinitely perfect, he cannot be the subject of additional perfection; and being *pure act*, he cannot be in a state of potentiality, i. e., he cannot pass from the condition of non-action to action, as is possible to beings that are perfectible, or which can pass from the state of *potentiality* into that of action.

Habits can be *acquired* by those agents only which are perfectible by *immanent action;* i. e., agents which intrinsically elicit their own action, it *remaining* in them, and perfecting them. The powers of such agents are not only the proximate and *active principle* of their own operation; but they are, at the same time,* *passive* in respect to this same operation; i. e., their *immanent* action affects them, for it perfects them. Hence, it is quite natural that, in *powers* whose action is *immanent*, the repetition of acts having the same or similar objects for their term, should gradually produce and complete for them the permanent effect, which we call *habit*, whose peculiar virtue is to give strength, promptness, and facility of action.

Those objects whose action is wholly *transient*, or which have no *immanent action*, do not *receive* any increase of perfection from their own acts, but they rather give it to the exterior object which is the term of their operation. Hence, such agents are not susceptible of that influence of *immanent* action, which causes the acquisition of habit.

* "It is necessary that the power in which habit resides, be both active and passive; for, it cannot be the proximate principle of eliciting acts, unless it be active; nor can it receive into itself habits, unless it be passive. But only that power is at the same time active and passive, which is able to elicit *immanent* acts: hence the subject of habit, must be capable of *immanent* action. This is confirmed by the fact that the act leaves the habit in that power in which the act is; because, it renders that very power, and not another one, prompt to operate. But, the habit remains in that power which is the proximate principle of such act; and, therefore, the act remains in the same also; hence, both the act itself is *immanent*, and the power, which is its principle, elicits *immanent action*. Whence it follows that the acts by which habits are produced, are such as, strictly speaking, have no effect outside of their own powers; which is proper to *immanent* acts."

"In brutes there are not habits distinct from the images in their fancy or their sensible impressions. The general reason of this is, that in all their acts *they are determined to one thing* (i. e., are necessitated to one, uniform mode of action, over which they have no real choice, or rational empire,) by force of the objects, just according as those objects are presented to them. But it seems more probable that the *internal sense* of man, *cogitative power*, (see page 87 of Applied Logic,) can acquire habit distinct from sensible ideas, giving facility, and inclining the power determinately to some acts. The reason is, because this sense in man is not absolutely *determined to one thing*, like fancy in the brute; for, it can be made, obediently to reason, to operate, or can be moved to determinate action." (Suarez Metaph., Disp. 44, secs. 1 and 3.)

It must be observed, however, that not all beings which have *vital* or *immanent action*, are susceptible of *habits*, in any *univocal* sense of the term. It is a fact well proved by general experience that the capability of *acquiring habit*, necessarily implies also the capability of *experimental knowledge* in the subject. Hence, since man has *intellectual* cognition, and brutes have that of sense alone, it is manifest that *acquired habits* in them can resemble only by *analogy;* or, these habits in them are proportioned in perfection to the respective cognoscive powers of man and brute.

It is manifest that when we consider the different powers in man as subject to his will, or to the empire of his rational nature, even his senses, under that respect, are *less determined to one mode of action*, or are less limited in the sphere of their action, and less subject in regard to their objects, than are the corresponding sensible powers of those agents, which have not this rational empire over their own acts. On this account, men's sensible powers are more susceptible of the *acquired* virtues, termed habits, than are those powers as they are in irrational animals.

INTENSITY OF QUALITIES, ACTS, ETC.

Compound sensible qualities, i. e., such as *beauty* or *ornaments*, which consist of several qualities, as color, figure, order, etc., coalescing into one; or, quality which is composed of them; also, habits and acts are all capable of *degrees*, or of more or less *intensity*.*

The *intensity*† or *intension* of a quality is said to be increased in degree when it is augmented or becomes more deeply radi-

* "Intensio actus fit per additionem gradus ad gradum." Action is intensified by the addition of degree to degree. It is convenient thus to conceive intensity to be increased, though it does not take place by *degrees* of increment which are actually distinct.

† "Intensio accipitur, prius et maxime usitato, pro mutatione illa per quam eadem qualitas magis ac magis in eodem subjecto secundum eamdem partem seu entitatem perficitur." (Suarez Metaph. Disp. 46.) *Intensity*, in its primary and most usual sense, stands for that mutation by which the same quality is more and more perfected in the same subject, according to the same part or entity of that subject.

cated in the *same subject*, or in the *same part* of the subject; as when heat is increased in a part only of the hand. But it is *remission* of the quality when the quality is correspondingly diminished in the same subject. There is increased *extension* of a quality, when, without leaving the former part of its subject, it passes or spreads to other parts; v. g., when heat spreads from the hand to the arm, without, however, leaving the hand; if it leave the *hand*, and go to the *arm*, this would not be *extension*, but *transmigration* of quality; if the quality leave some part, or parts of a subject, without leaving the whole subject, it would be *restriction of quality*. Hence, color, sound, etc., may be more or less *intense*, or *remiss*, may *extend*, *migrate*, etc.

General experience attests the fact as evident to all minds, that the vital acts whose direction is immediately under the will's control, are susceptible of a higher or lower degree as to intensity; and that their intensity or remissness much depends, in general at least, on the free action of the will itself. But since, as before observed, the action of the will is, by its nature, less evident to the understanding, *cæteris paribus*, than are the acts of cognition, it may often happen that, even when we know the species of its act, we are unable to see precisely and determinately the degree of its intensity; this does not occur in the same manner as regards the acts of cognition, which, being more evident, are more fully and accurately perceived. Yet, whenever the will's act is positively put, although remiss in degree, the nature or species of the act is completely determined, as is also its essential moral character, according to the nature of the objects. It is likewise impossible, in many cases, to decide with certainty as to whether the will has positively consented or acted at all, even when the objects proposed to its choice are evident before the mind. In important and practical matters, however, obscurity or rational doubt as to the will's fully *deliberate* choice, is scarcely possible.

The study of these obscure operations of the will is frequently called *the study of the heart;* and it is the chief means of becoming proficient in *the knowledge of human nature.*

Figure, as such, is incapable of degree; it may be larger or smaller; but this is difference of quantity, not a change in the degree of the figure as *such*. It requires no proof that *habits* and *acts* may be more or less *intense;* or, more or less *extensive*, in respect to their objects.

Substance, as such, is incapable of degree, but it may be greater or less in quantity;* and is capable of receiving successively *contrary* qualities; this, however, does not imply a difference of degree in the matter or essence of the object extended.

Difference of degree † does not change or destroy the essence of the quality of which it is predicated, or in which it obtains; no more than difference of quantity destroys or changes the essence of matter. ‡

* "Substantia non suscipit magis et minus; est substantiæ suscipere contraria." Substance is not, as such, susceptible of more or less, but it is capable of receiving contraries.

† "Gradus non mutat essentiam rei." The degree does not change the essence of a thing.

"*Magis et minus*, secundum quod causantur ex intensione et remissione unius formæ, non diversificant speciem. Sed secundum quod causantur ex formis diversorum graduum, sic diversificant speciem." (Div. Thom. Sum. I p., qu. 50, a. 4, ad. 2.) *More and less*, when caused by the intension and remission of one and the same form (quality or property), do not change the species of the object. But when they are caused by forms in different grades (different species) of being, they do diversify the species. As for example, the different degrees of *density* in air and water arise from the specific difference of air and water; so, in other words, the same quality may, in different objects, have different degrees of intensity, arising from the essential or specific difference of those objects, and thus furnish a means of distinguishing the species of those objects. But greater or less degree of the same color, v. g., in the *same object*, does not imply a change of the subject of that color in its specific nature; greater or less density of air under different degrees of pressure, does not imply a change in the nature of air; the same habit is not changed in its nature or species by being more or less deeply radicated in its subject, etc.

‡ Mr. Darwin, in his "Descent of Man," part 1, chap. 2, says: "We must admit that there is a much wider interval of mental power between one of the lowest fishes, as a lamprey, or a lancelet, and one of the higher apes, than between an ape and man." In this he assumes the power of sensation and that of intelligence to be different degrees of the same power; whereas, in fact, they have a *specific difference*. The *organ* is *material* in its functions, while *intelligence* is absolutely *immaterial*, and entirely super-sensible. A more rational contrast, and one founded on plain facts, could be made between a metallic toy monkey, and a real one, on the one hand; and a real monkey and a man on the other; in both cases the contrast would be very wide; but it would prove nothing in favor of his hypothesis. This is not the only instance in which Mr. Darwin is at fault in elementary first principles.

The doctrine of quantity and quality may here be summed up in terms that will now be readily comprehended: quantity, in the primary and general acceptation of the word, is an accident which is extensive of the substance which is its subject, giving it parts placed outside of parts, whence result greater or less size, and equality or inequality. As thus understood, it can properly be said to exist only in bodies which have dimension, or in material substance; from it there results real and substantial size, "quantitas molis," in these bodies, as greater or smaller. By translation, however, quantity is attributed to other objects, as virtue, habit, act, power, etc.; it is then *quantity of perfection*, "quantitas virtutis;" v. g., "Aristotle's genius was *greater* than that of Pyrrho."

But in the explanation here given, quantity is defined and described rather by its properties or accidents, than by its intrinsic essence. Quantity, strictly as such, or quantity, considered as to its essence, requires for the precise concept of it, only extension of parts, or parts outside of parts, in respect to themselves, not as *circumscriptively* occupying actual extension in space, though this circumscriptive extension in space is requisite for it to become subject to our senses: "quantitas, in essentia sua, est extensio partium in ordine ad se, non in ordine ad locum."

Quality includes under it all the positive accidents which are superadded to created substance, the effect of which is to give to it, when constituted in being, perfection and completeness in its mode, both of existing and operating. Powers, virtues, habits, and the like, which, it is evident, are necessary appendices of the substances to which they are connatural, are nevertheless extrinsic to the essence of the substance in which they reside, and are *qualities*, or they pertain to the category of *quality*. Quality, is by some defined to be, a certain absolute accident, adjoined to created substance, as the complement of its perfection, both in existing and acting: "qualitas est accidens quoddam absolutum, adjunctum substantiæ creatæ ad complementum perfectionis ejus, tam in essendo, quam in agendo."

Hence, *quantity* may be aptly termed the *measure* of substance; *quality*, the *disposition* of substance.* Quality is the *disposition* of substance, in that it disposes or constitutes it in such condition, that it is thereby perfected both in existing and operating.

RELATION.

Relation is the respect which one thing has to another; or, it is the order in which one thing is referred to another.† A *relation* implies a *subject* which is related or referred to another, the *term* to which the subject is related; and the *foundation or basis* of the relation; from it the relation really results; v. g., suppose two different bodies that have the same *shape or figure;* and the two bodies are respectively the *subject*, and the *term* of the relation; and the same *figure* or *shape* is the *foundation or basis* of the relation; v. g., "this orange has the shape of that lemon;" orange is the *subject*, lemon the *term* and *shape*, the *foundation* or *basis* of the *relation*, and the *relation* consists in the two being *alike.*

Relation is either *real* or *logical.* *Real relation* is that which objects have to each other independently of any knowledge or judgment we may have of it; as the relation of cause and its effect. The order, connexion, and mutual dependence, which exist among the works of creation are real relations, which exist independently of our knowing or understanding them.

Logical relation is one which the mind devises; as when it compares; v. g., a real thing to itself; or, conceives a thing as related to itself. In this case, the mind apprehends one object twice, and refers it to itself, as if it were two.

When the relation is *real* and *identical* in the *subject* and the *term*, it is mutual; v. g., "this *lily* and this *rose* are alike, since both are *white;*" "white," is *really* in both, and, therefore, the relation is *mutual*, and is said likewise to be of the *same denomination.* The mutual relation between *cause* and *effect*, *father*

* "Quantitas est mensura substantiæ; qualitas est dispositio substantiæ." (Div. Th., 1 p., qu. 28, a. 2.)

† "Esse relativi est ad aliud se habere." The essence of the relative is that it is referred to another.

and *son*, which are also said to be *co-related*, is not of the *same denomination*.

Relation is predicamental, or as one of the ten categories, includes only those relations which are between *real* objects. All the relations, likenesses, or respects of one real thing to another, which properly pertain to this category, are reduced by metaphysicians to three principal classes: 1st, relation of unity and number; 2d, of action and passion; 3d, of measure and measured.

Observe that all the ten categories or ultimate genera, include none but *real* entities; and hence, from among their *proper* subjects are excluded all *entia rationis*, or those entities that are merely creatures of the mind, though they be virtually founded in real objects; also such as have only *objective* being, i. e., which exist only in the intelligible concepts. Whence it follows that the relations that are devised by the mind, but which have no real being, as that between genus and species, between a thing and itself, and all the transcendental relations, are to be regarded as not properly pertaining to the *category* of relation.

Transcendental relations regard terms that transcend actual existence, or they are *metaphysical;* and, therefore, they run through all the categories. The relation between scientific knowledge and its objects, is *transcendental;* and by some it is also termed a *logical* relation; but the relation between a power apprehending, and the real object that determines its act, is *real.*

Much of our most valuable, as well as most interesting knowledge, regards these different species of relation. One of the most important of all these relations which furnish the mind objects for congenial exercise, is that of *cause* and *effect*, under the head of action and passion; it will be explained at some length, in the following chapter.

CHAPTER III.

ARTICLE I.

PRINCIPLE OF CAUSATION; OR, CAUSE IN GENERAL.

Whatever influences efficaciously in the production of a being, or a mutation in being, is a *cause;** and the result which is brought about by its agency or concurrence, is its *effect.*

The relation of cause and effect is not that of mere succession in time, or place, but it is that of dependence of the one on the other. The fact that the simplest minds can distinguish between mere *sequence* in time, or order, and the *dependence* of one thing upon another as its cause, shows how obvious to the human understanding is that distinction. It is not only evident that an effect cannot exist without a cause, effect and cause are co-relatives; but it is also evident to the mind that many things which are perpetually under our observation, actually have that relation of dependence.

Hume and other sceptics have denied all causation, and affirmed that what is thus understood is mere succession without any agency in what precedes, or any dependence in what follows after it.

The *Occasionalists* deny all efficiency in second causes, or creatures; and maintain that the reason or necessity for the existence of the effect, gives the *occasion* for God to *produce* that effect.

We know, however, on the testimony of consciousness, that we can act so as to produce results, or mutations, that really proceed from us; our senses receive influences that produce

* "Causa est principium *per se* influens esse in aliud." Cause is a principle which *per se*, i. e., by its own real operation, influences the existence of another thing.

changes or effects in them, and they give testimony to similar action and change in objects distinct from us. Since these facts are so manifest, and the conclusion so immediate, it is not wonderful that even a child understands clearly what is meant by "*make*," "*do*," or "*cause*."

While we have so distinct a notion of cause and effect as to their relation, we do not know in what the causality intrinsically consists. As substance and its powers are hidden from us, except so far as they are manifested by their operations, we can perceive their efficiency or causality in results only. We clearly distinguish between the two facts, "this comes *after* that," and "this comes *from* that," without being able to see how the action intrinsically proceeds from the power that produces it. But to deny this principle of causality, which is so clearly known under other respects, is to upset not only all science, but all our knowledge of anything.

Experience and the exercise of reason give among their first conclusions, the notion of dependence of one thing on another; and this relation is that of cause and effect. But limited reflexion suffices for coming to the general conclusion, "nothing is done without a cause; whatever has a beginning, must have had a cause." For, the mind readily perceives that whatever begins to exist, thereby acquires *what it had not before;* and this thing that it had not before, and which it acquires, must come to it from some agent that is distinct from itself; i. e., it comes *from a cause*. The peculiar and distinctive action of a *cause*, therefore, is, that it gives to another being what that being had not in itself, and which it thereby receives *from without* itself.

ARTICLE II.

DIFFERENT SPECIES OF CAUSES.

Since the influence of causality is exerted in very different manners; or, because the objects of its influence are specifically different, cause is divided into four distinct species, corresponding to the modes in which it produces its effect: namely, the *efficient* cause, the *final* cause, the *formal* cause, the *material* cause. They all agree in the general concept of causality, inasmuch as they all *concur* or *influence* in the production of effect; but, as said, their modes of influencing are specifically different.

The general distinction between the four causes will be best understood by an example in which their different modes of effecting or influencing will clearly appear; we shall, therefore, repeat a little more explicitly an illustration already given: A man makes a statue; 1st, he has an *end* in view which *causes* him to make the statue; 2d, he must have *material* out of which to make the statue, and that *material* or marble helps in its way to the *making* of the statue: it is the *material cause* of the statue; 3d, there must be an *agent* who can make or produce this statue out of the *matter;* this agent, or artist, is the *efficient* cause; 4th, the agent must put into that marble the *perfect form* which *makes* of it a statue; or, in other words, which determines its *specific nature*, as statue; and it is obvious that this *form influences*, in its way and degree, towards the *making* of the statue; it thereby becomes the *formal cause* of the statue. Hence, the *end* intended, the *agent*, the *matter*, and the *form*, all effectually help to produce the statue; but as their modes of concurring in the production of the effect are quite different, this gives rise to a division of cause in general into the four species above named. The statue is made *by* the agent, *of* the marble, *through* (*by means of*) the form, *for* the end intended or proposed.

The *efficient cause* is extrinsic to the effect; it is the first one that moves *physically;* for the *end* acts only *morally*, and the *matter* and *form* are dependent on the action of the efficient cause for their union; that is, for the effect. Hence, in material action, the *efficient cause* is that agent whose physical action begins the mutation in the object extrinsic to itself, which we term the effect. The subsequent union of the *formal* and *material* causes is dependent on this action of the efficient cause; therefore, as said, it begins the physical action, whose final term is the effect *intended.*

Hence, in *material* action, all four causes *always* unite, the *final*, *efficient*, *formal* and *material.*

In the action of simple or immaterial substance, only two causes may concur: namely, the *final*, and *efficient*; but an effect can not be produced by one cause alone.

The efficient cause must be either immediately, or mediately and virtually present to the object on which it acts, for nothing acts at a distance, "nihil agit in distans." It is evident that an agent cannot act *where* it is not, any more than it can act *when* it is not; for in either case it is really non-existent in respect to that object as a term of action. Hence, since nothing can act when and where it absolutely is not, a cause must be either immediately or mediately and virtually present both in time and place to the object on which it efficiently acts.*

Substantial *matter* and *form* cannot really compose the effect of man's spiritual or intellectual action; i. e., the mind cannot *per se*, by its own physical action, *transform* material substance. Judgment and reasoning have for the object of their action *truth*, which by analogy is called *matter*, and the understanding attributes to it *logical form* by action which is analogous to that by which an agent produces effects upon *substantial subject matter.*

A created agent cannot produce† new being, or cause a real

* "Motum et movens sunt simul." That which moves, and the agent moving it, are, as such, simultaneous.

"Agens et patiens sunt immediata, i. e., immediatione vel suppositi vel virtutis." That which acts, and that which receives the action, are *immediate*, either substantially or virtually.

† "Deus solus causat gradum essendi; quia primus omnium effectus est esse quod supponitur a cæteris tanquam fundamentum: sed Deus solus producit *esse*; seu illud esse quod diffusum est per omnes omnino perfectiones debet procedere ab altiori principio quam creatura. Agens particulare facit *hoc ex non hoc*, sed non facit *ens a non-ente.*" (Div. Thom., Summ. 1 p., qu. 105, art. 5.) God alone causes a *degree of being*; for the first of all effects is *being*, which is presupposed as the foundation of all else: God alone produces being; or, that *being* which is diffused throughout all perfections whatever, must proceed from a higher principle than a creature. A dependent agent can make *this out of non this*; (or *transform* one thing into another); but it cannot produce *being from non-being*.

grade or degree of essence; for this is, in its strict sense, *creation*, which is *pure efficiency*, or the action of the first cause, i. e., God. *Second causes*, i. e., created causes, being *dependent*, are not *purely efficient;* they can only *change* or *transform* subject matter; in other words, they require an object which actually determines and specifies their acts or efficiency.

The various manners in which the efficient cause acts will be readily and clearly understood if they be contrasted; for this purpose consider the following opposite modes in which it may operate: 1st, as *principal*, and as *instrumental* cause, which acts in virtue of its principal; 2d, as *necessary* and *free;* 3d, *physical* and *moral;* 4th, *remote* and *proximate;* 5th, *total* and *partial;* 6th, *adequate* and *inadequate;* 7th, *first** and *second;* 8th, *univocal;* i. e., whose effect is of its own species, as father and son; *equivocal*, i. e., whose effect differs from it in species, as *architect* and the *house* which he builds; 9th, cause *per se*, i. e., which directly, and of its own *real action*, *produces* its effect; v. g., "a vocalist *sings;*" "a penman *writes;*" *accidental* cause, or cause *per accidens;* as when a *vocalist paints;* he does not *directly as vocalist* paint, for vocalist is only accidental to one as *painting*, and has no influence at all on the effect.

The cause *per se*,† which *really influences* in the production of an effect is *one;* but the cause *per accidens* or *accidental cause*, which does not *really influence* the effect, is said to be infinite; the meaning of which will be readily understood by an example of it: if one should go from home for *the purpose* of buying something in the market, and on his way be *attacked by robbers*, his *intention of buying* could not be considered as the *one*, *cause per se*, of his *falling into the hands* of *robbers;* for, *any number*

* "Causa *prima*, quæ nulli subordinatur; *secunda*, quæ primæ subordinatur." The *first* cause is subordinate to no cause; a second cause is subordinate to the first.

† "Causa *per se* est *una*, et *proprie* dicta *causa;* causa *per accidens* nec est una, sed *infinita*, sed nec proprie dicta *causa*, sed *secundum quid*, seu *per accidens:* non est *proprie dicta causa, quia effectus per accidens* non habet *esse* proprie dictum." (Philos. passim.) The cause *per se* is *one*, and is *properly* termed a cause; the cause *per accidens* is not *one*, but *infinite*, nor is it *properly* called a *cause*, but is such only under some respect, or by accident; it is not properly termed a cause, for the *accidental effect* has not any existence properly so-called.

of reasons could have induced him to go to the market at that time; i. e., the cause *per accidens* of his being then attacked by robbers is not *limited* to this or that motive for his going from home.

It is in this sense that an *occasion* is sometimes rightly called an *accidental cause.** But it not unfrequently happens that an *occasion* or *opportunity* approaches more nearly to the nature of a *cause per se*, yet, however, without actually becoming a complete cause; in this case it is said to be an *imperfect cause*, since it *induces*, or *persuades* to action; but it is not a *perfect cause*, for it does not *produce* the effect. (D. Th., 2. 2., qu. 43, a. 1, ad. 3.)

The only reason why cause *per accidens* is denominated *cause* at all is that, whenever it occurs, it is in such case always conjoined with the thing which is *really* and *properly* the cause, and is then not separable from it. But neither the cause *per accidens*, *as such*, nor the effect *per accidens*, *as such*, has any *real entity;* † it is more correctly a certain respect only, of that which has reality and is a cause *properly* so-called.

The *final cause*, or *end intended*,‡ which is *objective good*, apprehended as such, acts first as a cause on the will, or rational appetite; for the *end* is an object of appetition, on account of its goodness, or it is a good which is desired and sought for, when it becomes an object of cognition.§ The *end intended* for irrational or necessary agents, must be referred to the author

* "Omne quod *est per se*, habet causam; quod autem est *per accidens*, non habet causam, quia non est vere *ens*, cum non sit vere *unum*. *Album* enim causam habet, similiter et *musicum; album musicum* non habet *causam*, quia non est vere ens, neque vere *unum*." (Div. Thom., I p., qu. 115, art. 6.) Whatever truly is, has a cause; what is, only as *accidental*, has no cause, for it is not truly *being*, since it is not truly *one*. *White*, has a cause, and *music* has a cause; but *white music* has no cause, for it is neither truly *being*, nor truly *one*.

† "Effectus per accidens proprie non *generantur*, nec *corrumpuntur*, nec *sunt* simpliciter, sed *secundum quid*." Effects *per accidens*, are not, properly speaking, *produced*, nor *destroyed*, nor do they simply *exist*, but only under a certain respect.

‡ "Finis est potissimum in unoquoque; i. e., finis est id quod principaliter intenditur in unoquoque." The *end* is chief in every thing; i. e., the *end* is what is principally intended in every thing.

§ "Nihil volitum nisi præcognitum." Nothing is wished, unless first known.

of their nature, by whom *it is determined* for them. The *end* or the *final cause* is the first of the four to act, and it causes the others to concur and to execute, the efficient cause being the second to operate. The *end* is the *first** in the *intention;* but it is the *last* in the *execution;* i. e., it is the *effect intended*, and the effect intended is the end which is last attained, and in which all rest.

The *end*, when considered as to the different relations it may have to the intention, is *proximate* or *remote; mediate* or *immediate;* and *ultimate* or *not ultimate.* These opposite relations will be easily understood, if it be borne in mind, that an end may be desired either for *its own sake;* or, on *account of something else*, that is desired; in the first case, it is strictly and properly an *end;* in the second, it is really a *means* to an end.

As the will by its own spontaneous natural action can wish *good* only, since *good*, as such, is its *essential object;* it is not free to wish *evil*, as such; or, in other words, by its nature it is necessarily determined to desire *good;* and, as regards the desire of this *good in general*, it is not free, but obeys the necessary law of its nature.† Hence, it is evident that this *good as absolute, or good in general*, is strictly an ultimate end, which is presupposed to all other ends, which can be intended or desired by the will. These truths being understood, it will be easy to perceive the consequent truth, that there can be no choice or election as to this ultimate end, since the will is predetermined to it by the necessary law of its nature as a power of appetition. The will is physically unable to love *evil* for itself or *as evil;* it can love *evil* only when apprehended and presented to it, *as good*, under some respect. In respect to this ultimate end, all other ends are *mediate*, or have the nature of *means* in reference to it. In regard to certain *intermediate ends*, the will can deliberate, suspend or change. Hence, man's responsibility for his actions depends upon the use he makes

* "Primum in intentione, est ultimum in executione." What is first in the *intention*, is last in the *execution*.

† "Minus malum, est aliquod bonum." Less evil, is some good.

'Malum sub ratione boni, potest fieri objectum volitionis." Evil, under the respect of good, can be the object of volition.

of his power freely to choose the *means of good;* and he becomes morally *good*, or *bad*, according as there is, or is not, real rectitude in his intention as regards those means which he employs for the attainment of this good. Hence, the obligation arises also for him to know what is *good*, and what is *evil*, in all the objects thus subject to election or choice.

Distinguish between the *end* of the *act or work*, and the *end intended*, or the *good* to be gained by the *work*.

Distinguish, also, between the *end* which *necessitates* action in the will, and the *end* which it can freely *elect* or *choose*. It is *good* which *causes*, as an end; but its *apprehension* is an indispensable *condition*.*

ARTICLE III.

MATERIAL CAUSE; FORMAL CAUSE.

As the terms, *matter* and *form*, *material cause* and *formal cause*, are much used in philosophy, law and ethics, for the most subtle, as well as for the most important distinctions, it is necessary that they should be clearly understood. For this object, it is deemed useful briefly to state in this place the philosophical theory that gives origin and meaning to these terms.

According to the Aristotelian or *peripatetic* philosophy, which has had much to do in moulding both the thought and the higher language of all civilized nations, *material substance*, of which the earth is made, consists essentially of two principles, *matter* and *form*. *Matter*, without the form, could have no determinate existence at all; it would be a mere *potentiality* for actual existence; but could not, as such, really exist. The *form*, which is the principle of *activity*, and of all *specific nature* or *essence*, unites by composition with matter, and actuates it into real existence; and, at the same time, gives to it

* "Bonum ut apprehensum est objectum appetitus." Good as apprehended is the object of appetition.

its *determined* and *specific* essence; i. e., makes, by union with it, *material substance.**

At the beginning of the world *matter* and *form* were *con-created;* i. e., passed from their causes into existence at the same time. Taken separately, they are both incomplete being; they are for each other, and, when they have the essential conditions for actual existence, they necessarily unite; and, being united, they remain in union, unless separated by force. Some forms are more deeply radicated in matter than others are.

Matter, as such, therefore, has no species; it is the *form* that determines species, and constitutes it such. Hence, since there exist many species of *material substance*, there must be many species of *forms*, that are actually existing. To understand this, it must be observed that, when the world was first created, material substance was diversified with many species or forms, and made to possess within itself at the same time many other forms *potentially*,† which may be educed from it by a competent *efficient cause.*

Matter, therefore, is the *subject* in which are contained *potentially*,‡ like an *effect* is precontained in its *actually existing cause*, many *substantial forms*, which may be educed from it by an *efficient cause;* and these *forms* that are educed from the matter, where they existed *potentially*, take the place of, or displace actual forms; which actual forms are not thereby simply annihilated, but are *re-immersed* in the *matter*, or they revert to the state of *potential being*, in matter.

The vital principle in organic beings, is a *substantial form;* v. g., the *vegetative principle* in *plants*, the *brute soul*, *anima*

* "Materia, quatenus est primum subjectum, est una et eadam in omnibus rebus." (Suarez Metaph.) Matter as the first subject in material substance, is one and the same in all things.

† "Materia est infinita in potentia ad formas." (Summ. I p., qu. 7, art. 2.) Matter is infinitely capable of receiving its forms.

‡ "*Esse in potentia*, hic non est ea mera *possibilitas*, quæ est *potentia objectiva;* sed esse in potentia involvit *subjectum* aliquod *reale*, cujus sinu res sit contenta, quæ dicitur *esse in potentia.*" To exist *potentially*, is not that mere possibility, which is only *objective*, (exists only in the concept of it); but to be potentially, involves a *real subject*, in which it is actually contained.

belluina in brutes, or animals of every species, man excepted, are *substantial forms educed from matter;* as also the principle that gives to crystals their specific nature, is substantial form. They return to matter, or are re-immersed in it, when dissolution, or death takes place. This eduction of new forms from matter, and the re-immersion of old ones into it, always suppose the agency of an *efficient* cause.

Since the operations of the *brute soul, anima belluina,* are *purely organic,** brute actions do not transcend the power of purely *material substance;* and, therefore, they are entirely *from* matter, and wholly *for* matter; and hence, brute souls cannot exist separate from matter. But the actions of intelligence and volition in the human soul, are from a principle that is not organic; they are inorganic or entirely *super-sensible*† in their species, or transcend the powers of material nature; and, therefore, the substance that possesses intellect and will, is essentially and specifically *immaterial.* Hence, though the human soul does inform or actuate matter by entering into composition with it, yet it is not *educed from* matter, and at death by dissolution, it is not re-immersed into matter; but it is a substantial form that can and does exist separate from matter, or, then exists *per se;* or, to use the term by which this mode of existing is expressed, it *subsists;* it is not said, however, in that state of existence, to be a *person,* because it does not *completely subsist,* being by its nature ordained to union with the body.

The human soul is by its nature fitted and ordained to unite in composition with matter; but yet it does not, like inferior substantial forms, completely depend for its existence on matter.

It follows, therefore, that there are *forms* which are *complete,*

* "Natura uniuscujusque rei ex ejus operatione ostenditur." (Phil. passim.) The nature of a thing is known by its action.

† "Anima humana non est forma in materia immersa, vel ab ea totaliter *comprehensa,* propter suam perfectionem. Ideo nihil prohibet aliquam ejus virtutem non esse corporis actum." (Div. Thom., 1 part, qu. 76, art 1, ad. 4.) The human soul is not a form that is immersed in matter, or that is totally *comprehended* by it, on account of its perfection. Therefore, nothing prevents some of its virtue from being no act of the body; i. e., some of its action is not action of the body, or the body has no share in it.

and *subsist*, but do not inform matter, and, therefore, have no relation to, or dependence on, matter; as, angels. For, if there are *incomplete forms*, *a fortiori*, *complete* ones should actually exist; and there are forms that are *incomplete*, and yet can *subsist*, but they inform matter, and are by their nature or essence ordained for union with matter; as, the human soul; it can exist separate from matter, but its only connatural and normal state is that of union with matter.

All accidents whose presence in, or absence from, material substance does not change the species of their subject, are *accidental forms;* as, *quality*, greater or less extension, figure, features, etc.

From this brief and incomplete outline of the peripatetic *theory* of material substance, it must appear evident that *matter*, as a *cause*,* is *receptive*, and *passively retentive;* or it *sustains*, as a *subject;* and that *form*,† *causes* by giving determinate *existence*, *nature* and *action* to the compound which it constitutes by union with *matter;* and thence it is, that all specific nature, and all action, are attributed to the *form*.

Hence, the *material cause*, is the *subject* upon which the efficient cause acts, to produce its intended effect.

The *formal cause*, is that reality, of whatever kind it may be, which the efficient cause by its action induces, or brings into actual being in that subject matter.

The change produced in the subject by the efficient cause, may be either *substantial* or *accidental*, i. e., the form induced, may be either substantial or accidental.

By analogy, other objects, as metaphysical and logical truth,

* "Quemadmodum materia est in toto (composito) principium *patiendi;* ita et forma est principium *agendi;* seu totum, ratione materiæ, patitur, et ratione formæ agit, seu totum agit *ut quod*, forma *ut quo*. Est totum quod existit, est, subsistit. etc." As matter is the principle that *receives action*, in the compound; so, the form is the principle of *action;* or, the whole object, *acts*, in virtue of the *form*, *suffers* action in virtue of its *matter;* or the whole is that *which* acts, the form that *by* which it acts; the whole is what exists, subsists, etc.

† "Omnis ratio boni. pulchri, ordinis, perfectique a forma venit; quia eo ipso quod est actus substantialis hæc omnia ipsi conceduntur." (Div. Thom., 1 p., qu. 76, art. 1.) The whole nature of the good, beautiful, order, perfection, comes from the *form;* for, since it is the substantial act, these are all attributed to it.

genus, species, etc., are termed *matter*, and, therefore, are conceived as susceptible of *form;* v. g., "rational animal," may be regarded as having *animal* as matter, and *rational* as form; since "rational" constitutes with *animal* as quasi *matter*, *man*. Hence, matter and form are regarded by analogy as likewise having *causal* influence in objects of the intelligible order.

These terms, therefore, have extensive application; but *the mode* in which the *matter* and *form cause*, is always the same; i. e., by *composing* the effect; the form giving its *denomination* or specific name to the effect, and the *matter* receiving and sustaining the form.

An example will illustrate the analogical use of these terms: a man, who is *unintentionally unjust* to another person, does *material* injustice, but not *formal* injustice; for, it is the *intention*, as right or wrong, that gives to actions their specific moral or *formal* nature.

From the preceding observations, it is manifest that the definition of cause has its most proper application to the *efficient cause.* It was, perhaps, on this account that the ancient stoics contended that the efficient cause is the only one which is truly and properly a cause at all. But it is undeniable that, as already shown, there are more causes than one, truly distinct from each other, and which have, in their mode and degree, real influence in producing many effects.

There cannot be an actual effect* which is produced by *only one* cause; for there can be no *efficient* cause, without the *final* cause; and *vice versa*, there can be no *final cause* without the *efficient* to which it is presupposed, as the first of all causes; and hence, for the production of an actual effect, both must concur.

The cause, by its nature, is prior to its effect;† but as to the

* "Nullus est effectus in rerum natura qui unicam tantum habet causam, formaliter loquendo." (Suarez Met. disp. 26, sect. 3, no. 3.) There is no effect which strictly has but one cause.

† "Causa est prior effectu prioritate *a quo*, seu ratione dependentiæ." The cause is prior to the effect, in the relation of dependence.

"Causa in actu, et effectus actu, sunt simul." The cause and effect as actual, are simultaneous.

"Posito fundamento et termino, consurgit relatio." When the basis and term are put, the relation simultaneously regards them.

relation *actually existing* between them, they are simultaneous; or they begin to exist formally as such at the same time; for, when the *basis* and *term* of a relation are put, it simultaneously *relates* the two to each other; or, it arises at the same time for both the *actual cause* and its *actual effect.*

Every effect has within it some degree of perfection, which gives to it a certain similitude to its cause; but the resemblance may be only that of analogy, as when the cause is *equivocal;* v. g., the *architect* and the house which he builds with its *design;* the perfection which is in the *house*, resembles the *intelligent mind*, by analogy only.

The effect is either *virtually* or *formally* precontained in its cause; and, therefore, it is really from the cause. In the first case, the cause is *equivocal*, i. e., of a different species from the effect; in the second case, the cause is *univocal*,* i. e., of the same species as the effect.

An effect that has the *material* cause, requires the three others also. But we may actually know one or two causes, and yet be ignorant of the remaining ones. Since no being can act at a distance, "nihil agit in distans," it is an *essential condition*, or a *conditio sine qua non*, that the agent and object acted on, be either *mediately* or *immediately connected.* But, take care to observe that a *condition*, how essential soever it may be for the *action* of a cause, has not itself any *real causality;* and, therefore, it is an error to confound a *condition* with the *cause* that depends on it; or to attribute to it any real *agency* in producing the effect.

The *exemplary* cause, or the *ideal* or *type* in the mind, by which an intelligent efficient cause is directed in producing an effect, may be referred, under different respects, to the efficient

* "Causa *univoca*, æqualis est effectui in essendo, nobilior ratione dependentiæ; causa æquivoca, est vel *principalis*, vel *instrumentalis; principalis* superat effectum in essendo; *instrumentalis* superatur ab effectu, nisi sumatur ut *condivisa principali*, tune enim influit per virtutem inferioris ordinis.'' (Suarez Met. Disp. I7, sec. 2, no. 19.) The *univocal* cause is equal to its effect in essence, but more noble as regards dependence; the equivocal cause is either *principal*, or *instrumental;* the *principal*, exceeds its effect in essence; the *instrumental* is inferior to its effect, unless as *precisely distinguished* from the principal, for, thus taken, it influences by virtue of an inferior order, and is a partial cause only. It is more noble than its own *proper* effect.

and to the formal cause; namely, either as perfecting the agent for action; or as, in some manner, *extrinsically forming* the effect.*

ARTICLE IV.

PERFECTION OF BEINGS; THE FINITE AND INFINITE; THE KNOWLEDGE OF THE INFINITE IS LOGICALLY DERIVED FROM THAT OF THE FINITE.

A thing is perfect, when nothing is wanting to complete it in fulfilling the proper end† of its being; due respect being had as to whether that *end* be temporary, i. e., by way of transition to another; or, fixed, and unchangeable, as a state. The *perfection*, and the *goodness* of a thing, are *really* the same; yet, in the concept, or logically, the perfect is presupposed to the good; for, in thought, we found the idea of a thing as being *good*, upon its perfection.

Perfection is *absolute* or *relative; absolute perfection* includes all realities that can enter into the concept of *infinite perfection; relative perfection* includes all those realities that are required to constitute any particular species of complete finite perfection.

Simple perfection is that, from the very concept of which is excluded all positive imperfection; as "justice," "intelligence," etc. The *mixed* perfection includes in its essential concept the idea of perfection which is *mixed* with *imperfection;* as, v. g., *reasoning*, which implies the absence of simple intelligence. Hence, reasoning is, under different respects both a perfection and an imperfection. Reason can come to the evident knowledge of truth, not known as self-evident, only by *demonstration*, or by *discourse of reason*; *simple* intelligence perceives the same truth intuitively, i. e., without the less perfect

* "Dispositio concurrit in genere causæ materialis: subjectum facit magis receptivum." Disposition concurs by way of the material cause: it makes the subject more receptive.

† "Ultima perfectio rei est in consecutione finis." The ultimate perfection of a thing, is in the attainment of its end, or reaching its destined end.

process of *reasoning** to it; by the simple apprehension of an essence it acquires a knowledge of all that can be affirmed, or denied, by way of real property, in respect to the object. In other words, simple intelligence does not know truth by *composition* and *division*, as reason does; or, what is the same, by *synthesis* and *analysis*, for it does not know *predicate* and *subject* first as separate, but sees the one *in* the other. Distinguish, therefore, between knowing a thing *after* another, *in* another, and *from* another; the first is common to finite intelligence and reason; the second, pertains to simple intelligence; the third, is the *peculiar and distinctive operation of reason.*

The *finite* is what has *limits;* the *infinite,* is what has no *limits.*

The infinite is either *actual,* or it is *potential infinite.* The actual infinite actually has all perfection without *limit.* This is possible only in *one God.* The *infinite potentially,* is actually *finite,* but can be *increased without limit.* The *infinite actually,* cannot be increased, and cannot be subjected to measure, or number.

Finite added to finite cannot produce infinite; and, therefore, the actual infinite does not consist of extension or multitude.

No finite being can be conceived so great, but that a greater one may be conceived as possible.

Creation actually infinite is impossible: 1st, because that which *begins* cannot become *infinite;* 2d, because *potential infinite* cannot become *actual infinite;* or, neither that which can be *finished,* nor that which cannot be *finished,* can become infinite.

* "Ad discursum intellectualem proprium, et formalem, requiritur quod unum cognoscatur ex alio; id est, quod ex alio prius noto deveniatur in cognitionem alterius posterius noti quod erat prius ignotum; sicque quod una prior cognitio sit causa posterioris, sive quod ex priori unius cognitione pariatur cognitio alterius, præcedatque prior cognitio posteriorem, si non in tempore, saltem natura et causalitate." (Billuart de Angelis, Tract. 3, art. 3, sect. 3.) For discourse of reason, properly and formally such, it is required that one thing should be known from another; i. e., from one thing previously known we come to the knowledge of another thing afterwards known, but which was previously unknown; and thus that a prior cognition is the cause of an after one, or that from the prior knowledge of one thing is born the knowledge of another, and that the prior cognition precede the posterior one, if not in time, at least by nature and causality.

The philosophers, who teach that the human mind has naturally a more or less *immediate intuition of God*, deny the possibility of knowing the *infinite* through the *finite*.

The chief reason *a priori* which they allege for this impossibility of concluding the infinite from the finite, is that "the conclusion cannot be greater than the premises from which it follows as a consequent."

But their proof of the hypothesis that the human mind naturally has an immediate intuition of God, seems to rest mainly on two erroneous arguments: 1st, the misapplication of a canon of logic; 2d, a misconception of the fact of actual experience. They argue, that since the idea of an infinite being cannot be derived *a posteriori*, for the conclusion cannot exceed the premises, therefore, because as a fact, we have that notion, we must have it as an *a priori intuition*.

But the canon of logic referred to, forbids a greater *extension as to quantity* in the conclusion than was in the premises; but not *greater comprehension*. If the prohibition held true of both, then there could be no reasoning at all from truth known, to truth unknown. Since the conclusion attributes to a subject a predicate which is not attributed in the premises, the subject of the conclusion has greater *comprehension* in the conclusion, than it had in the premises, especially when the predicate affirms perfection, or denies imperfection.

Also, when we reason *a posteriori*, or from effect to cause, the effect may have been either *virtually*, or *formally* precontained in the cause; in the case in which we reason from an effect to its *equivocal*, or *super-eminent cause*, we pass from what is *inferior in species*, to what is *eminently superior* in species; v. g., when we reason from the *house* to the *architect*, from the *painting* to the *artist*, which is legitimate reasoning, we always conclude from an *inferior* to a *superior species* of being.

Hence, conclusion from the *finite* to the *infinite*, as its *super-eminent* cause, gives a conclusion of greater *comprehension*, though of less *logical extension*, than the premises explicitly and directly expressed, but yet, it is both consequent and legitimate illation.

It is to be assumed that no sane philosopher denies that the human mind, as a fact, does reason *a posteriori*, or from effect to cause, by means of the real relation between cause and effect.

There is no object of cognition which the mind perceives with more facility, or which is more connatural to human intellect, than the real relation of cause and effect. Evidences of dependence lead us daily to refer numberless *effects* to their *causes*, and this we have done from the earliest exercise of reason. In the same manner, the mind can see evidences in the visible world around us, of its dependent and contingent existence; and, as the idea of limitation or finiteness is most simple, its object being so immediate and so obvious to the mind, it is clearly within the powers of human reason, to prove to itself the finiteness of the visible world, in the same manner in which it proves any object to be limited or finite.

Hence, the mind of man, by its native power of reasoning, and without any intuition of God, can argue from what it knows and sees for itself: "There is no *effect** which is not produced by *sufficient cause;* the visible world is an *effect*, and, therefore, the visible world is produced by an adequate cause."

The intellect, then, is naturally competent to perceive by its own light, both that the visible world is *finite*, and that it is an *effect;* for it is mutable, therefore, contingent, and, consequently, may lose or acquire being, which are distinctive marks of the finite. It may ask itself, what is a "sufficient cause" for such an effect.

Reason would lead the mind to attribute to that "sufficient cause"† perfections pre-eminently superior to those of the

* "Non datur effectus sine causa: nihil est quod rationem sufficientem cur sit non habeat; hæc axiomata non confundenda sunt. Juxta primum, nihil efficitur sine causa; juxta secundum, nihil est, seu existit sine ratione sufficiente: primum non pertinet ad Deum, cum Deus non habeat causam; secundum pertinet ad Deum, cum sit ratio sufficiens cur debeat admitti quod Deus existit." There is not given an effect without a cause; there is nothing which has not a sufficient reason why it exists; these axioms should not be confounded. By the first, nothing is effected without a cause; by the second, nothing is, or exists without a a sufficient reason: the first does not apply to God, since God has no cause; the second does pertain to God, since there must be a sufficient reason why it ought to be admitted that God exists.

† "Si objiciatur, 'effectus finitos, quales sunt creaturæ, non exigere causam infinitam;' id conceditur de eorum causa secundaria, sed non de causa primaria,

effect argued from; v. g., *priority* to all other causes, therefore, existence *a se*, and the *infinite* perfections of all kinds, which flow logically from admitting a *first cause that is independent or absolute.*

The very words, *infinite*, *immense*, and all the names of God which are *negative* in form, indicate the natural process by which the human mind forms its concept of absolute perfection, as expressed in the very structure of language; for, the *negative* names of God, show that the *positive*, out of which they are formed, was *presupposed as affirming the finite premises* of which they express the conclusion.

Suarez* observes the fact that, "in all things pertaining to God, it is more difficult to know the manner in which they are in him, than it is to know the manner in which they cannot be in him;" i. e., it is easier to know *what God is not*, than it is to know *what he is.* This is the reason why it not unfrequently happens that *negative terms* are employed to enunciate the divine perfections.

The accepted significance of these *negative names*, shows also, that the concepts for which they stand, were formed in the mind by the *removing* of imperfection, and the consequent *addition* of perfection. This concept of *infinite perfection* in God, as the first cause, we actually make more and more comprehensive by study, reflexion, and meditation, as we grow in years.

As a matter of *experience*, we have not that primitive intuition of the infinite, or immediate intuition of God.

Had the human mind naturally any such intuition of *ens creans existentias*, as the first great thought, which is the foundation of all other thoughts, it should have, it would seem, its own *proper name* in every language, which would be known to

quæ sit omnium causa a nulla causata; hanc enim esse infinitam necesse est." Distinguish the effects in visible nature as proceeding *from second causes*, from that respect of them which exacts for them, moreover, a *first* and *unproduced cause*. No effect absolutely depends on a second cause, for the second cause is itself dependent on the first cause.

* "In omnibus divinis rebus, difficilius est cognoscere quomodo sint, quam quomodo non sint." (Suarez, 2 opuscul, lib. 1, cap. 8.)

all, and understood by all; for it would necessarily and most *distinctly be seen* as constituting the basis of all human thought, of perception, judgment and reasoning. But, as a fact, it has no such *name*, commonly recognized as pertaining to it, in languages, and it fulfills no such function in human thought; on the contrary, the terms employed to enunciate it, which are not agreed upon, even in philosophy, offer to us an hypothesis which is obscure and difficult to be comprehended, because not only it does not declare, but it even contradicts, the facts of experience.

Whatever may be the best philosophical explanation, the *fact of experience* is, that the progress of the mind is from the *singular and concrete objects* that through the senses determine its action, to the *intelligible*, expressed to it by the *idea or concept;* from the *indeterminate idea* of *essence* and being in general* to the *indefinitely great;* and, by *remotion* of all *limit*, and the *addition* of all positive *perfection*, to the *infinite*, or to *absolute being*, as the only sufficient cause of all else.

Hence, to affirm that the human mind cannot naturally infer the *infinite* from the *finite*, is not *logically correct;* and to affirm that the human mind has naturally and originally the *immediate intuition of God*, or, of *absolute being*, or, *ens creans existentias*, is not true as a *matter of fact.*

In the conclusion of a syllogism, the terms may have more *comprehension*, or their concepts include more *essential perfection*, than they expressed in the premises. The *infinite*, as a conclusion from the *finite*, expresses less logical *extension*, but more *comprehension*, or *perfection*, than is explicitly in the premises; for, whether the predicate attribute something positive, or deny some imperfection, the conclusion is the synthesis of a subject and predicate not made in the premises; and its sub-

* "Intellectus noster; dum de potentia in actum reducitur, pertingit prius ad cognitionem universalem et confusam de rebus quam ad propriam et specialem rerum cognitionem: sed perfectus modus cognoscendi, non prius attingit universalem quam specialem cognitionem." (Vide Div. Thom., 1 p., qu. 14, art. 6.) Our intellect, when it goes into action, attains to a universal and confused knowledge of things before it does to proper and special knowledge; but the perfect method of knowing does not first attain to universal, and then to special cognition.

ject is thereby increased in comprehension. The absolute infinite is not such by *extension;* i. e., by continuous or discrete or logical *quantity;* but it is such by *comprehension of all perfection.*

A desire to effect a unification of knowledge, or a coördination of all cognitions, by a simple principle, has led many to adopt a theory that identifies the *ontological* and the *psychological* orders; but, as a fact, they are not identical in the actual nature of things; i. e., the order of our cognitions is not from the first Being, to the works of that being; but it is naturally just in the reverse order; that is, it proceeds from his works to Him.

The argument by which the existence of *absolutely perfect and real being, entis realissimi,* is claimed to be validly deduced from the *idea* of such a being, involves a double middle term; v. g., "he that has a *true idea* of absolutely perfect and real being, thereby knows that being to exist; but there is in every mind, which comprehends the expression, *absolutely perfect and real being,* the *true idea* of such a being; therefore, from the very *idea* of such a being, it follows that the mind may and does know it as really existing."

The phrase, "true idea," is here ambiguous; and, in fact, it has two objects in the premises;* in the first, or in one mind, the *idea,* it must be supposed, formally connotes its object as actual or real; in the second, or in the other mind, it legitimately expresses only the *concept of an intelligible object,* in which *actual existence* is neither affirmed nor denied; i. e., it exists in the second mind only *objectively,* as it is termed; or, for one mind, the existence is *real;* in the other, it is *ideal* only: it needs not to be said that, if the *existence* of the object were merely *ideal* in both minds, then the argument would be simply nugatory.

* "Ex hoc (ex idea Entis quo majus et melius cogitari nequit), non sequitur quod intelligat, id quod significatur per hoc nomen, *esse in rerum natura,* seu, ut dicunt, *existere in actu exercito;* sed existere dumtaxat *in apprehensione intellectus,* seu, ut dicunt, *in actu signato.*" (Billuart, 1 p., qu. 1, art. 1.) From this idea it does not follow that the intellect perceives its object as *real,* or as actually existing; but it exists only in the *apprehension of the intellect,* or only in its sign, the concept.

Since the conclusion must follow the weaker part of the argument, it can affirm nothing more, in this case, than the concept of an intelligible object, whose *objective truth*, or *esse in rerum natura*, actual being, remains to be proved. Illation from the *purely ideal*, as such, to the *real*, is not valid; if it were, then any absurdity could be *logically* demonstrated *a priori*, or from the idea of it, to be truth.

An object in the mind is *purely ideal*, when the notion of it which the mind has is merely a concept of what is not known by it as real; the mind acquires this idea by simply apprehending the term or terms by which the object is expressed in language, and its idea is, therefore, not derived from the object, as it is in itself really and extrinsically to the intellect, whether by means of evidence or testimony.

If, in the syllogism given above, we suppose the *idea* to connote the object as *in actu exercito*, or *real* in each mind, then, considered as *reasoning*, the *argument* is still more absurd; for, it is a vicious circle in which the same thing, though assumed to be *self-evident*, is proved by itself as reason, *idem per idem*, and it would be equivalent to this: "He that knows God to exist, knows God to exist; but Peter knows God to exist, therefore, Peter knows God to exist." In fact, truth which is intuitively evident, neither requires nor admits proof; nor, therefore, can it be directly subject to rational discussion.

"But," it is further said, "he that has the idea of absolutely *perfect* being, in which the existence, *in actu exercito*, actual existence, of such a being, is not affirmed, but it is included only, *in actu signato*, i. e., only ideally, has a *false idea;* and thus the mind would *err per se*." The *idea* in the case supposed, would be *false* by *privation*, or *negatively;* but it would not be false *positively;* therefore, the mind would not *err per se*; for, it would simply be *ignorant* of a truth which is not yet manifested to it by the evidence of that truth; this would be *ignorance*, but not *error*. From this it would merely follow that the existence of God is not, as regards us, *per se* known, or self-evident, but requires proof.

The old philosophers acutely and precisely enunciate the

distinction between that *necessity of actual existence*, as it is in absolutely perfect being, *in ente realissimo*, i. e., in God; and as it actually is in relation to our intellects or our cognition of it, in the following terms: "propositio, *Deus est*, per se nota est quoad se, sed non quoad nos;"* the proposition, *God exists*, is *per se* known, as regards itself, but not as regards us.

A proposition is *per se* known as regards itself, but not *per se* known as regards us, when it has no medium of proof *a priori*, nor is its truth directly and immediately evident to us on first apprehending the terms. Such proposition is also said to be *immediatc*, in the sense that its predicate is *immediately* of the subject, or there is no *medium* between it and the subject, through which it agrees with the subject; but the predicate is included in the very nature of the subject, as its definition, or as a part of its definition. In case, however, that it is not self-evident to us, or *per se* known as regards us, the essence or quiddity of the subject does not become known to us, by the mere first apprehension of the terms that enunciate it; but it must be demonstrated to us by means something extrinsic to it, which is better known to us. *It evidences itself*, though our minds are not capable of *immediately* and directly receiving that evidence, but it must be conveyed to them through a medium which is extrinsic and *a posteriori* by which this evidence is, in some respect, *reflected* upon our minds.

That which is *per se* known, as regards us, or is self-evident

* "Propositio, *Deus est*, est per se nota *quoad se*, sed non *quoad nos:* illa propositio non est per se nota quoad nos, in qua quidditas subjecti ex prima et communi apprehensione terminorum nobis non innotescit, sed indiget *discursu* ut nobis innotescat, quia tunc non potest statim nobis innotescere an prædicatum conveniat subjecto; atqui quidditas Dei nobis non notescit nisi per discursum." (Billuart 1 p, qu. 1, art. I; vide page 139.)

"Cum ergo propositio per se nota et immediata idem sint, dubitari non potest quin multa sint per se nota in se, quæ non sunt per se nota nobis. . . Sunt quædam veritates in se immediatæ; i. e., sine ullo medio inter prædicatum et subjectum, quas non nisi per aliquod medium (extrinsecum) intelligere valemus: v. g., quantitas est entitas accidentalis." (Suarez Met. Disp. 29, sct. 3, no. 32.) Since a proposition which is *per se* known, and a proposition which is *immediate*, are the same thing, it cannot be doubted that there are many things *per se* known, as regards themselves, but which are not *per se* known as regards us; there are certain truths which are immediate in themselves, i. e., without any medium between the subject and the predicate, which we are not able to understand unless through some medium; v. g., quantity is accidental entity.

to us, is seen and assented to by our minds, on first apprehending the terms, and without any reasoning, whether *a priori* or *a posteriori*; v. g., "A whole is greater than its part." But while the proposition which is *per se* known as regards itself but not as regards us, possesses, in itself, the most perfect of all *objective evidence*, and the most absolutely necessary truth, in itself; yet, our imperfect intellects do not attain to it *immediately*, but do so only by *reflex knowledge* from other things, which are connected with it logically. Of this kind is the proposition, "God exists;" and of this kind, also, are many of the highest and most universal truths, as remarked in respect to the proper object of wisdom or philosophy, on page 139.

Hence, to sum up what was said in regard to the argument by which the existence of God is claimed to be proved from the mere idea of absolutely perfect being, *entis realissimi;* either this idea connotes its object as actually existing, *in actu exercito*, or it does not; if it does, the argument in proof of it is useless, and is nothing more than a vicious circle. If the idea does not thus connote the object in *both* minds, then either it thus connotes the object in neither, or in one mind only; in the first case, the argument is simply nugatory; in the second, it is merely an equivocation, as is every argument which concludes from the *ideal*, as such, to the *real*.

The *existence* of absolutely *perfect being*, or of the *infinite*, must be learned otherwise than from the *mere idea* of it, or by the equally preposterous argument from the possibility of such a being; and, in fact, it is strictly demonstrable only *a posteriori*, or by reasoning from effect to cause.* The existence of absolutely *perfect*, *necessary* or *infinite being*, cannot be demonstrated *a priori*; for, there is no principle *prior* to such being from which it comes, it being the *first of all principles*.

All the demonstrative proofs of God's existence by natural reason are *a posteriori*;* and they are all reducible to the argu-

* "Deum esse est demonstrabile non *a priori*, seu per causas, sed *a posteriori* seu per effectus: prima demonstratio dicitur *propter quid;* secunda, *demonstratio quia*. (Philos. passim.) The existence of God is not demonstrable *a priori*, or through causes, but *a posteriori*, or by effects; the first, is called demonstration *propter quid;* the second, demonstration *quia*.

ment for the necessity of a *first and independent cause.* The proof derived from *motion*, the argument for the necessity of *unproduced being*, for *absolute being*, etc., are, in reality, but different modes of showing the necessity of a *first cause* that exists *a se.*

ARTICLE V.

NECESSARY AND CONTINGENT BEING; OF ORDER; IT CAN BE INTENDED BY NONE BUT AN INTELLIGENT BEING.

A thing is *absolutely necessary*,* whose non-existence is intrinsically impossible; a thing is *contingent*, whose non-existence is possible.

God alone is absolutely necessary, in the strictest sense of the words; all other necessary being or truth, the eternal essences of things, metaphysical truth, as, v. g., "a part is less than the whole," etc., must be conceived as, in some manner, *deriving* their necessity, or depending for it on a presupposed Being whose necessity is still more strictly absolute, as it is under all respects underived and independent; and, therefore, their necessity, immutability, etc., are less strictly absolute. The necessity which is predicated of them is by some appropriately styled, metaphysical necessity.

Hence, *metaphysical necessity* belongs to objects, which, in their very nature, could not be otherwise than they are; v. g., the *triangle*; the *circle*; or *necessary truths* in general. It is antecedently and absolutely required that, if they really exist, they be conformable to their essential concept; but their *actual existence* as *real* things, "in rerum natura," is *contingent*; i. e., depends on a free cause.

Physical necessity, is that which is *consequent* upon physical law; and is, therefore, *contingent* also, in some respect; v. g.,

* "Necessarium est quod ita existit ut deficere non possit. Contingens est quod potest esse et non esse." A thing is *necessary*, which so exists that it cannot cease to exist. A thing is *contingent*, which so exists that it can cease to exist.

it is *physically* necessary that fire burn, that the sun rise to-morrow, if the stability of their physical laws be not suspended by Divine intervention. It is *a physical fact* that the sun rose yesterday morning; and, as it now has *consequent* necessity, and is no longer actually contingent being, the truth of that fact is really *metaphysical*, under this respect of it.

Absolutely necessary being, can neither have a beginning nor an end. For, what begins to exist, depends upon some *condition* for its existence; and, therefore, its being was not *absolutely necessary*; and also, if it cease to exist, its being is not absolutely necessary either; for, what comes to an end, could have only conditional or dependent being. Hence, being that is *absolutely necessary*, cannot be conceived as actually *in a state of possibility*, and it is, therefore, *eternal*. But all *contingent* being was in a state of possibility before it began to exist.

Necessity is either *antecedent* or *consequent*; v. g., it is *antecedent* necessity for every circle to be round; every rectilinear triangle to have three angles, whose sum is equal to the sum of two right angles; it is *consequent necessity* that the sun rose this morning, and, under another respect, it is also necessary that it will rise to-morrow; the *necessity*, in the latter case, is *consequent* upon the *hypothesis* that the law of the world's motion will not be changed before that time. The *circle* and *triangle* are *contingent*, in respect to their actually existing, as *real* beings.

No contingent being can exist, unless brought into existence by some cause, i. e., some being distinct from itself. The efficient cause of its beginning to exist, must be *extrinsic* to itself; for, if the sufficient reason of its existence were within itself, or intrinsic to it, then its existence would not be *contingent*, but *absolutely necessary*; or, in other words, the supposition can be made only of *unproduced* being.

A thing may be *produced* in two ways: 1st, by *creation from nothing*;* 2d, by being formed or made out of something else.

* "Creatio est rei productio ex nihilo *sui, et subjecti.*" Creation is the production of a thing from nothing absolutely; i. e., from nothing that is presupposed as subject matter out of which it is *formed*, or *educed*.

A being is made or produced out of something else, when it is made by the efficient cause, out of some subject matter which is extrinsic to the cause; v. g., an oak produces another oak; an architect builds a house, etc.

A being may be *destroyed* also in two ways: 1st, by *annihilation* or *absolute reduction* to *nothing;* and 2d, *by dissolution* into the elements out of which it is made, by which the *whole*, as such, perishes.

Simple substance, or a being that does not consist of parts, and that exists *per se*, i. e., alone, or not as *inhering*, cannot be produced out of pre-existing substance. For, by reason of its *simple* essence, it cannot be formed out of pre-existing *parts*, since parts are incompatible with its simple nature; it cannot be produced from material substance; for that would not be its *production*, since its *existence per se* in that substance must be presupposed to its *eduction from* it; and in which, not being an accident, it did not *inhere;* and on which, not being a constituent part, it did not *depend* for being. Finally, it cannot be educed from another *simple substance;* for since a simple substance is not *compounded*, it cannot separate a *substantial part* from itself. Hence, simple substance that exists *per se*, can begin to exist only by creation from nothing.

*Order** is a perfection, by which multitude is reduced to complete unity; it so disposes of its like and unlike constituents, that each has its appropriate place in respect both to the parts and to the whole. When the proportion of relations, on which order is founded, is perfect, according to the specific nature of the object thereby formed; then that object is, under different respects, *perfect*, *good*, or *beautiful* in its own species.

Order is referable to the relations of time, place, material substance; to things moral, social, and intelligible; and, in general, to any object in which we conceive relations of parts among themselves, and to the whole.

* "Ordo parium dispariumque, sua cuique loca tribuens dispositio." (S. August.) Order is the disposition of like and unlike things, giving to each its proper place.

"Compositio rerum aptis et determinatis locis." (Cicero.) Order is the arrangement of things in apt and determinate places.

Any order in action, proves the author of it to be intelligent; because the intention and production of it require the exercise of judgment. By the order in men's actions and conversation we perceive daily the evidences of judgment exercised by them; of *ends* deliberately *intended*, and of means compared, selected, and coördinated for their accomplishment.

To *intend*, is properly an act of the will; it is an *efficacious desire of an end*, which is, therefore, formally sought for by appropriate means; or, it is an act by which the mind *tends* to an *end wished for*. The selection and arrangement of the means to that end, require practical judgment.

The ape can warm himself at the fire which is made for him; the dog can mount upon the chair that is already near the window, and thence jump to the window; but neither can the one select means to keep the fire alive; nor can the other combine separated and absent objects, so as to put them in the relation to each other of stiles; for both acts would require a comparison of abstract and concrete relations; i. e., judgment.

Instinct deals with certain actually established and *concrete* relations of things, and when those relations cease to exist, or are essentially changed, it is powerless to devise entirely different means from its determined ones, or to combine and employ a new species of means.

To select and combine means, to establish new relations, to devise means to an end which were not employed before, are acts of judgment that are proper only to rational natures. Hence, order or design gives complete evidence that its proper cause was an intelligent agent.

There is order also in the works of the beaver, the bee, etc.; but they give no evidence whatever of *intending* it, which is an act of intelligence; or that they exercise judgment in the *selection* and *use* of the means.

Cognition which is purely of sense, or organic, and limited to singular objects, and concrete relations; action, which, in respect to the production of order, as such, is merely mechanical; fully explain their causality, and are all that can be attributed to them as agents. The intelligence and judgment, clearly discernible in their work, we must refer, through the law of their nature, to the author of that nature. They can accomplish an *end determined for them*, by *determined means*;* but they cannot substitute means of different species; or, as their action is *determined to one thing* by natural law, they cannot *select* another end, or other means, equally good, or better, but must, circumstances being the same, always do the same thing, in the same *specific manner* and *degree*, and by the same means; for they can know only the *singular*, and can apprehend and retain only concrete relations; they are not capable of transmitting improvement as a species, are not perfectible, either in their knowledge, or their mode of action.

"*Determinatum*† *ad unum*," means *limited or determined to one mode of acting*, without any real choice or rational empire over the agent's own action; when the object is actually presented, it cannot remain really indifferent as to action or non-action, or be free to choose the object, or choose the contrary, but is necessitated by the object to *do what it does*.

There is, indeed, order in the action of all natural agents;

* "Cognitio et appetitio *animæ rationalis*, sunt illimitatæ; dum, e contra, *materia* determinata est ad unum; anima autem belluina est *materialis*." Rational cognition and appetite, are unlimited; but matter is determined to one thing; its capacity to receive and contain, is determinate and limited; of such is the brute soul, which is *material*.

† "Natura determinata est ad unum; sed voluntas se habet ad opposita. Voluntas dividitur contra naturam, sicut una causa contra aliam, quædam enim sunt naturaliter, quædam voluntarie. Est autem alius modus causandi proprius voluntati quæ est domina sui actus, præter modum qui convenit naturæ, quæ *est determinata ad unum*. Semper naturæ respondet *unum*, proportionatum naturæ: naturæ enim in genere respondet aliquid unum in genere, et naturæ in specie acceptæ respondet unum in specie; naturæ autem individuatæ respondet aliquid unum individuale. Eorum igitur voluntas principium est, quæ possunt sic, vel aliter esse. Eorum autem quæ non possunt nisi sic esse, principium natura est." (Div. Th., 1 p., qu. 12, a. 1, et 1, 2 p., qu. 10, a. 1, ad. 3.) Nature is determined to one thing; the will is capable of opposites. The will is the opposite of nature, as one cause is the opposite of another, for, some things are natural, some things are voluntary. There is also one mode of causing, proper to the will as supreme over its act; a different one agrees with nature which is *determined to one thing*. There is always one object corresponding to nature, proportioned to nature: to nature in general, corresponds some one thing in general; to nature taken as a species, answers a species of object; to individual nature, corresponds an individual thing. The *will*, therefore, is the principle of those things that can be either one way, or another; *nature* is the principle of those things that can be only one way.

the *intention* of it, however, is not referable to them, but to an intelligent cause which is above them, and anterior to them.* Order and unity, attained by appropriate means, are manifest in the crystal, the mineral, the vegetable, the brute animal, in all objects around us; but the true cause and design of it, we cannot ascribe to those objects. For order, as such, can be *intended* and formally *effected* only by an intelligent cause; and the concurrence of irrational agents in producing it, is only instrumental and mechanical.

Hence, none but an intelligent cause can *per se* produce order; for order essentially implies judgment; man, by the exercise of reason, produces order in thought, word, and work; but the order that is in his physical *nature* as a substance, is from God: "Ordo rectæ rationis est ab homine, ordo naturæ est a Deo."

To investigate this order with the design which it evinces, as manifested in the works of creation, in the means apportioned and directed to ends which are discernible in all of them, constitutes what is termed the study of *final causes.* As before remarked, the final cause is the highest and the most noble of the causes; for, it bespeaks the intelligent principle that gives motion, direction and efficacy to all the other causes, since they are subordinate and subject to it, and are, therefore, dependent on it in operating. Hence, its objects furnish the mind congenial and elevated knowledge, since they acquaint it with the ends for which the different works of creation are destined, as shown by their action; and, by consequence, no study depending on the mere light of reason, can give us more perfect views of the author of their existence.

When Bacon and others say that the study of *final causes,* according to the manner in which they are discernible in the nature of things around us, is arrogant, and tends to atheism, their fear and warning come, perhaps, from misguided reverence

* "Ovis fugit lupum ex quodam arbitrio quo existimat eum sibi noxium; sed hoc judicium non est sibi liberum sed a natura inditum." (Div. Thom. 1 p., qu. 59, art. 3.) The sheep flees from the wolf by a certain choice in which it esteems the wolf hurtful; but this judgment is not free, but is implanted in it by nature.

to God; "æmulationem Dei habent, sed non secundum scientiam."* All things are parts of the volume which creation forms, and it is open before us that we may read, and learn to know the existence and the perfections of its Author, as shown in his works. As the bees of Mount Hybla sip honey from the very flowers that give to reptiles deadly venom, so, that which teaches wisdom to the well meaning, may be turned to evil aims by the ill-disposed.

In the operations of natural law, there is never mere accident, or purely fortuitous event; for, irrational agents have no action except in obedience to the law of their nature, imposed on them by the author of their being. Their action, though various, is orderly; their mechanism, though complex, has unity, and nature never fails either in the coördination of her means or in the attainment of her ends; "natura nunquam deficit in necessariis." Hence, such study of the creatures around us not only tends to knowledge that is true, and high, and wise, but at the same time gives us conclusions that are infallibly certain.

* "They have a zeal of God, but not according to knowledge." (Rom. x.) See page 56.

END OF ONTOLOGY, OR GENERAL METAPHYSICS.

ALPHABETICAL INDEX.

www.ingramcontent.com/pod-product-compliance
Lightning Source LLC
LaVergne TN
LVHW050525100826
845148LV00002B/446

* 9 7 8 1 4 2 5 5 2 0 5 6 4 *